K–12 TEACHERS IN THE MIDST OF REFORM

Common Thread Cases

Traci Bliss
Idaho State University

Joan Mazur
University of Kentucky

Merrill
Prentice Hall

Upper Saddle River, New Jersey
Columbus, Ohio

Library of Congress Cataloging-in-Publication Data
K–12 teachers in the midst of reform : common-thread cases / [edited by] Traci Bliss, Joan Mazur.
   p. cm.
  Includes bibliographical references.
  ISBN 0-13-937327-6
   1. Elementary school teachers—United States—Case studies. 2. Elementary school teaching—United States—Case studies. 3. School improvement programs—United States—Case studies. I. Bliss, Traci. II. Mazur, Joan.
LB1776.2 .K22 2002
371.1'00973—dc21

00-049548

Vice President and Publisher: Jeffery W. Johnston
Executive Editor: Debra A. Stollenwerk
Editorial Assistant: Penny S. Burleson
Production Editor: Mary Harlan
Design Coordinator: Diane C. Lorenzo
Cover Design: Ceri Fitzgerald
Cover Art: SuperStock
Text Design and Illustrations: Carlisle Publishers Services
Production Coordination: Terry Routley, Carlisle Publishers Services
Production Manager: Pamela D. Bennett
Director of Marketing: Kevin Flanagan
Marketing Manager: Krista Groshong
Marketing Coordinator: Barbara Koontz

This book was set in Novarese by Carlisle Communications, Ltd. It was printed and bound by R. R. Donnelley & Sons Company. The cover was printed by The Lehigh Press, Inc..

Photo Credits: All images supplied by the authors.

Merrill
Prentice Hall

10 9 8 7 6 5 4 3 2 1
ISBN 0-13-937327-6

To Edward F. Reidy, Jr.,

June 20, 1947–August 2, 1999,

who served as

Deputy Commissioner in the Kentucky Department of Education through

the formative years of change in the 1990s

K–12 *Teachers in the Midst of Reform: Common Thread Cases* was made possible through the generous support of:

    The Bell South Foundation, Atlanta, Georgia
    The Gheens Foundation, Louisville, Kentucky
    Kentucky Educational Television, Lexington, Kentucky
    The University of Kentucky/University of Louisville Joint Center for the Study of Policy

Foreword

Why read and use these case studies? First and foremost, they are extremely well done. We readers are provided with narratives and thick description of authentic lives of teachers. The rich detail in each case is supplemented by pieces of evidence that exemplify sound teaching activities and students' work. These actual accounts of teachers are designed to delve into the problematic aspects of everyday teaching. Dewey noted that a problem is anything that "perplexes and challenges so that it makes belief uncertain," and, indeed, these case narratives perplex and inspire. They also challenge through the use of case exhibits and structured case inquiry. We are given questions that pose problems with the case situations and challenge our first interpretations. Each case bibliography invites us to learn more about the theoretical underpinnings of the issues illustrated. Through the use of these cases, we learn about the efforts of individual teachers and increase our knowledge of the intricacies of classroom lives. Teachers' activities are embedded in complex webs of interconnections, so that in examining the practice of one teacher, we learn about the teacher's community, classroom, students, parents of the students, and colleagues. We learn what happens when change is attempted. Let me be more specific.

A colleague refers to these cases as studies of teachers in the *mist* of reform. Although initially appealing as a play on words, further reflection confirms the appropriateness of thinking about the *mist* of reform. Reform efforts are generally promulgated in the language of policy—a language hyperbolic and grand but lacking detail and a language that can lead one to feel enveloped in a mist when planning daily activities needed to reach such visions for change.

These case studies serve to clear away some of the mist, to illuminate vistas of actual changes that teachers undertake to implement proposed improvements. K–12 *Teachers in the Midst of Reform* cases are referenced to one set of reform ideas, the Interstate New Teacher Assessment and Support Consortium (INTASC) principles. However, because these standards are consistent with current reform standards produced by various national organizations, they have universal application. Cases that mirror the struggles of actual practice help us to think through the myriad implications of infusing standards in today's classrooms. Portraying these situations is a unique and important service and one that makes this book valuable to a wide range of educators.

In my work preparing students to teach secondary science, agriculture, or mathematics, I want to ready my students for the contexts they will encounter when they leave our preservice program. As a teacher educator, I want to nourish their youthful enthusiasm and idealism and their visions of themselves as contributing to change.

And yet, I want them to realize that change will be difficult; it will require a level of commitment they may not anticipate. I worry I sound cynical. The case studies in this book help, both by describing remarkable successes and by deepening our understandings of the reasons that contribute to less successful change efforts.

My particular focus is the teaching of science, and at the outset I wondered if I would find the cases describing elementary teaching or other subjects irrelevant. In fact, I found quite the opposite. Just as one learns about one's home culture by working in another, reading such a variety of cases deepened my insights and invigorated my understanding of secondary teaching. Highlighted are the similar issues across teaching contents and the professional commitments all teachers share. The authenticity of these accounts will do much to enliven the profession.

Deborah Trumbull
Cornell University

Preface

PURPOSE OF THE BOOK

When groups of teachers come together to analyze practice, either as novices or those proficient in their craft, the vitality of the analytic process depends upon the richness of the practices being examined. Our goal in creating this compendium of true teacher stories is to help catalyze dynamic learning communities. When teachers collectively engage in analytic problem solving and take action based on fresh but well-reasoned insights, they constitute the types of communities for which these cases are designed. Whether in university classrooms, district professional development contexts, or Professional Development School sites, or on the Internet, these authentic accounts beckon systematic reflection. What went well and why? What would I have done differently, under what circumstances, and with what potential consequences? What theories and research support my decision making?

APPROPRIATE COURSES

The ten cases featured here, selected from our two earlier volumes, have proven effective catalysts for analytic thinking in mixed groups of K–12 educators. Each case shows the consequences of teacher action in the face of a complex problem. As such, these cases have been used as supplemental readings to raise and explore key issues in such diverse undergraduate and graduate courses as Inquiry, Thinking and Knowing, Philosophy of Education, Theoretical Foundations of Pedagogy, Curriculum, Change Strategies, and Analysis of Practice and Supervision. These kaleidoscopic tales invite the use of multiple lenses for examination and, hence, fit well in a range of courses. In teacher education contexts, professors often use the cases for courses that focus on one's philosophy of teaching. For them, the cases illuminate how philosophies and/or teaching approaches (such as those described in *Approaches to Teaching* by Fenstermacher and Soltis, Teachers College Press, 1998) play out in practice and may either contribute to or detract from the teaching/learning context. At the graduate level, including doctoral courses, we have found them extremely useful in curriculum courses because real curriculum is seen in real contexts.

Standards

How do performance standards come alive in unique combinations? Using the INTASC matrix on page xxii, you see how standards are embedded in each case. The interplay between specific performance standards and actual classroom practice is the basis for thoughtful discovery: how and why does this occur? At the conclusion of every chapter, discussion questions are linked to relevant INTASC standards. Furthermore, opportunities for reflective practice (INTASC Standard #9) are abundant within these stories. The subjects of the cases themselves show varying commitments to reflective practice, which are applicable to the broad spectrum of K–12 teachers. For example, the reflective process used by the teachers in "Stagnant Pools and Flowing Waters" is relevant for any teacher, regardless of subject area or years of experience.

How These Cases Came About

Case subjects were selected based on recommendations from their peers and other prominent educators in reform contexts. The cases are not intended to be "models" of standards-based practice but rather to provide windows into the provocative pedagogical issues embedded in the standards. They are examples of real practice.

Our commitment as case authors has been to accurate documentation such that embracing a specific approach to change becomes the reader's choice. During extensive observation and interviewing, we encouraged teachers to discuss their experiences and important insights. Questions were open-ended, and we spent much time clarifying the meaning of what we saw and heard. The development process was collaborative throughout, with a mutual commitment to authenticity. In five of the ten cases, we use the real names and contexts of the teachers involved. Each principal character made his or her own decision about anonymity and authenticated the case events and descriptive accounts. As a group, the case subjects have given countless hours to be observed, interviewed, and videotaped.

Support Materials

The Instructor's Quick Guide is a useful tool for those new to facilitating case discussions and to promote the development of learning communities through the analysis of practice. Selected cases are available in multimedia format on a CD-ROM to facilitate distance learning communities. Both are available from the publisher.

ACKNOWLEDGMENTS

The eighth case in this volume, "Staying the Course," features Christy Sullivan, who maintains her vision of what makes students lifelong writers despite the challenges of change. Christy's story provides valuable insights into reflective practice as she strives to embody what John Dewey referred to as the "attitude of wholeheartedness."

During our seven years of researching, field testing, and producing the teachers' stories contained here and in earlier volumes, our own wholeheartedness was nourished by the unfailing support of a handful of individuals. Foremost among them is our mentor, Judith Kleinfeld of the University of Alaska, whose commitment to high standards never failed to inspire us. Sharon Brennan and Linda Levstik of the University of Kentucky; Liz Hobson, formerly of Kentucky Educational Television; Judy Buzzell of Southern Connecticut State University; Deborah Trumbull of Cornell University; Leslie Graitzer of the BellSouth Foundation; our editor, Debbie Stollenwerk; and our graphic designer, Nita Kaufman, have truly "stayed the course" with us in defining our horizons and making the real experience of teachers dynamic vehicles for analyzing practice.

Our current and former graduate students have given generously of their time and most importantly their enthusiasm. Our heartfelt thanks to Toni Bishop, Stefanie Brimacomb, Susan Brodie, and Jenny Lynn Varner.

Two educators deserve special mention.

Early on in our careers, Eliot Eisner helped shape our quite different but complementary paths. For Traci, the first seeds of these cases were sown as Professor Eisner's teaching assistant at Stanford. There she developed her commitment to qualitative research that focuses on curriculum content and rich descriptions of contemporary classrooms. For Joan, Eisner's influence began during her study of visual modes of representation with Geri Gay at Cornell's Human-Computer Interaction (HCI) Group, where she became dedicated to understanding the many qualitative complexities of narrative and the power of storytelling.

Ed Reidy, an extraordinary teacher to whom this book is dedicated, was a prominent leader in Kentucky's systemic reform and in national debates about student standards and assessment. His unreserved support for a case approach to professional development emanated from his commitment to a learning community paradigm. Few things delighted Ed more than seeing teachers eagerly learn from one another's journeys. In the words of Soren Kierkegaard, Ed had "an eye which ever young and ardent sees the possible" (from "Either/Or" in Vol. 1 of *Diapsalmata*, 1843, translated 1987 Copenhagen: E. Munksgaard).

Reference: Fenstermacher and Soltis, J. (1998). *Approaches to Teaching*. New York: Teachers College Press.

We also wish to thank those who reviewed this book for their helpful comments and suggestions:

Frank Bickel, State University of New York, Oswego
JoAnne Buggey, University of Minnesota
Judith Buzzell, Southern Connecticut State University
Jeri A. Carroll, Wichita State University
Leigh Chiarelott, Bowling Green State University
Joseph G. Claudet, Texas Tech University
Jeanine M. Dell'Olio, Hope College
Jean Dennee, Eastern Illinois University

Sandra L. DiGiaimo, University of Scranton
Mary Lynn Hamilton, University of Kansas
Kenneth Howey, Ohio State University
Todd Kent, University of Virginia
J. Gary Knowles, Ontario Institute for Studies in Education for the University of Toronto
Stephen Lafer, University of Nevada, Reno
Debra Bayles Martin, San Diego State University
Betty Jo Simmons, Longwood College
Elizabeth Simons, Kansas State University
William M. Welty, Pace University

ABOUT THE AUTHORS

Traci Bliss, Ph.D., is an associate professor of curriculum studies and teacher education at Idaho State University. She has served as a state policy advisor to the National Board for Professional Teaching Standards and helped draft the INTASC Standards. She is the Director of Idaho Classrooms of Accomplished Teachers sponsored by the J. A. & Kathryn Albertson Foundation.

Joan Mazur is an associate professor of instructional design and technology at the University of Kentucky. She is widely published in such diverse journals as the *Journal of Teacher Education* and the *Journal of Computer-Mediated Communication*, continuously focusing on the integration of technology and researching its effects in a variety of educational contexts.

CONTRIBUTORS

Jennifer Bell is an assistive technology specialist and directs a federally funded Assistive Technology Project at the University of Kentucky.

A. Edward Blackhurst is Professor Emeritus in the Department of Special Education and Rehabilitation Counseling at the University of Kentucky. He is past president of the Association for Special Education Technology.

Teri Brown is principal of a Northern Kentucky high school and a doctoral candidate at the University of Kentucky's Department of Administration and Supervision.

Judith B. Buzzell is an associate professor of education at Southern Connecticut State University, the author of several case books, and Connecticut's Multicultural Educator of the Year for 1999.

Caroline Fahrney is a school psychologist in a suburban high school in Illinois.

Gretchyn K. Furlong has taught in rural and urban elementary schools at various grade levels. She is currently a consultant to school districts in the development of specialized educational plans.

Harper Fouts Kelly has been an award-winning elementary school teacher for 11 years. She currently teaches multiage primary in Anchorage, Kentucky.

Linda Kreisler is a high school English teacher with 10 years of experience. She teaches in an urban district in North Carolina.

Jane Clark Lindle is a professor in administration and supervision at the University of Kentucky. She also serves as the co-director of the University of Kentucky/University of Louisville Joint Center for the Study of Educational Policy.

Catherine M. Murray is a high school special education teacher in Pocatello, Idaho.

Michael O'Donnell is a high school journalism teacher in Blackfoot, Idaho.

Brenda Overturf is a middle school language arts teacher in a suburban area of Kentucky. She has more than 20 years of experience in education.

Billie Jo Rylance is an assistant professor of special education at the University of Wisconsin at Oshkosh.

Gina Schack is an associate professor of education at the University of Louisville.

Brief Contents

Contents

CASE 3
Arts on the Line   57

Traci Bliss with Catherine M. Murray

Patsy Cox teaches at Portland, a highly diverse urban elementary school in a state committed to systemic reform. Cox has always integrated art in her teaching without the assistance of an art teacher but in close collaboration with her colleagues. Consistent with the state reform goals, she embarks on intensive training in a new curriculum approach, Different Ways of Knowing (DWoK). Despite initial reservations, by the second year of the program, Patsy sees how valuable the curriculum is, because it emphasizes integrating learning experiences through key themes. The principal of Portland is stunned to learn that Patsy has decided to move on and is concerned about the success of the new program.

CASE 4
Caroline Never Smiles   79

Jennifer Bell, Billie Jo Rylance, Traci Bliss, and A. Edward Blackhurst

Throughout her early elementary years, Caroline, a student with multiple physical disabilities, enjoys academic success in the regular education classroom. As she approaches middle school, her grades start to plummet, she becomes increasingly isolated from her peers, and the assistive technology device that has been specifically designed for her remains on the shelf. Some of her regular education teachers are astounded to discover how little they really understand one of her disabilities: Moebius Syndrome. When Caroline's mother begins expressing her frustration over Caroline's downward spiral, several issues emerge about teachers' responsibilities for special needs students. Is it too late for Caroline to regain lost ground?

CASE 5
On the High Wire   109

Brenda Overturf and Gina Schack

A team of middle school teachers at various stages in their careers designs an interdisciplinary student-centered unit based on the work of James Beane. The unit allows students the freedom to explore issues of concern to them within the broad topic of transitions.

   The students react positively to the unit, demonstrate increased motivation, and have fewer behavioral problems. Although the teachers are pleased with their students' performance, several voice their concerns about the student-centered teaching approach. How can teachers allow students to shape the content and progression of a unit and still be sure that certain concepts are being covered? What are appropriate assessments in a student-centered curriculum?

CASE 6
"I Don't Think I Can Teach This Again"   133

Judith B. Buzzell

Leslie Jenkins faces the prospect of teaching *Adventures of Huckleberry Finn* with trepidation, although she has taught it for the past two years. Twain's classic recently came under fire in her state. African American parents in the nearby urban district condemned the novel for its use of the word "nigger." The superintendent in that district subsequently removed the book from the eighth-grade curriculum, citing racial tension and potential damage to students' self-esteem. Moreover, many teachers admit that the book's context, dialogue, and sophisticated satire can be difficult for young students to comprehend.

   Leslie is aware that although the book has stirred controversy and censorship many times since its publication, it is generally acknowledged as one of the great American novels.

   How, Leslie wonders, can she prepare her class of "average" ability students to understand this classic literary work? Is she sufficiently prepared to deal with the controversial issues that may emerge?

CASE 7
Compromise and Defeat: A Power Struggle at Watermill   163

Teri Brown, Traci Bliss, Jane Lindle, and Michael O'Donnell

Watermill Middle School was notorious for its extensive discipline problems. In an effort to improve the school, the district hired Jack Carnes, an enthusiastic administrator determined to make significant changes as the new principal. He helps to radically change the curriculum and instructional practices at Watermill and earns a statewide reputation as a successful, reform-minded administrator.

   Watermill had an active School-Based Decision Making Council before Carnes became principal. On the surface, Carnes adopts the council's procedures, but many council members believe Carnes has subverted the council's power by making independent decisions concerning new faculty hires and school restructuring.

   How can teacher and parent representatives diffuse Carnes' power, especially since he is held in high esteem by the community and throughout the state? What recourse do teacher and parent representatives have to ensure their voices are heard? Are their expectations realistic?

CASE 8
Staying the Course   175

Linda Kreisler and Traci Bliss

Christy Sullivan immerses herself in a full-time summer Writing Project, which helps shape a transformation of her once traditional approach to teaching English. What for Christy is a new approach to teaching writing requires extensive preplanning, frequent conferences with individual students, and continuous feedback.

The resulting increase in Christy's workload causes her to frequently fall behind in her grading and other administrative duties. The parents of one student complain to the principal that they have not been properly informed of their daughter's performance throughout the semester. In response to this parental concern, Christy's principal demands she stay on top of her grading and record keeping.

Christy believes her new teaching approach is extremely successful and that the heart of the problem is too few English teachers. Can she continue to develop her new curriculum while meeting the demands of her principal and her students' parents? Moreover, will she?

Traci Bliss and Caroline Fahrney

After a career in medical research, Jason Gordon becomes a biology teacher in a tight-knit department that has received several accolades for reform. Jason believes in a building-block approach to teaching biology, with strong emphasis on critical-thinking skills. Although Jason is highly successful, especially with students who have difficulty learning, he feels ostracized by other members of the department who advocate more of a discovery approach to biology.

Despite several years of teaching in the same school and the wholehearted support of the principal, Jason still doesn't have his own classroom, and his strained relationships with colleagues continue. Should Jason try to move to another school where he might feel more appreciated? If he stays in his current position, what can be done to improve the situation?

Traci Bliss

Tenth-grade student and avid football player Mark Mattioli demands to be transferred from Elaine Temkin's U.S. History class because he finds her emphasis on critical thinking and use of primary source reading assignments too demanding. The award-winning Temkin convinces Mark to stay in her course, and with her help and encouragement, his performance shows improvement.

Mark takes a new interest in historical issues and controversies and soon becomes enthused and outspoken in class discussions. However, Mark continues to pursue an active social life, and after-school activities interfere with his course work.

Can Elaine motivate Mark to truly excel in her class instead of just getting by? Will Mark's initial success in Elaine's class carry over to the next school year and to other courses? Furthermore, should the approach she used to help Mark with his reading be used with the entire class?

I S S U E S   M A T R I X

Issues	Common Thread Cases				
	Case 1 Reading, Writing, and RAM	Case 2 Stagnant Pools and Flowing Waters	Case 3 Arts on the Line	Case 4 Caroline Never Smiles	Case 5 On the High Wire
Assessment	•	•	•	•	
Administrative Support	•	•	•	•	
Block Scheduling					•
Collegiality Issues	•		•	•	•
Critical Thinking		•	•		•
Diversity	•	•	•	•	
Heterogenous Grouping	•	•		•	
Individualized Instruction	•	•		•	
Inquiry			•		•
Integrated Curriculum/ Interdisciplinary Instruction		•	•		•
Learning Environment	•	•		•	•
Multiple Intelligences	•	•	•		
Parent Involvement	•	•		•	
Portfolios	•		•		
Professional Development	•		•		
Reflective Practitioner	•	•	•		•
Rural		•			•
School-based Decision Making	•				
Small Group/Cooperative Learning	•	•			•
Student Motivation	•		•	•	•
Students with Special Needs	•	•		•	
Suburban	•			•	•
Team Teaching/Collaboration	•	•	•		•
Technology/Media Integration	•		•	•	
Thematic Teaching	•			•	
Urban			•		
Writing Process/Writing/ Across the Curriculum	•	•			

	Case 6 "I Don't Think I Can Teach This Again"	Case 7 Compromise and Defeat: A Power Struggle at Watermill	Case 8 Staying the Course	Case 9 Will the Real Reform Please Stand Up?	Case 10 When Is Enough, Enough?
		•	•	•	
	•				
			•	•	•
					•
	•		•	•	•
			•	•	•
		•	•		•
	•			•	•
			•	•	•
	•	•	•		
		•			
			•	•	
	•		•		
			•		
		•			
	•		•	•	•
	•		•	•	•
	•			•	
				•	
				•	
	•		•		
					•
	•		•		•

INTASC MATRIX

	Common Thread Cases			
INTASC Principles	**Case 1** Reading, Writing, and RAM	**Case 2** Stagnant Pools and Flowing Waters	**Case 3** Arts on the Line	**Case 4** Caroline Never Smiles
Principle #1 The teacher understands the concepts, tools of inquiry, and structures of the discipline(s) he or she teaches and can create learning experiences that make these aspects of subject matter meaningful for students.				
Principle #2 The teacher understands how children learn and develop, and can provide learning opportunities that support their intellectual, social, and personal development.	•	•		•
Principle #3 The teacher understands how students differ in their approaches to learning and creates instructional opportunities that are adapted to diverse learners.	•	•	•	•
Principle #4 The teacher understands and uses a variety of instructional strategies to encourage students' development of critical thinking, problem solving, and performance skills.	•	•	•	
Principle #5 The teacher uses an understanding of individual and group motivation and behavior to create a learning environment that encourages positive social interaction, learning, and self-motivation.	•			•
Principle #6 The teacher uses knowledge of effective verbal, nonverbal, and media communication techniques to foster active inquiry, collaboration, and supportive instruction in the classroom.	•			•
Principle #7 The teacher plans instruction based upon knowledge of subject matter, students, the community, and curriculum goals				
Principle #8 The teacher understands and uses formal and informal assessment strategies to evaluate and ensure the continuous intellectual, social, and physical development of the learner.		•	•	
Principle #9 The teacher is a reflective practitioner who continually evaluates the effects of his/her choices and actions on others (students, parents, other professionals in the learning community) and who actively seeks out opportunities to grow professionally.		•	•	
Principle #10 The teacher fosters relationships with school colleagues, parents, and agencies in the larger community to support learning and well-being.	•	•	•	•

	Case 5 On the High Wire	Case 6 "I Don't Think I Can Teach This Again"	Case 7 Compromise and Defeat: A Power Struggle at Watermill	Case 8 Staying the Course	Case 9 Will the Real Reform Please Stand Up?	Case 10 When Is Enough, Enough?
	•	•				•
		•		•	•	
		•			•	•
		•		•		•
	•		•	•	•	•
		•	•		•	
	•	•			•	
	•			•		
	•	•		•		
	•		•		•	•

Reading, Writing, and RAM

STARTING OUT

"If only I'd known what to do with them. I was a total amateur. I'd hardly ever used a computer let alone tried to incorporate one of them into my classroom!"

Fourth-grade teacher Vicki Lugo had been eager to transfer to Solana Santa Fe (SSF), a new elementary school in the large urban-adjacent district of Solana Beach, in San Diego County bordering the Pacific Ocean. The diverse student population and the new high-tech facility offered challenges that Lugo sought to energize her teaching. Also, she was eager to work with principal Marge Copp, a former colleague whose skills she'd come to respect. The school was finished in late July, barely a month before the students would arrive. Lugo confronted her first hurdle as soon as she'd unlocked the door of her new classroom: A networked computer station and printer hummed quietly next to her desk.

In addition to this station, three more computers arrived soon after the start of school, a donation from a parent whose company was upgrading. Although she'd had little computer training herself, Lugo was convinced that elementary students needed both language and computer literacy to succeed in the 21st century. The donations pushed the issue, and Lugo knew she must capitalize on the opportunity. Still, she found herself with 26 students, some valuable equipment, and no plan for technology integration.

Enlisting the help of Janet Golden, the school's technology lab teacher, Lugo worked nights and weekends to get her skills up to speed. By mid-year she had developed a range of strategies for integrating technology. "Every technology skill must have a curriculum connection" became her mantra. As the first year progressed, Lugo saw her goals take shape through a fourth-grade language arts curriculum infused with technology applications and linked to literacy skills. Using rubrics from a continuous assessment reading program as guidelines, Lugo required students to spend more than half an hour each day using the computer to work on reading or writing proficiencies.

The central program was Kid Works (www.mwcdrom.com), an integrated software package containing a word processing program, a spreadsheet, and a database. Lugo developed an on-line pen-pal program called Key Pals (see Exhibit A). In Key Pals, students used e-mail to communicate with students in other schools who were reading the same books or gathering data on cooperative projects. Students in different schools discussed commonly read books and met literacy goals such as discovering themes, identifying with characters in a story, and offering evidence for generalizations. The district's Internet policy required parental permission, which was easily obtained since district security measures prevented students from accessing objectionable materials. Because all parents agreed to let their children participate, monitoring student access was not a problem (see Exhibit B). It didn't take long for Lugo to be convinced that her many hours of planning were justified.

"The results kept me going, especially the successes with average students," she said. "So often we spend so much time with high or low achievers. The computers make it possible to individualize instruction, but, more important, the kids are self-motivated. . . . They keep learning on their own. Once kids got their computer skills certificate from Janet Golden, their confidence soared. They helped other students and were invaluable resources to the teachers."

Spurred by their accomplishments and the principal's wholehearted support, Lugo and Golden also designed "Tech Camp" for SSF's summer enrichment program. Tech Camp offered students a variety of integrated activities to build technology skills. For example, students could use a HyperCard stack for book reports. Opportunities also existed for students to use a digital camera or scanner to explore alternate ways to represent information. For $225, students attended Tech Camp daily for two weeks; scholarships were available for those students who were eligible for free or reduced-price lunch during the school year. Initially developed for fourth, fifth, and sixth grades, Tech Camp was so successful that parents demanded a similar program for children in the primary grades.

A BREAK FROM THE CLASSROOM: THE DISTRICT LANGUAGE ARTS MENTOR

Lugo's success did not go unnoticed, and she was appointed the district mentor teacher for language arts. She was in demand at all of Solana's five schools for her expertise in literacy and technology. Lugo spent her days racing between schools and tutoring teachers in computer applications. However, after her second year, Lugo returned to the fourth-grade classroom.

"I realized I could make more money tutoring students after school and still have time left for a life. I loved solving problems and working with teachers who were excited about using technology and integrating language arts, but it was just too much of a grind."

Working with young children again, she focused on eliminating obstacles to learning through the use of technology. Fourth graders did not have the necessary keyboarding skills, and Lugo felt she was spending too much time teaching basic computing. Also, she'd complained to the principal that too many of her students now came in with below-grade-level reading and writing skills. This situation was unacceptable, especially in a district with the resources of SSF.

OUTMANEUVERED: MARGE COPP'S PROPOSAL

A few months after Lugo's return to her fourth-grade classroom, first-grade teacher Sharon O'Brien came to Lugo for moral support. The principal, Marge Copp, was pressuring her to apply for a federal Title VII grant to provide intervention for minority students and also to train as a Reading Recovery teacher for the first grade. O'Brien was interested but didn't want the administrative responsibilities. "I'm still excited about working with the first grade," she told Lugo. "You've got to come with me to see Marge. You know how much I want to learn Reading Recovery, but don't let me get hoodwinked into doing this." Lugo understood. She had been impressed by the Reading Recovery results discussed at conferences she'd attended over the years. Like O'Brien, she had wanted for some time to be prepared in Reading Recovery but had not had the opportunity, and she was well aware of the time required to administer grants. O'Brien scheduled an appointment, and they met with Copp the following week.

Marge's proposition was deliberately designed to appeal to the professional interests of both teachers as well as their interest in collaboration. They could team teach the first grade. In the morning, Lugo would have the majority of the students while O'Brien pulled out Reading Recovery students for intensive literacy development. In the afternoons, O'Brien would teach math to all the children, and Lugo would administer the Title VII grants and provide professional development in technology for other teachers. The following year they would switch roles: Lugo would learn Reading Recovery, and O'Brien would teach language arts and manage the considerable documentation required for the grant. Lugo and O'Brien exchanged glances and perplexed looks. They were intrigued by the possibilities. Lugo spoke first: "This gives us a whole new angle to consider." Copp gave them a week to decide.

"Marge had outmaneuvered us," Lugo said after they had agreed to Copp's proposal. "She gave us an opportunity to team; we could both accomplish our long-term professional goals to become trained in Reading Recovery—all with the flexibility to integrate technology with the academic skills our students so badly needed. But I was worried. Could I take what I'd learned about integrating technology in the fourth grade and make it work in the first grade? Would it be too confusing to teach technical skills along with literacy development? How could we manage to do it all?"

VICKI LUGO

Vicki Lugo is a dynamo who, according to colleagues and parents, energizes those around her. Her more than 25 years of experience have coalesced into a "can-do" attitude—confidently approaching any project, no matter how daunting. "I've been at this a long time," Lugo says enthusiastically, "and things will always work out one way or another!" Her dedication to raising student achievement is characterized by an openness to change and to new techniques. Her initial use of computers was spurred by the potential to increase individual participation and develop independence in learners—two goals that have become increasingly important to Lugo.

Lugo grew to value diversity and productivity during her own elementary school years in the 1950s. Through eighth grade, the 21 students in her class were a self-contained community at the only school in a small rural farming community in the Sacramento delta. As an Anglo-American, Lugo was in the minority of a class consisting of Filipino, Chinese, Japanese, and African American students. She remembers teachers emphasizing student performances in every aspect of the curriculum.

"We were always working on individual and group performances, and they were topics that engaged us—in social studies, for example, we'd make huge topographical maps of other countries. The expectation to demonstrate what we knew was not limited to academic subjects. Before any student could graduate, she or he had to show the ability to read music and also pass a basic swimming test. After all, we lived on the Sacramento River!"

At Santa Catalina High School, Lugo developed interests in diversity and Spanish. As a junior in college, she attended a university in Mexico City, where she met her future husband. They later agreed that their two children would have dual citizenship. "Over the years, we've almost always had a Mexican exchange student living with us. It has been great for our family, and it has helped us to stay bilingual, which is so valuable in my teaching."

As a result of her own educational experiences, Lugo has always believed that students must have authentic materials. In teaching her students to read, she uses a variety of books rather than basal readers. Sharon O'Brien, Lugo's partner in the first-grade experiment, credits Lugo for broadening her own teaching methods. When O'Brien started at SSF, she'd been using standard workbooks and seatwork for seven years. O'Brien was "wowed" by Lugo's holistic philosophy and her skill at integrating literature, field experiences, and art projects into language arts.

"I was stunned," she said. "Vicki's room was brimming over with books, art projects from field trips, and displays of students' written work . . . I'd never seen students producing so much, reading so much, or enjoying themselves so thoroughly. I was scared to let go of my structured workbooks, but Vicki quickly convinced me that students could learn immense amounts on their own with proper guidance, monitoring, and structured activity."

Lugo's teaching style has been characterized by one parent as a "refreshingly no-nonsense approach" to teaching literacy. In fact, Lugo is convinced that her current approach exemplifies good teaching. She believes that teachers are largely evaluated on what she calls the "fluff" activities that hook kids, but do little else, and "canned" lessons that look good to official observers. Lugo adamantly refuses to hand in five-step lesson plans before her biannual evaluation. "I've told them, 'Come to my classroom for the morning, and after I'm done we can discuss what happened.' We will focus on how I monitored students and adjusted activities to correct problems or moved students forward who were achieving their goals. This is the heart of teaching—constantly adjusting the curriculum so students are always succeeding."

THE COMMUNITY AND THE SCHOOL

Suburban Solana Beach, north of San Diego, is a community with about 2,300 students in five elementary schools. Here, as in many border communities, one sees dramatic contrasts in lifestyle in the various socioeconomic strata.

Before SSF opened in 1993, a community task force (composed of parents, teachers, and professors from the nearby state university) explored how to best meet the needs of what would be a highly diverse student body. Despite the controversy, the committee decided the school would offer Second Language Acquisition via an English Immersion Program rather than the district's current Transitional Bilingual Program. The majority of the committee members were convinced that for students to achieve, they needed to be fluent in English. To promote communicative goals for all students, Spanish as a second language would also be offered. Teachers who embraced these approaches were encouraged to apply to the new school as transfers. O'Brien and Lugo, both bilingual, jumped at the opportunity to teach at SSF.

Solana Santa Fe is a modern, single-story school for grades K–6. The vestibule is vibrantly decorated with a seashore motif. Starfish, shells, and seaweed are interspersed with displays of student work from a tide pool exploration project. At the center of the display, a computer station's monitor repeats an attractive screen that invites visitors to use the CD-ROM program on the tidal ecosystem.

Marge Copp, the school's first principal, chose technology, parental involvement, and diversity as themes for her new school.

"Few principals can build the school community from the ground up as the physical plant is being constructed. I felt I had a golden opportunity to shape a school that is truly a community . . . a place where everyone had access to a highly technological learning environment. I insisted the school have the wiring infrastructure to support high-speed computing, even if the computers were not initially available. I wanted that foundation and capacity from the beginning."

Despite her goals, Copp's vision was often blurred by the realities of school life. Although her plans included extensive on-site professional development for teachers in technology, faculty interest was lukewarm. "I'm not actively resisting computers," said a veteran teacher who transferred to SSF because of her interest in working more closely with parents. "It's just that I can't find the time." Also, despite the guiding principles of diversity and community, the school has no Hispanic faculty members (although half, like Lugo, are bilingual). Furthermore, common planning time is not built into the schedule.

The faculty members relish the opportunity to share ideas with one another. One experienced teacher, new to the school, said, "At my old school I was the star, but here everyone works together, and all are superstars. I just blend in with the crowd." The tight-knit faculty credits their team spirit in part to a five-day retreat that Copp scheduled before the school opened. It was expensive, and no other new school has been given this opportunity.

Copp's emphasis on parental involvement means parents are expected to monitor children's work at home and become active in the school community. For example, beginning in first grade, parents may be required to read with their children each night or to work on math activities such as counting change and writing numbers. Parents also are strongly urged to participate in orientation and support activities, such as the following:

- *Orientation*: A two-day workshop during which parents learn how to contact teachers and how to ask questions about their child's progress.
- *Support*: Two workshops for parents to participate in the "Rolling Readers" program, in which they listen to their children reading books daily; numerous counseling and tutoring programs available through parent request or teacher referral.
- *Communication*: A Web site (http://www.sbsd.sdcoe.k12.ca.us); a districtwide newsletter; bilingual teachers; a telephone in every room for home/school communication.

To accommodate the Hispanic parents and to further encourage involvement, informational flyers are bilingual, and instructional materials, such as books on tape, are available in Spanish. Through resources such as the tapes, parents can help SSF achieve its curriculum goals. Teachers regularly design innovative classroom units, and there is general acceptance of new approaches. Lugo benefited from this atmosphere of teamwork, innovation, and support as she embarked on the design of her integrated technology curriculum.

DESIGNING THE FIRST-GRADE TECHNOLOGY CURRICULUM

Lugo's decision to move to first grade had occurred quite unexpectedly at the end of her fourth year at SSF. Thus, she had not attended the two in-service workshops on the integrated software program for first graders. She would have to tackle the appropriate programs on her own. After heading the Tech Camp that summer, she had only one month to learn the programs, review the curriculum CDs and other on-line materials, and plan the year.

Lugo knew that creating an environment in which students could produce quality papers and illustrated texts had been key to her fourth graders' successes, but first grade was different. First graders might have limited computer experience, and she could expect only emergent literacy skills. Could she design a motivating curriculum that targeted their needs? She also faced another problem: Only half of the incoming first graders had been introduced to a computer and some on-line drawing tools in kindergarten.

Lugo began by identifying each student's literacy skills using the Accelerating Literacy developmental reading stages (see Exhibit C). She incorporates skill development into math, science, social studies, and literature experiences. For Lugo, students would demonstrate dimensions of early literacy through several skills, such as listening to and enjoying a range of stories and books, expressing curiosity about the use of writing in communication and reading words in context, attending to modeling of story structure, and predicting story events. As the year progressed, students would use CD-ROM informational materials and other subject-area instructional software with the goal of producing several written works. Activities included writing and constructing different versions of stories. She would use two computer programs, Kid Works (www.mwcdrom.com) and Kid Pix (www.broderbund.com), to match these skills with activities. Also, based on her experience with unprepared fourth graders, Lugo insisted on teaching correct keyboarding skills from the outset, using a self-paced keyboarding program geared for young children, Mavis Beacon Teaches Typing for Kids (www.mindscape.com).

Lugo knew first graders needed repetitive tasks, but these had to be highly motivating. The correct mixture of exploration and structure was required to capitalize on children's natural curiosity while building their skills. Fourth graders could be shown the programs or skills once and then take off on their own, but first graders need continual monitoring and support to learn. Parent helpers in technology would be essential.

Finally, after working nonstop for all of August, Lugo finished her yearlong technology plan. The goal was for students to use technology as a tool for daily learning. Ten objectives defined the skills students would acquire throughout the year; each month was carefully planned to meet the objectives incrementally (see Exhibit D). Lugo agonized over the completed plan: Would it work? Would such young children lacking fine motor skills actually be able to learn keyboarding and use the programs independently? Would they use the computer to represent various aspects of their work as the fourth graders had done so easily? Could she get the needed parent support? Also, Copp, whose vision had launched the new school and who had set the teaming plan in motion, had taken a position as the district curriculum supervisor. In the midst of one of the bigger transitions in her professional life, Lugo could no longer rely on Copp's expertise when problems arose.

ROOM 4: THE FIRST-GRADE LEARNING ENVIRONMENT

Lugo and O'Brien share the first-grade classroom that easily accommodates their 26 students. Seven computer stations are arranged around the perimeter of a 10-foot by 12-foot alcove adjoining the main room. The computers are networked to a printer in the classroom and are also linked to the Internet via the school's wide-area network (WAN). Additional technological resources can be found in both the Media/Library Center and the computer lab. The lab's 15 stations, additional software and CD-ROMs, and full-time instructor make it possible to increase students' access to on-line resources and individualized assistance.

Lugo's students use their classroom computers for most of their work. Parents were kept informed via a bilingual newsletter and phone calls to ensure they understood the rationale behind the extensive computer work. Lugo determined she would need six parents to assist daily in the computer area and recruited volunteers during the second week of school at "Back to School" night. She prefers parents who have relatively few computer skills.

Computer hardware, features, and functions

Computer Hardware	Source of Equipment	Computer Features	Function for Students
2 Macintosh Performas	School district	Color monitor, 16-MB RAM, sound cards, and recording microphone	Create text documents, create graphics, record and play sound
5 Macintosh Performas	Parent donations	Same as above	Same as above
Apple color ink jet printer	School district	Networked color printer	Same as laser printer, but color; can print from any computer
Internet modem connection and LAN	School district	Dial-up Internet access, dedicated phone line for school	Communicate with students in other schools via e-mail

"The best volunteers are those with no experience. I tell parents they need to smile and have lots of patience; that is the initial requirement. It's an opportunity for parents to learn these computing skills, and this keeps them motivated. I keep the parents just a bit ahead of the children, so they can stay confident. Once they realize that they don't have to know everything and that the children often know as much or more than they do about the computers, they're fine. It's a big step for parents."

Karen Hedlund, a computer volunteer, believes she has learned as much as the students about technology.

"We're all learning so much from Vicki," she said. "I was really nervous at first, but now, if I'm stuck helping a child, I just ask if anyone knows how to help . . . we work together . . . the kids are just as responsible for getting the work done as we are. It really makes students proud to solve a problem an adult can't figure out."

Lugo notes the secret to engaging parents lies in the tasks the teacher selects and assigns to volunteers. "Volunteers need a job that matters to the children's learning—then they are committed. I'd love to give them the routine tasks like setting up stations or correcting papers, but that won't keep them coming back, and it certainly won't interest them while they are here."

Ellen Martin, each of whose three children have had Lugo in the past three years, agrees. "I love volunteering," she said. "The time I put in frees up Vicki and Sharon to spend time with the children on new skills and specific problems. I check up on the daily 'Read to Me' assignments, I encourage the children to read, help them sound out words, and work on meaning by pointing out pictures or other contextual clues. If someone is struggling, I report problems to Vicki, so she can work with students one-on-one."

Lugo began the year with basic skills: turning on the computer, keyboarding, and accessing programs. She posted instructions for children and parent volunteers (see Exhibit E). When introducing a new program, she taught it to the children in small groups. With each child seated at a computer, she talked him or her through it, going slowly and checking to make sure all were following. The first graders needed and enjoyed repeated opportunities to try program options such as opening or saving a file. "Learning a new program can take a week of half-hour sessions at the computer," Lugo said, "but after the continuous repetitions and examples, students take over—they rarely forget how to use the programs." Nonetheless, a parent volunteer works in the computer alcove every day to provide whatever assistance the children may need.

Students spend a minimum of 30 minutes each day using a computer to refine silent and oral reading skills as well as writing. Social studies and science CD-ROMs are integrated into the language arts curriculum. Also, on many days during the afternoon math program, O'Brien uses computer programs such as Math Blaster or the Kid Pix "stamps" feature in which students group graphics of plants or animals into exciting patterns and meanwhile develop their observation skills.

Lugo does not play down the challenges of integrating technology. "Computers can be a hassle for a teacher. There are equipment failures and mechanical problems. It can take several minutes to discover that the computer is not working because the plug is loose in the outlet." She emphasizes, though, that the results have justified the additional time. Features of the programs, such as drawing tools, can help students see concepts and develop skills in powerful and creative ways.

"Students are completely engaged, actually doing the work. They read and write and research topics for much longer than I could get them to do without the computers. They like the control and are so proud: especially in first grade—it's *legible*. We have a wall with their written computer work posted. They often arrive early to gaze and point out their own papers and read 'the wall,' which displays others' work."

Teaching with Technology

Lugo claims the technology that is part of her daily lesson plans has been instrumental in formulating her current teaching philosophy.

"The use of the computers has totally changed the way I see my students and how I teach," she said. "I'm guiding them rather than directing. They learn so much on their own. I used to plan out each activity for them, step by step. Now I structure the activity so they can take those steps on their own, find their own way. Students will ask questions—if they know it is okay and expected. It's so much more meaningful, and it shows they are thinking. But it can be risky."

"The key to my new approach is to constantly monitor students. If I see someone staring at the computer, I go over and see if he or she is stuck and needing some attention. The beauty of the individualized instruction the computers provide is that while others are highly engaged, I have time to spend with students one-on-one. For example, I can be freed up to read aloud with one particular child each day rather than the usual twice a week."

The key to Vicki Lugo's approach to integrating technology and literacy activities is to constantly monitor students.

Six of Lugo's 26 students are Spanish-speaking, and some of their families move frequently. Often families with several children share a residence with relatives. According to Lugo, these extended immigrant families tend to be stable, with half of the mothers at home. Others in Lugo's class live in large homes in Solana Beach and have a low percentage of working mothers. Although these upscale families provide many opportunities for their children, parents are often absent, and the children are frequently in the care of nannies. Thus, the majority of these first graders are eager for attention and look to adults at school for consistent structure, encouragement, and motivation. Lugo observed that computers make it possible to teach intensive yet individualized foundational skills that require the active participation of all students.

"I think we're doing too much fluff in the younger grades," Lugo said. "I'm not opposed to fun, but it needs to be purposeful. Students need intensive reading and math work. After all, if they aren't on level for reading, they are going nowhere in this highly competitive district. A teacher can spend 45 minutes cutting out construction paper or writing a worksheet to plan for an experience that only lasts 10 minutes, must be initiated by the teacher, and has questionable learning value for students. On the other hand, a teacher can spend 20 minutes of planning time creating a lesson so that students can read or write independently on the computer for up to 30 minutes with a cognitively challenging language activity."

Lugo believes that developing skill-proficient first-grade learners is her main job. She reflected back to the days when she used a more structured basal approach.

"When I did basal reading programs, we were supposed to teach children 185 skills! At mid-year I checked my records. Were we even close to the 70-some odd skills in which each student was supposed to be proficient? With that system, we were always focused on what kids didn't know, not what they did."

Now Lugo reports that continuous assessment—a key to keeping students moving along the literacy continuum—is a manageable task. The Kid Works program is a vital assessment tool because it keeps a progressive data log of each student's work in an ongoing portfolio (see Exhibit F).

A TYPICAL DAY: GETTING DOWN TO BUSINESS

When Lugo's and O'Brien's first graders come flooding into the classroom at 8:15, Lugo has already been there for an hour supervising the fourth-, fifth-, and sixth-grade Hispanic students. They use her classroom computers for the federally funded math/science computer enrichment program she administers for the school.

Each day begins with the same routine, which Lugo believes is essential to good management. Students put their belongings in their cubby slots, exchange their "Read to Me" book (taken home every night to read with their parents) for the new take-home book, and sit down at their assigned round tables to review the day's activity plan. Although the content changes, students rotate daily through the following six areas:

• Journal or free write
• Desk Work: brainstorming or group critiques
• Silent reading
• Read aloud to a parent volunteer to check comprehension of the previous night's "Read to Me"
• Spelling work
• Computer work

Beginning at 8:45, groups composed of various skill levels rotate through the stations in half-hour intervals until the 10:30 recess. Following recess, the rotations then continue from 11:00 to 12:30. During this time students meet with O'Brien for Reading Recovery,[1] or they work individually with Lugo as needed. Each day, Lugo systematically assesses progress by kid watching and keeping anecdotal records as they work alone or in groups.

As students in the computer rotation take their seats in the alcove, Lugo and a parent volunteer check the students' handwritten materials for typing into the computer. Instructions for the day's work are briefly clarified and students begin. For example, during the first month of school, students worked on their first computer assignment, a self-portrait. First they filled in the blanks on a hard-copy handout: "My name is _____ ; I like to _____ ." They then typed this into the computer with hands placed correctly on the keyboard. Finally, students used the draw program to sketch a self-portrait. As the year progresses, the assignments become more cognitively challenging. Student progress is assessed using the Accelerating Literacy Model (see Exhibit C).

---

[1] Fifty percent of the Reading Recovery students are Spanish speakers who receive instruction in alphabet recognition and sight words.

In this classroom, technology helps to solve motivation problems associated with practical aspects of literacy achievement. Lugo uses the classroom computers to combine the needed skill repetitions, which otherwise could become tedious or boring, with tasks that maintain students' interest. The kids can use color graphics or variable font sizes to keep their focus on words and meaning. "They love it," Lugo reports. "Students can type the word BIG then increase the font size so that BIG appears on the screen." Additional computer time can be highly motivating for students with specific needs.

For example, one ESL student, Emmelyne, had severe inattention and low literacy skills. Additionally, she did not qualify for Reading Recovery because her skills were just slightly higher than the cutoff. As soon as Lugo observed that she was beginning to match pictures to initial sounds and catching on to the rereading strategy, Emmelyne was rewarded with additional computer time to add clip-art pictures to her writing (see Exhibit F). Motivated to practice, Emmelyne's incentive to write words that matched the illustrations she'd inserted had a significant effect. Lugo recorded a marked increase in her vocabulary on her Accelerating Literacy Reading Portfolio.

Uriel, a shy Hispanic boy who spoke virtually no English initially, worked with O'Brien each day in Reading Recovery. He had trouble remembering vocabulary, and his writing skills were poor. Uriel worked for long periods of time on modeled writing prompts such as fill-in-the-blank stories. Lugo's anecdotal records showed that Uriel remembered vocabulary from the modeled writing prompts he'd put on the computer (see Exhibit F), and he was given additional time in the alcove. The on-screen display seemed to provide the reinforcement he needed to visualize sentence patterns and remember words in context. Lugo and parent volunteers coordinated their efforts to closely monitor and reinforce his vocabulary and comprehension skills.

Emmelyne shows her enthusiasm for using the computer to illustrate her writing.

Matt, an advanced reader, seemed to be able to read any material he was given. Placed immediately in the most accelerated of the six reading groups, he remained there throughout the year. However, Lugo observed two issues concerning Matt's skills: (1) he lacked creativity and had difficulty comprehending and summarizing all he had read; (2) he often became bored and constantly needed new, stimulating work to stay engaged. Using a program called Storybook Weaver (www.broderbund.com), Lugo was able to spark Matt's creativity. The program uses dramatic graphic backgrounds and an assortment of fantasy characters that can be cut and pasted together to form creative story lines. To keep Matt engaged, Lugo assigned him additional computer work related to a language arts–math project. He used the database program in Kid Works to compile the statistics on students' favorite foods as part of a unit on data collection, description, and representation (see Exhibit F). By the end of the year, Emmelyne, Uriel, and Matt were at grade level for all skills. Lugo noted how these very different students thrived: "The technology enabled me to use multiple paths to literacy for getting through to these kids—each with a very different problem." Though she felt confident that Matt and Emmelyne would be successful in second grade, she worried Uriel might backslide without constant follow-up and support.

These students' successes demonstrate Lugo's belief that it is critical to teach to students' individual learning styles and to provide computer materials that allow them to explore their linguistic, mathematical, or artistic talents.

"At the computer, each child can manipulate text, play with shapes and draw pictures, select illustrations, or listen to sounds that heighten their attention to language forms and vocabulary. It is an intense experience that goes hand in hand with the other immersion activities that are part of my approach. Students have to *think* about writing, reading, and hearing language, and with the computer it's easy, fun, and they can show what they know."

TECHOSAURUS

By May, Emmelyne, Uriel, Matt, and the other first graders had completed all the work assigned for the year. As a reward, students could request a topic of their choice. They chose dinosaurs. Lugo's four-week unit served as a capstone for the year's literacy and technology work. The room decorations and displays were changed. The wall-mounted papier-mâché tide pool from a previous unit was transformed into a prehistoric landscape, and dinosaurs appeared amidst the crepe paper vegetation.

The dinosaur unit used all the language arts activities and regular stations with which the students had become so familiar. The children learned about dinosaur characteristics, their ecosystems, and their habitats through dinosaur sticker stories and free writes on dinosaur facts. They learned songs and poems about dinosaurs, made a class mural showing the three periods of dinosaurs, and used an interactive CD-ROM program "Learning about Dinosaurs."

The culminating activity of the Dinosaur Unit required students to invent a dinosaur and list its characteristics, the period in which it lived, and its environment—including food sources and natural predators. Using the draw tools in Kid Works, students sketched the imaginary dinosaur and its habitat and then transferred the project to the Kid Pix program, where it could be presented as a slide show.

Lugo confessed her amazement at the children's progress and ability to produce the illustrated texts on the computer. "I have friends who can't yet use the word processing and draw programs to accomplish what these six- and seven-year-olds have done," she said. "We have to check continually to make sure they are using correct keyboarding, but essentially there were no skills planned that they did not learn. And they have been so creative!"

High expectations were the critical element. Lugo believes that if she and O'Brien had limited the possibilities for students or not insisted they read, write, and use the computers daily, the students' achievements would have been quite different.

A COLLEGIAL DILEMMA

Lugo and O'Brien began debriefing on the year's experiment in mid-May. Although both felt an enormous sense of achievement and professional growth, each had a serious concern. Lugo was worried about the continuity of instruction for the first graders. Could next year's instructors maintain the technological skills her students had acquired? The second-grade teachers were using computers but not at the intense level of integration students had come to expect in her class. She had insisted, for example, on combining keyboarding skills with simple narrative coherence. Would both these essential skills continue to improve, or would they languish or disappear with a lack of practice and technology integration? How could she bring up this touchy subject with colleagues?

O'Brien was concerned about the following year when, according to the deal they'd struck with Marge Copp, she and Lugo would reverse roles. Lugo would handle the Reading Recovery in the morning, and O'Brien would provide the technology integration for the literacy immersion program. Could she maintain Lugo's high academic standards? Could she get up to speed with the computers? Even though she had adequate computing skills, she believed Lugo's were far superior—especially in the seamless way she managed instructional computing. Lugo was so cool with mechanical problems; she never seemed to get rattled. O'Brien planned to spend the summer polishing her skills and practicing technology lessons, but she still worried that her lack of confidence would hinder students' technological foundations.

Also, a new principal, Julie Burke, was due to arrive in August. The landscape had changed. Burke was perceived as supportive of teachers and very involved with students, but by her own admission, she didn't have the technology expertise of her predecessor, Marge Copp.

REFERENCES AND SELECTED BIBLIOGRAPHY

AskERIC Virtual Library. http://ericir.syreduc/Virtual. One of the leading Web site repositories of lesson plans on the Internet, contributed by teachers.

Balajthy, E. (1991, February). Keyboarding, language arts, and the elementary school child. *The Computing Teacher,* 40–43.

Banks, J. A., & Banks, C. A. (1991). *Handbook of research on multicultural education.* New York: Macmillan.

Blair, T. R., & Jones, D. L. (1998). *Preparing student teachers for pluralistic classrooms.* Boston: Allyn & Bacon.

Buckleitner, W. (Ed.). (1998, Winter). *The elementary teacher's sourcebook of children's software* (Vol. 4, p. 31). Patterson, NJ: Active Learning Associates. (In this piece, Dr. Olsen, a research scientist at SRI International, does not recommend keyboarding to be formally introduced until third grade.)

Cochran-Smith, M. (1991). Writing processing and writing in elementary classrooms: A critical review of related literature. *Review of Educational Research, 61*(1), 107–119.

Collaborative Ideas Web site. http://www.k12.wv.us/wschool/html/lesson/collab.htm. This Web site provides a list of online projects in which your students can participate.

Cuban, L. (1986). *Teachers and machines: The classroom use of technology since the 1920s.* New York: Teachers College Press.

Delpit, L. (1995). *Other people's children: Cultural conflict in the classroom.* New York: New Press. Distributed by W.W. Norton.

Robyler, M. D., & Edwards, J. (2000). *Integrating educational technology into teaching.* Upper Saddle River, NJ: Merrill/Prentice Hall.

Rancho Santa Fe Web site. www.sbsd.sdcoe.k12.ca.us.

Tatum, B. (1997). *"Why are all the Black children sitting together in the cafeteria?" and other conversations on race.* New York: Basic Books.

E X H I B I T   A

Key Pals Project

Vicki Lugo used the Key Pals project in the fourth grade for reading critiques and exchanges. First-grade students used the Key Pal project in this exhibit to collect data for Matt's database project (see Exhibit F). Note in week five (5) instructions to use the "Advanced or Super User" levels refer to the "At East" security and management system used at SSF.

Class _____

Your Name _____

Key Pal's Name _____

Week 1: Sending a message

- Find your **mailbox.**
- Enter your **password.**
- Put your key pal's name in the **subject bar.**
- **Address** your message. (Whose class are you sending it to?)
- Type in the following information:

Hi,
My name is _____ . My favorite color is _____ .
I am _____ years old.
From,
_____ (type your name)

- **Send** your message.

Week 2: Reading a received message and sending a reply

- Find your **mailbox.**
- Enter your **password.**
- Find your name and click twice on the paper **icon** to open your mail.
- Read your message.
- Click on **Reply.**
- Select **Memo.**

- Type in the following information:
  Dear (*key pal's name*).
  My *favorite food is* _____ . My *birthday is* _____ (Date).
  _____ (*Type your name*)
- **Send** your message.

Week 3: Receiving a message/Closing/Starting a new message/Zap Shot picture

- Find your **mailbox.**
- Enter your **password.**
- Find your name and open your mail.
- Read your message.
- Close the message window.
- Select New.
- Put your key pal's name in the **subject bar.**
- **Address** your message.
- Type a message of your choice to your pal.
- **Send** the message.

Week 4: Using the info

Database: How to sort (rank) the information

The following info can be determined for each of the participating classes or just the "home" class. The info has been defined by class so that it can be used for additional projects if desired.

Class _____

What was the favorite color? _____ (#?) _____

What was the favorite food? _____ (#?) _____

What month has the most birthdays in it? _____ (#?) _____

What is the most common age? _____ (#?) _____

Week 5: Viewing our key pal pictures

- Have computers at Advanced or Super User level so the desktop is available.
- Gain access to the appropriate **server** for the home base of the key pal.
- Double click on the Server icon to open the menu.
- Go to the Zap Shot folder where photos are stored.
- Open the folder for your key pal's class.
- Double click on the photo **icon** and "Meet your Pal."

Week 6: Using the info (Continued)

Option 1: Pictographs

Using a draw program, students can create columns and then stamp in appropriate visual responses to the data. They will have to determine the names of the columns and what they are trying to demonstrate. This can be very structured or open-ended depending on the class and the amount of "charting" experience they already have. See the following example.

Favorite colors in Vicki Lugo's class

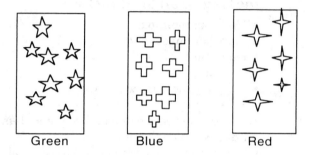

Green   Blue   Red

Option 2: Venn Diagram

A Venn diagram can be used to show which students have things in common. Each student should have a blank Venn diagram chart, a class list, access to the database, and a pair of scissors. Looking at the data, the students can place the information in the appropriate space. See page 32 for student example of Venn Diagram.

E X H I B I T   B

Parental Permission Form for School Internet Use

Solana Santa Fe, like most schools, requires parental permission for any student use of the Internet. The following form was developed to address concerns about the appropriateness of materials used and supervision of students using the Internet.[1]

Solana Beach School District
Acceptable Use of Internet and Information Systems Contract

We are pleased to offer students, faculty, and staff of Solana Beach School District access to the district computer network for electronic mail, the Internet and other information systems. This access is limited and is subject to District policies, rules, regulations, and restrictions, as they may be adopted and amended from time to time. This use is also subject to all applicable laws.

No student will be granted access without written consent of the student's parent or guardian. That consent can only be given by signing and returning this contract to the District. PLEASE READ THIS DOCUMENT CAREFULLY BECAUSE IT WILL BE A BINDING CONTRACT WHEN SIGNED.

Access to these resources through the district is a privilege, not a right. Notwithstanding any provision in this contract, the district may revoke access at any time by giving written notice to the parent or guardian.

When using the District's computer network, the student's behavior can affect the other students as well as the employees of the District and the public. A student's activities while using the network must be in support of education and research, and consistent with the educational objectives and the rules and regulations of the District. In addition, a student accessing the Internet and other information systems, using District network equipment and facilities, is responsible for all on-line activities which take place as a result of the student's access. No access is permitted without the permission of and the general supervision of an employee of the District. IMPROPER USE OF THE NETWORK WILL RESULT IN THE CANCELLATION OF THE STUDENT'S ACCESS PRIVILEGES AND REVOCATION OF PERMISSION TO USE THE NETWORK, AS WELL AS DISCIPLINARY ACTION BY SCHOOL OFFICIALS.

What is improper use is defined in district rules and regulations, which may be amended from time to time. By the way of example and illustration only, the following is a list of some of the uses which are unacceptable:

- using impolite, abusive, offensive, or otherwise objectionable language in either public or private messages;
- using the Internet or other resources for sending or retrieving confidential, illegal, obscene, or other material unrelated to the educational objective for which access is granted;
- placing on the Internet or other information systems material which is confidential, illegal, obscene, or unrelated to the educational objective for which access is granted;
- sending, receiving, copying, or changing copyrighted materials without first obtaining all required permission;
- knowingly or negligently allowing any other person to obtain the student's password;
- using another person's password;
- damaging, destroying, removing, copying, or abusing any district equipment, including but not limited to computers, modems, printers, and software.

Retain Top Portion for Your Information

Return Bottom Portion to Your Child's School
Parent/Guardian's Agreement

As the parent or guardian of the student identified below, I have read and carefully considered this Contract. I have also had a full opportunity to discuss this matter with school officials and to familiarize myself with the nature and content of the Internet and other information systems available through the District network system. I understand that employees of the District may not always be able to prevent and restrict access to controversial and sensitive materials on the Internet and other information systems.

I give my consent to the District granting this access to my child. I release the District and its employees from any responsibility or liability resulting in any way from my child's use of this access privilege or based on any materials the student acquired or sees as a result of access by the student or others. I also agree to accept full responsibility for supervision and control of my child if and when my child has access to the Internet or any other information system without using any District network system or equipment. I understand that the District and its employees have no relationship to such nonschool use. I understand that I can revoke this consent only by written notice, delivered to the school administration. I understand that the District also can revoke this access at any time, upon notice to me.

Parent/Guardian   _____ **Date** _____

_____   No—I will not permit my child to use Internet services.

Student's Agreement

I understand and agree to abide by the principles and guidelines of this contract.

Student's Name (please print)   _____

Student's Signature   _____   **Date**   _____

Teacher's Name   _____

E X H I B I T   C

General Description of the
Accelerating Literacy Model

A sample student record for developmental reading stages is shown in this exhibit. Lugo uses the comments section and additional sheets to record anecdotal records on literacy progress. In first grade she is evaluating from Stage early 0 through Stage 3.

Accelerating Literacy
Kindergarten through Sixth
Walker Enterprises
650 Columbia St. #415
San Diego, CA 92101 (619) 237 9836
(888) 253-5450 Fax: (619) 236 9576
www.literacy-for-all.com
Evaluator: Dr. Rena Walker

General Description

The *Accelerating Literacy* (AL) Model provides teachers with the base of knowledge they need to teach reading and writing preschool through sixth grade. The AL Model meets the needs of all students, including those who are bilingual, considered to be at-risk, gifted, or have special needs. Data collection procedures, data analysis, instruction, critical thinking, assessment benchmarks, and students' literacy development are articulated across the grades. *Accelerating Literacy* emphasizes balance in three areas: Curriculum (math, social studies, literature, science); literacy (read-aloud, shared reading, guided process reading, silent sustained reading, modeled writing, and guided process writing); and processing (using semantics, syntax and graphophonics to construct meaning). *Accelerating Literacy* presents the necessary components of balanced instruction to demonstrate how district grade-level text, literature, trade books, and the basal readers are put together to form a cohesive instructional PK–6th grade program. The AL staff development model has three components—training, implementation, and coaching. These pieces work together and provide students with effective, consistent instruction.

In Brief

Accelerating Literacy, a preschool through sixth-grade literacy model, was developed by Rena M. Walker. Introduced in southern California in 1990, AL has been successfully used in more than 1,000 schools to date.

Goals

The model assists teachers in establishing benchmark standards, identifying student's needs, establishing consistent instructional expectations, assessment procedures, and monitoring students' achievement across the grades. An increase in teachers' effectiveness and efficiency of instruction is evidenced within a few months of implementation. The model has been found to be effective in all types of schools, including Title I, in urban and rural settings. Participation of parents is recommended and explained through Reading Clubs and Read-to-Me Programs. Data analysis computer software is provided. Schools utilize their grade-level text and books/stories found in basal series, literature, and trade book collections.

Results

Students' achievement gains have been documented by participating schools. A self-monitoring system is presented in AL to provide teachers with easy access to pertinent data so they can make instructional adjustments and revisions. Teachers and administrators have consistently reported that students are more actively engaged in processing print and more motivated to read and write. Teachers improve their decision-making through analyses of student data. The initial step, analyzing and collecting baseline data, is presented in the AL Model as follows: Kindergarten and first grade students are assessed on print awareness, and listening/speaking development. Students are then staged developmentally in reading, writing, listening, and speaking. Second through sixth grade students are initially placed in reading through information gained from oral reading records and comprehension assessments. A Reading Class Profile Sheet for each class is developed (computer assisted) and used by the teacher to plan effective instruction in guided reading and components essential to balanced instruction. Each student's data is placed on reading and writing portfolios and used in parent, administrator, and teacher conferences.

E X H I B I T   D

Lugo's First-Grade Technology Plan

Lugo's yearlong technology plan shows the progression of technology skills, beginning with keyboarding basics and progressing through the use of more complex programs. Students are assigned to computers and learn the basics of navigating and inputting information using Kid Works during the first two months. Additional tools and resources are then added. There are tools for generating texts and representations of information (such as Storybook Weaver and draw programs) as well as content CD-ROMs (such as the Rain Forest CD).

Technology Plan for Vicki Lugo, First Grade, SSF

Goal

Students will use technology daily, as a tool for learning.

Objectives

1. Students will have the ability to use all fingers when typing.
2. Students will gain a knowledge of draw programs, Kid Pix and Kid Works.
3. Students will be able to manipulate font, size, and location of printed text.
4. Students will be able to write sentences and stories on Kid Works and then illustrate them. They will be able to change fonts and print their work.
5. Students will be able to use Super Print to make cards or posters.
6. Students will be able to write a story with a beginning, middle, and end on Storybook Weaver.
7. Students will be able to enjoy a Discis Book on CD-ROM.
8. Students will be able to manipulate an informational CD-ROM.
9. Students will continually work on Reading Maze (a phonics program), Word Munchers, and Jack and the Beanstalk.
10. Students will be exposed to and use two or three math software programs.

September

- Begin drawing programs.
- Begin writing.
- Begin keyboarding.

Activities

I. Assign students to computers.
II. Teach how to turn on and how to use At Ease.
III. Teach how to get into Kid Pix (this was learned in kindergarten) Free Exploration.
IV. Teach Kid Works (see instructions, Exhibit E).
   The students write:
   My name is _____ .
   I like to _____ .
   Then the student does a self-portrait.

October

- Begin keyboarding on Kids Keys.
- Begin word processing; teach how to change fonts so that students begin to recognize letters written different ways.
- Continue drawing.

Activities

I. Frame sentences: *A jack-o'-lantern is* _____ .
II. Frame story: *This is a bat. A bat has* _____ . *A bat has* _____ . *A bat can*
   _____ . *A bat can* _____ .
III. Halloween poetry
   _____ *here,*
   _____ *there,*
   _____ , _____ ,
   everywhere.

December

- Introduce Super Print.
- Continue with keyboarding.
- Introduce Word Munchers.

Activities

I. December is . . . (done in Kid Works and illustrated).
   December is a time for

   _____ ,
   _____ ,
   _____ ,
   and _____ .
II. Students will make a Hanukkah or Christmas card using Super Print.

January

- Keyboarding for five minutes at the beginning of each computer session.
- Introduce Jack and the Beanstalk story writing in small groups.

- Introduce Storybook Weaver.
- Introduce Math Blaster—math.

Activities

I. Resolutions for the New Year (the last words of the second and last lines rhyme)
It's 2001
La, la _____ ,
This is the year I'll
_____ !

II. Winter stories (poem done in Kid Works and illustrated)
Winter is when . . .
_____ are _____ ,
_____ are _____ ,
_____ are _____ ,
and _____ are _____ .

III. Descriptive writing, "My Snowman," with illustration

February

- Continue with keyboarding, Reading Maze, Word Munchers.
- Emphasize Storybook Weaver so that the students really begin writing stories on their own.
- Begin e-mail Key Pals; work with this in the lab and in the class.
  - Use the Internet with the rain forest study.
  - Math word problems on Kid Works.

Activities

I. Storybook Weaver stories.
II. Have students type stories from their journals in Kid Works.
III. Students make Valentine's Day cards for their parents in Super Print.

March

- Story Writing.
- Continue with Key Pals, Reading Maze, Jack and the Beanstalk, and keyboarding.

Activities

I. Rain forest stories on Storybook Weaver

II. Rain forest animal stories
A _____ lives in the rain forest. (Then the student writes three sentences about the animal of choice.)

III. Database work in the lab

April

- Let students have more free choice about using the computer.
- Emphasize the use of Storybook Weaver for writing software.
- Continue with keyboarding, Reading Maze, and writing software.
- Introduce Thinker Things—math.

Activities

I. Spring vacation story writing. Given the topic sentence, *"During Spring vacation I did many things,"* the students add three to four sentences and end with *"I had a fun vacation."* (These are not illustrated but printed on pastel-colored paper.)
II. Storybook Weaver stories about the ocean.
III. Tide pool animal stories—each student writes a story about the tide pool animal of choice. These are illustrated and done in Kid Works.

May

- Keyboarding, Storybook Weaver, and Jack in the Beanstalk.
- CD-ROM used for information on dinosaurs.
- Introduce Learn About Dinosaurs.
- Introduce Count Down—math.

Activities

I. Acrostic Poem—each student chooses an ocean word to go with each letter of his or her name.
II. Dinosaur stories; description and illustration of an invented dinosaur.
III. Father's Day cards in Super Print.
IV. Label dinosaur pictures on Learn About Dinosaurs.

June

- Free choice.
- Practice using Kid Works and printing independently so students can be tutors next year.
- Use Kid Pix to produce a slide show of the creative writing dinosaur descriptions.

E X H I B I T   E

Kid Works Instructions

Lugo spends several weeks teaching an integrated software package to first graders and parent volunteers. Her technique is to show students in a step-by-step fashion, constantly monitoring their understanding and performance. Instructions are displayed at all times by each computer station for reinforcement of skills and to assist volunteers as they subsequently work with students. Notice that in addition to the technical skills, literacy development such as listening to the story is also included.

1. Sign in.
2. Select Story Writer, write your story, and save.
3. Select Go, highlight Story Illustrator, draw, and save.
4. Select Go, highlight Story Writer, select open, and highlight the story you want to print.
5. Read your story.
6. Put the cursor at the beginning of the story and choose your picture from the picture box at the bottom of the screen.
7. Select Go, highlight Story Player.
8. Listen to your story and then print if it sounds right. If not, you need to fix it; go back to the Story Writer to edit your story. Then go to step 7.

E X H I B I T   F

Samples of Student Work

Samples of student writing and representational work using computer tools are as follows:

1. Emmelyne's patterned writing poem "December is a Time for . . ."
2. Uriel's acrostic (also called a name poem) using ocean words to match the letters of his name.
3. Matt's database of favorite foods for Lugo's class with three representations of the data (the numeric data sheet, a Kids Stamps diagram, and a Venn diagram generated using the Kid Works word processing and draw program).

Emmelyne's illustrated December poem.

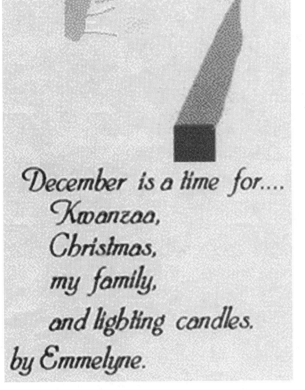

December is a time for....
Kwanzaa,
Christmas,
my family,
and lighting candles.
by Emmelyne.

Uriel's acrostic (name poem).

Urchin   Rock
Ray   Octapus
Isopod   Jelly
Eel   Abalone
Limpet   Shark

URIEL   ROJAS

nu	Class Lu	Lugo Birth M	Class Lugo Fav (	Lugo Age	Lugo Favorite Fo	Class Hayes
01	Elyse	July 4th	green	6	Pizza	Megan
02	Brianna	Nov. 6th	green	7	Pizza	Lexi
03	San	March 15th	green	7	Pizza	Justine
04	Alexandra	Sept.	Pink	6	Pizza	Jaclyn
05	Jena	Feb 8th	blue	7	Pizza	Alexa
06	Brooke	Feb 17.	blue	7	Pizza	Karli
06t	Brooke	- -	- -	- -	- -	Seung Yeon
07	Ilana	March 20th	blue	6	Pizza	Allie
07t	Krysta		Blue	6	Pizza	Blaire
08	Chantal	Aug. 14th	blue	6	Pizza	Kenzie
09	Emmelyne	Sept. 11	pink	6	Pizza	Katie
10	Charles	March	red	7	Spaghetti	Kelli
11	Edgar	Dec.	green	7	Oranges	Vincent
12	Timothy	Feb 24	green	7	Macaroni & Cheese	Jerrud
13	Makoto	Nov. 17	green	6	Watermelon	Spencer
14	Tyler	Feb 21	red	7	Chicken Noodle Soup	Christopher
15	Garrett	June 27	blue	7	Pizza	Nathan
15t	Garrett	- -	-	- -	- -	Brandon
16	Stephen	June 19th	red	6	Pizza	James D
17	Uriel	April 19	white	6	Pizza	Eric
18	Casey	Sept. 6	green	6	Pizza	Tyler
19	Christophe	April 5th	green	6	Pizza	Alex
20	Rafael	April 12th	Red	6	Strawberries	Graeme
21	Matthew	May 19th	Red	6	Pizza	Kenneth
21t	Matthew	- -	- -	- -	- -	James R.

Database for Lugo's class.

Matt's chart of the
"favorite foods" data.

Matt's Venn diagram of the
most common class
responses.

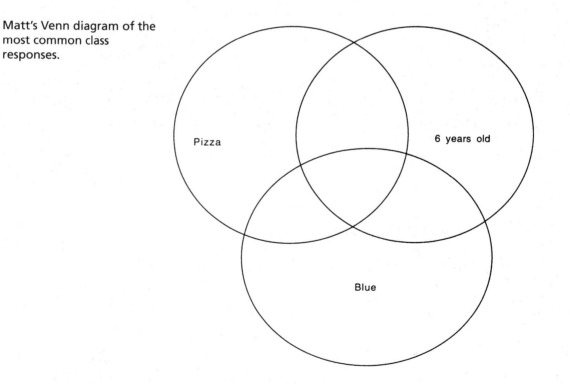

DISCUSSION QUESTIONS

1. What is Vicki Lugo's philosophy of teaching?
    *   How did her philosophy evolve from her own educational experience?
    *   How is technology integral to her philosophy?
    *   How might her approach be translated into other subject areas?
    *   How might her philosophy be limiting for diverse learners? For example, is the notion of independent learning (rather than collaborative learning) culturally dependent?
    *   How might a teacher with a different philosophy (less holistic) utilize the strengths of this approach to teaching literacy?
    *   How might a constructivist teacher critique Vicki's philosophy and curriculum?

2. Lugo notes that learning to use computers can be time-consuming and mechanical difficulties can cause classroom implementation problems.
    *   Give examples from the case that illustrate these two potential problems.
    *   Might there be a positive side to occasional mechanical problems? What might children learn from mastering technical problems themselves or observing their teachers do so?
    *   How realistic is it to expect teachers to continually upgrade their technology skills? With other demands on their time, which demands should take priority and why?

3. Lugo notes that one particularly strong argument for using computers in first grade is to enhance the legibility of children's handwriting.
    *   What are the advantages and disadvantages of using computers to address this problem?
    *   Consider children's fine-motor development, for example. How might the use of computers delay or enhance the development of fine-motor skills?
    *   What essential skill is being highly developed without the limitations of manuscript printing? How might such skill development be important in more holistic instruction?

4. Lugo notes that teaming is a key factor in her success. She works with O'Brien and Golden and also includes parents in her "classroom instructional team."
    *   What are the advantages and disadvantages of this strategy? How does this approach relate to valuing diversity? Explain.
    *   How might a teacher who does not have the extensive parental and professional resources achieve similar technology/literacy integration to support instructional goals?
    *   Discuss the pros and cons of the Lugo–O'Brien team.

- Given the success of the current arrangement, should the plan for next year be modified so that the teachers don't switch roles? Weigh the apparent benefits of their professional development versus the children's apparent best interest.

5. Parental involvement is emphasized at SSF and in Lugo's classroom.

   - Discuss the advantages and disadvantages of such extensive parental involvement.

   - In Lugo's classroom, parents participate primarily in support roles. What might be advantages and disadvantages of involving parents in the planning as well?

   - Does the policy of promoting diversity and parental involvement differ from the actual practice as in SSF? In Lugo's classroom?

6. Determine whether Lugo's use of technology is developmentally appropriate.

   - How is *developmental appropriateness* defined at the early childhood level?

   - In what ways did Lugo use technology to promote the following, and how developmentally appropriate were they:

     - children's learning of information
     - children's exploration and discovery
     - children's learning of concepts
     - children's social interaction
     - What other ways might she have used technology to enhance these areas?

   - How might Lugo use computer technology to affirm the language backgrounds and cultures of nonnative English-speaking children?

7. Consider Lugo's curriculum in general.

   - How justified is her emphasis on language arts? Take into account factors such as the children's grade level, socioeconomic backgrounds, and linguistic backgrounds.

   - What other areas of the curriculum might she be sacrificing, and what potential losses exist for the children?

   - Consider Lugo's emphasis on skill development. To what extent is her approach appropriate given children's varied developmental and instructional needs? Give evidence from the case to support your position.

8. Lugo is concerned about the second-grade teachers' use and integration of technology into the curriculum.

   - In traditional areas such as mathematics, reading, and social studies, teachers carefully consider the scope and sequence of the curriculum. Should there be a scope and sequence in technology education? Explain why or why not, and if so, how might this be implemented?

   - How might Lugo address her concerns with the teaching staff? What are the politics of such a situation?

9. Lugo and O'Brien emphasize the building of individualized literacy skills. By the end of the case, all of their students have met the grade-level requirements. To what extent can their success in promoting literacy be attributed to their use of technology as opposed to other aspects of their program such as Reading Recovery or extensive parental involvement?

10. Assess if Lugo's (and SSF's) approach of assimilation (for example, replacing Spanish language strengths with English immersion) rather than acculturation (for example, using Spanish language strengths to learn English concepts) presents limitations for diverse learners such as bilingual students or ESL students?

11. Assess the various avenues that Lugo and the school provided for diverse populations. Do these opportunities adequately meet the needs of the student body?

CASE 1

Discussion Question	Corresponding INTASC Principle
4,5	**10** The teacher fosters relationships with school colleagues, parents, and agencies in the larger community to support learning and well-being.
6	**2** The teacher understands how children learn and develop, and can provide learning opportunities that support their intellectual, social, and personal development.
6	**3** The teacher understands how students differ in their approaches to learning and creates instructional opportunities that are adapted to diverse learners.
7	**5** The teacher uses an understanding of individual and group motivation and behavior to create a learning environment that encourages positive social interaction, active engagement in learning, and self-motivation.
7	**6** The teacher uses knowledge of effective verbal, nonverbal, and media communication techniques to foster active inquiry, collaboration, and supportive instruction in the classroom.
7,8	**4** The teacher understands and uses a variety of instructional strategies to encourage students' development of critical thinking, problem solving, and performance skills.

Stagnant Pools and Flowing Waters

THE SQUEAKY WHEEL GETS GREASED

While monitoring the groups' projects in our primary classroom, I caught Gretchyn's eye as we watched Shellie wait for the others in her math group to finish a math project. She rested her chin on her hands and watched David, who was attempting to add 4 + 4.

"O.K., I've got four in my head," he said haltingly as he raised his hand before him, "and I put four fingers up—one, two, three, four . . . four! 4 + 4 equals four!"

With a sigh, Shellie agreed to help David, who was still stuck at the beginning of the project. Her math story problem adding 8 + 8 was written, drawn, and already colored as was Teresa's. Teresa looked at Shellie and shrugged, "I know what you mean."

Shellie's experience was of particular interest to us, since we had recently overheard another group member, Chelsea, stomp her foot and exclaim, "All we do is unfix cubes and bears!"

The girls' comments stuck with us—and uncomfortably so. We had recently moved two boys, Robbie and Tommy, from a "Younger" ("Y") group to the "Older" ("O"), more advanced group for a variety of reasons, including their discontent with the rate of group progress. We were becoming increasingly uneasy with the idea that we may have shown favoritism to the two boys and overlooked the needs of the three girls. For the most part, Shellie, Teresa, and Chelsea sat politely and participated at the appropriate times in the "Y" group, while the two boys, when they finished their work early, would huff or announce loudly that they needed something else to do. Moreover, the three girls were effective partners for the students who did not catch on quickly. After considering the issue, we realized that it was not in the girls' best interest to move them up to the "O" group. Although they were indeed too advanced for the "Y" group, they did not yet have the skill level of the "O" group. The underlying problem of stagnant groups in math was too big an issue to tackle in mid-year . . .

Her math story written, drawn, and colored, Shellie waits in frustration as the boys in her group work through their problems.

THE SCHOOL

Our school, Southside Primary, was built nearly 30 years ago. It stands alone—some might say isolated—in a historic section of Shelbyville, Kentucky, just across the tracks and about two blocks from downtown. Like the other two city schools, the facility reflects its age. Attempts to update the building's appearance have been minimal, focusing on the outward appearance (repainting or retiling, for example) rather than on basic structural needs. Individual classrooms are not only small but also noisy because of the lack of sound barriers such as tile ceilings or carpeting. The one structural change supporting statewide reform has been the installation of doors between classrooms: this promotes a cooperative atmosphere between children and teachers.

Visitors to Southside usually describe the school as inviting and child-oriented. The walls are covered with vivid student-made projects, writings, and graphs, adding warmth and vitality to each hallway. Most classroom doors are open, and the halls buzz with children's voices. Parent volunteers can be seen in the hallways with small groups of children, in the classrooms reading or writing with an individual child, or in the resource room preparing materials for the teachers. There is very little turnover among our colleagues at Southside. While some have been here as few as four years, a number of others have taught exclusively at Southside for almost 30 years.

During the first year of its inception, the School-Based Decision Making (SBDM) council voted to adopt the multiage classroom model for Southside. This model, originally mandated in Kentucky, consisted of grouping first through third grades together. Two years later, the council voted to change the name of Southside Elementary School to Southside Primary School, reflecting its commitment to multiage classrooms.

Because the principal has instilled a sense of professional freedom in the faculty, teachers eagerly experiment with new ideas. However, despite their interest in innovation, most faculty members were not enthusiastic at first about grouping these grades together for the primary program. Some teachers were determined to stay within the one-grade setting, while others were willing to try two ages together but not three. Despite this initial reluctance, however, each team has worked hard to make the program succeed within the classroom family concept. Because teachers were allowed to choose their own partners for team teaching, a genuine sense of colleagueship began to emerge. Gradually the entire faculty became more team-oriented, spending time together and sharing anecdotes that highlighted concerns and celebrated successes.

THE CLASSROOM

Before Gretchyn and I became team partners, our classroom had been used as two special education classrooms. As soon as we learned that we would be together in a primary classroom, we petitioned the SBDM to remove the wall between the two rooms to create one large primary classroom. Once the wall was removed, other problems with the aging room, such as pipes protruding from the ceiling, presented an opportunity for testing our creativity. One solution was to hang short paper streamers of all colors from the pipes, which made the basement-like atmosphere of the room more festive and inviting.

Because flexible grouping is such a vital component of the primary classroom, the room is currently arranged to facilitate many different groups to meet in a variety of situations. Two area carpets help divide the open space. An immense blue carpet is positioned on the right side of the room. Four horizontal red stripes help guide as many as 45 children to find space to sit. Rarely, however, do we have a common lesson with all our students together—we found that children at these ages have a difficult time being attentive in such a large group. In front of the blue carpet is an imposing bulletin board with the words "Workshop Wizards" posted brightly at the top. The board guides and organizes us as well as our students through the many workshops scheduled each day. Under each workshop heading are invitations to mini-lessons, individual conference schedules, and other pertinent information.

In the far left corner of the room a smaller red carpet provides space for at least 25 children to gather. The red and blue carpets are the cornerstones of our room, because they allow us to teach all students simultaneously. The red and blue carpets have other functions as well. The red carpet serves as the class library; the blue carpet, bordered at one side by a sturdy wooden loft painted bright green and yellow, is a part of the Theater Center. The loft resembles an oversize bunk bed with a comfortable mattress where the children can curl up to read and write. The bottom of the structure serves as the theater. In the other corners of the room are the art, discovery, and technology centers (see Exhibit A).

Our classroom arrangements create a physical space where students can organize their time, work on their own interests, and move in and out of activities while being easily monitored by and immediately accessible to us at all times.

THE STUDENTS

"Diversified" describes the mix of children in our classroom. The children represent a range of ages, backgrounds, and abilities. Twenty percent of the students are African American.

The students range in age from five to ten throughout the course of the year. Depending on birthdays, some five-year-olds spend half of the day in our primary classroom after being in a traditional kindergarten classroom in the morning. Other five-year-olds, turning six in the fall, stay in our room full time. At the other end of the spectrum are nine-year-olds in their final year of multiage grouping. Students may also turn ten in our classroom if they need another year in the primary program to meet the exit criteria before entering fourth grade.

Many of our students work on their family farms. During harvest season, they frequently bring us fresh vegetables, and during tobacco season they often come to school with their hands stained from the stripping process. There are also students whose parents work in local factories or urban Louisville. These parents rarely see their children during the school week due to late-night shifts. Some students' parents who are doctors, nurses, and health administrators at the local hospital have been very involved and supportive of school reform because of their own experiences with health care reform.

Our students also represent a wide range of learning profiles. Three students are hearing impaired; one of them can hear only in her left ear. A second, profoundly deaf as a result of meningitis, relies on a full-time interpreter in the classroom—who also willingly helps all children. The third student has partial hearing, which is greatly improved with hearing aids. Five students identified as potentially gifted meet twice a month with the district's gifted teacher in our classroom. Four of the students identified as learning disabled work daily with the special education teacher. Twelve students receive individual and small-group tutoring from Chapter One aides in reading and writing.

THE MATH GROUPING: EMERGING PROBLEMS

After Shellie's complaint of having to continually wait in math groups, we gradually accepted the fact that we were not adequately addressing individual differences in math. This was a difficult realization because individualized learning was something we had prided ourselves on in the language arts program.

We had organized our math program the same way for the past two years. We divided our students into two math groups: The "O" group who were p3's and p4's (previously second and third graders) and the "Y" group who were p2's (previously kindergartners and first graders). The grouping had seemed to work well in the first year, so we continued with the same organization. During the second year, Tommy and Robbie were demonstrating the necessary skills to move into the O group. For example, in cooperative groups with the Y group, Tommy would make comments such as "Gosh, would you hurry up?" or he would build symmetrical spaceships with pattern blocks, which he finished well before the other students. Tommy's good friend Robbie was a gifted student who was fluent in his math problem solving. We both were astonished when he was able to calculate the difference between the gravity of Mars and the gravity on Earth; he was then able to communicate to this group, "That means that you would be three times lighter on Mars than you are on Earth!"

Parents' concerns were also a key issue. Gretchyn was well aware of the pressure from Robbie's mother. "She thought that Robbie's math skills were too high for the Y group," Gretchyn recalled. "She would constantly tell me how bored he was in math. Because of her communication with me on this issue, I became more convinced that Robbie would benefit from being moved up. Likewise, I felt pressure from Tommy's mother, who repeatedly compared Tommy to Robbie.

Our goal has always been to serve the individual needs of our students in a multiage, multiability classroom. We knew that to meet our own expectations, Tommy and Robbie should be moved up into the O group.

AN UNRESOLVED ISSUE

We had never given much thought to moving other children to the O group. With the exception of Tommy and Robbie, children in the Y group were willing to cooperate with few complaints and seemed to be progressing at a developmentally appropriate pace. When we discussed whether to move Shellie into the O group, we decided against it. This group was working on two- and three-digit subtraction with base ten pieces. We believed this was too advanced for Shellie and that the move would most likely frustrate her. She had certainly been working hard in the Y group, and she was learning how to add double-digit numbers.

I asked Shellie's father whether his daughter had said anything at home that would lead him to think that she was unhappy with math. He shrugged off the issue. "Shellie seems to be doing fine right where she is," he said, "and even if she is bored, she'll have to learn how to find something to do to keep herself busy." He thought it was good for her.

Moving one child up in the middle of the year did not seem to be the answer. But what was? We decided we would figure out how to change math for the following year but knew we had no choice but to finish the current year as it was: stagnant groups for math and groups that ebbed and flowed for reading and writing.

THE FLOW OF READING AND WRITING

We were uneasy about this organization of our math program into two essentially inflexible groups. By contract, our reading and writing programs allowed us to meet the developmental needs of each child as they occurred. As Gretchyn noted, "Our Reading and Writing Workshop fits our model of how an ideal primary classroom should work."

On a typical day, several children read and write either independently or in small groups. Other children use the computers to publish their own stories. We conduct mini-lessons in various areas around the room in groups of five. When not working with a small group, we meet with individual students as they create their writing projects.

"I just feel so good about the way our workshops are going," Gretchyn said. "Since we use very systematic anecdotal records based on observations, products,

Harper Kelly and Gretchyn Furlong meet daily to exchange classroom observations and insights and to adjust instruction based on continual assessment.

and conferences to decide what areas the students need help in, we can place them in the appropriate small group. By staying current with each child's progress I think we're making it possible to develop all the necessary skills without their being labeled or held back by a permanent attachment to a particular group" (see Exhibit B).

One aspect of our assessment system that I find particularly effective is individual conferencing with students. In fact, I have mentioned to parents on several occasions, "My favorite part of the Reading and Writing Workshop is when I get a chance to have a conference with the kids. It gives me a chance to see where they really are, not where I think they are. They always lead me in new directions and opportunities for individual achievement."

Gretchyn nodded in agreement as she added, "I like the whole idea that no one child is stuck in one reading or writing group. Each kid is working at his or her own pace and skill level. When we put them into groups, they're almost always multiage. The question is, though, why does the Reading and Writing Workshop seem to meet the developmental needs of all the children, while math commits children to fixed groups regardless of their current skill level?"

REFLECTIVE WATERS

As Gretchyn and I dug deeper into this question during our summer reflective time, we discovered the component that made the Reading and Writing Workshops run so smoothly: flexible grouping strategies. Reading and writing activities are designed to create a true workshop atmosphere with the constant grouping and regrouping of students. Using a workshop structure with continuous assessment allows us to meet the needs of all our students in one classroom setting.

Before tackling the now-obvious missing component from our math program—flexible grouping—we decided to rename math time "Math Workshop." Although a change of name may seem superficial, it signified to us a change in mind-set. Once we committed to the concept, we knew we had to make it a reality. We now associated math with the many successes that had been exclusively for language arts.

The next step was to develop an approach that would make the math workshop concept feasible. While we already had some goals in mind, we had to develop strategies for reaching them. One framework I had read about in the book *How Big Is the Moon?* was "exploring math in relevant and meaningful contexts" (Baker, Semple, & Stead, 1990, p. 7). The authors of this book, primary teachers in a New Zealand multiage classroom, helped children "choose what, how and with whom they will explore their math options" (p. 36). This scaffolding structure encouraged children to choose the appropriate level of challenge and movement. Students welcomed the opportunity to self-monitor. Through it they gained courage and confidence to take risks in areas where they might have previously felt reluctant.

As Gretchyn recalled, "the book demonstrated the philosophy we were attempting. Orchestrating a classroom always involves a delicate balance of risk-taking, accountability, and responsibility toward the students. *How Big Is the Moon?* gave us specific strategies and examples of ways to maintain this balance within our newly created math workshop."

We also incorporated the Kentucky Early Learning Profile (KELP), which is an instrument for "documenting individual student learning, development, and growth during the primary program." KELP provided a rubric for gathering anecdotal records as well as additional structure for student conferencing (see Exhibit C). The math section provides learning descriptors and concepts (see Exhibit D). This assessment tool helped us place students into one of three specific groups of developmental needs: beginning, developmental, and independent/advanced groups. Moreover, because assessment is current and ongoing, it is never static or predetermined in what group a child will be placed.

A DAY IN THE LIFE OF MATH WORKSHOP: PROJECTS

"Let's get to the blue carpet!" With that call, some 43 students scramble to take their places.

"It's project time!" a few students call out. Quickly, Gretchyn and I facilitate student generalizations about project work:

- Good projects have to serve a purpose.
- We need projects to show we know stuff in here.
- We've been thinking about good projects all year.

Then we draw out the group in brainstorming "candidate project" ideas such as these:

- How many marbles have we earned in the marble jar?
- Who has lost teeth, and how many have they lost?
- University of Louisville basketball fans vs. University of Kentucky basketball fans?

Then we query them:

- Why would that be a good project?
- How would you measure something like that?
- Will that serve a purpose like we talked about earlier?
- What purpose did you have in mind?

Some nominations from the floor find their way onto "the final list," while others are agreeably withdrawn by the students who suggested the concepts, enthusiasm having waned as a result of peers' questions.

And then the really critical process begins in the minds of the students—namely, "What's *my* topic?" and "Who is in *my* group?" Gretchyn and I are deliberately directive in this process. By the time students move to their newly designated group, all seem to be on track and involved with the tasks at hand. Gretchyn and I ensure this by checking carefully for understanding. While the focus of this workshop day is group planning, it is evident that students are already eager to move ahead, voicing their desires with, "Can we get started collecting our data?"

The first steps of student work are critical. Students often want to rush through this planning process. But if the project group has not adequately thought through the topics they must address, the process can quickly become chaotic. We have specific questions to guide the students' work as we move from group to group, asking them in detail how their research is going to proceed. Also, when we conference with students at this time, we may ask simply, "What question are you trying to answer with this project?" In some cases, students struggle for a moment as they try to articulate their purpose. These first critical steps help ensure that all students thoroughly understand what it is they are asking before they begin collecting data (see Exhibit E).

STUDENT REFLECTIONS

When asked to compare last year's math curriculum with this year's, the students began with a dissection of the grouping patterns. They described last year's patterns as being one of Youngers and Olders, ". . . except," as every group noted, "for Tommy and Robbie. They went up because they were real smart." Two students hypothesized that these two math wizards probably "got lots of extra help at home," while another added that "he could beat either one of them in football or soccer." Last year's grouping received some interesting praise such as, "We got to use more real things in math last year. Like when we were studying fractions, we used apples and crackers. Do you think we're going to get to use them again?" Tommy and Robbie quickly pointed out that even when they were placed in the 'O' group last year, the work still was not hard enough. No mention was made of why other students did not "move up" or the issues of gender exclusion, with which we had struggled. The impression from the students was that "age grouping" was simply the way things were done last year.

Then we discussed the new grouping pattern begun this year. Every student interviewed preferred the new arrangement. Comments such as "I'm like a teacher on pluses and minuses because I'm really good at that," and "I get to teach how to work with strips" indicate that the occasional role of "student as teacher" was valued by the students themselves. Significantly, three of the more advanced students mentioned that they had learned something from the less advanced students.

The children also noted our apparent commitment to change. Nine students indicated that we would do math differently next year because "they always do new things for us every year."

We recorded our own responses to the students' reactions. Gretchyn suggested, "There is a sense of safety within this structure. The students feel free to make occasional mistakes so they will take more risks. Obviously, they feel more confident when there is flexibility."

I was quick to agree: "All children believe they can learn better by reinforcing math concepts with other children. Of course, we need to make sure that the reinforcement is accurate and that the faster students are challenged to enhance their skill development."

CRYSTAL CLEAR AND FLOWING

We knew that the ultimate assessment of our new approach would be the individual progress of Shellie, Teresa, and Chelsea, the students who had precipitated the transformation. Throughout the year, we had kept a keen eye on whether the girls were being challenged, becoming more aggressive in talking about math, and able to work in groups appropriate to their developmental needs. I noted in the margin of my teacher record, "I have found that by writing anecdotal records, I am able to observe exactly what the children are demonstrating—not what I think they can do. Therefore, the children are being placed in groups that are much more appropriate than before."

In her own written comments, Gretchyn noted that "If you take one child and follow him or her through the year so far, you will find that he or she has been in a multitude of math groupings. For example, Shellie has been in the Independent/ Expanded group for the past week during our exploration of fractions. However, she was in the Developing group to help her progress in understanding subtraction facts. Once we noticed her subtraction concepts were developing quickly, we even moved her and two other children into the Independent group in the middle of the week. We noted that this flexibility helped all of our students to develop more efficient strategies in learning basic facts they didn't have."

Flexible grouping was now working in math with the same kind of success we'd seen in language arts. Parents noticed the differences as well. At a parent conference, I asked Shellie's father what he thought of our new approach and how he thought Shellie was doing in math this year compared with last. He was amazed at the enthusiasm she was showing at home. He commented, "One day she couldn't wait to show me how she could find fractions all over the house." She now really enjoys math, even though the program is harder!

This is not the end of our change in strategies. We must continue to explore the best ways to group and regroup students based on individual needs. We realize that next year's students will bring a whole new set of needs to the learning environment. By continually assessing each student and by reflecting on our approach, we know new challenges will emerge. The key for us will be to be sure our teaching is developmentally appropriate and to offer equitable opportunities for all in our classroom.

REFERENCES AND SELECTED BIBLIOGRAPHY

Adams, T. L. (1998). Alternate assessment in elementary school mathematics. *Childhood Education*, 74(4), 220–224.

Anderson, R. (1993). The return of the nongraded classroom. *Principal*, 72(3), 9–12.

Bailey, S. M. (1993). The current status of gender equity research in American Schools. *Educational Psychologist*, 28, 321–339.

Baker, D., Semple, C., & Stead, T. (1990). *How Big Is the Moon?* Portsmouth, NH: Heinemann.

Burns, M. (1992). *About teaching mathematics*: A K–8 resource. Iowa City, IA: Math Solutions Publications.

Dever, M., Zila, R., & Manzano, N. (1994). Multiage classrooms; a new way to learn math. *Principal*, 73(4), 22–26.

Grossman, H., & Grossman, S. H. (1994). *Gender issues in education*. Boston: Allyn & Bacon.

Jeanroy, D. (1996). The results of multi-age grouping: An elementary principal documents the outcomes of meeting students' developmental needs. *School Administrator*, 43(1), 18–19.

Linn, M. C., & Hyde, J. S. (1989). Gender, mathematics and science. *Educational Researcher*, 18, 17–27.

Micklo, S. J. (1997). Math portfolios in the primary grades. *Childhood Education*, 73(4), 194–199.

Mills, C. J., Ablard, K. E., & Stumph, H. (1993). Gender differences in academically talented young students' mathematical reasoning: Patterns across age and subskills. *Journal of Educational Psychology*, 85, 340–346.

Richardson, K., & Salkeld, R. (1995). Transforming mathematics curriculum. In S. Bredekamp & T. Rosegrant (Eds.), *Reaching potentials: Transforming early childhood curriculum and assessment*. Vol. 2 (pp. 178–192). Washington, DC: National Association for the Education of Young Children.

Slavin, R. (1982). Student teams and comparisons among equals: Effects on academic performance and student attitude. *Journal of Education Psychology*, 70, 532–538.

Slavin, R. (1982). *Cooperative learning; student teams: What research says to the teacher*. ERIC Document Reproduction Service No. ED 294–926. Washington, DC: National Education Association.

Floor Plan of Classroom

This floor plan shows the activity centers in Harper Kelly's and Gretchyn Furlong's multiage, multiability primary classroom.

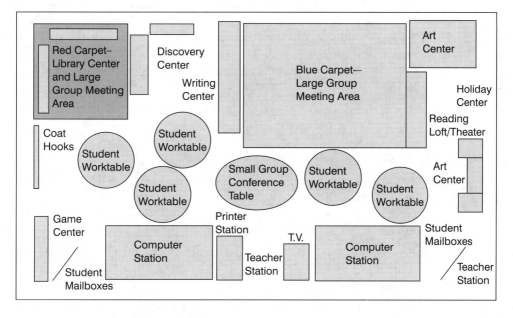

EXHIBIT B

Excerpts from Teachers' Anecdotal Records

PHILLIP

Math

8/21

Coming up to me: saying "I forgot how to count" but when asked, "How many is this?" he said, "30." "How did you know?" "I counted." Worked one on one, w/ 10 strips counting by ones. Picked up a clock twice while working with strips. Counted by 1 with prompt.

9/15

4 − 2 = 6. Put up two groups of 4, then took away 2 fingers = 6! I put down one group of 4, he took away 2, then said "2-Oh!"

9/23

Phillip was able to write the math sentence 8 − 3 = 5 by himself when I held up the manipulative picture.

10/28

Shaded in the number 32 when asked to shade in 24. We worked on 32 yesterday.

10/30

Had drawn many ways to show 10, but only one way to show 24. "24 adding 8 equals 32." Circled 12 twos to make 24. Wrote 2 + 2 twelve times.

10/31

Very easy to talk to about math! Counted "20" 5s in the whole math. How many are 24? Counted "1, 2, 3, 4. And one 4!" Wrote 5 + 5 + 5 + 5 + 4 = 24. Tried to count by 5s. 5, 10, 20, 40. Do you know how to count by 5s? "No"

11/11

Can count by 10s, 5s with some trouble. Counts by 25s with help. Counts mixtures with help.

Writing

9/12

Sat right down & began writing. Some sight words evident: toys, with, bat. Many inventive spellings, but phonetically correct: Days = Daz. Some words w/out vowels: hm (him).

10/24

Phillip is working on putting periods where his voice stops.

10/26

Writing about another story he had read. . . . We brainstorm an original story. Shows lots of capitals. Will go back and fix.

11/9

Wrote I PLAYD tic tac toe. it was fun. Mini-lesson: capitals—when i stands alone, or after period, went back and fixed his own piece.

SAMANTHA

Math

8/29

Figured out how 5 is an odd number. "Because if you break it in the middle, it's not even on both sides. You have to break in half."

8/30

Smiled and raised her hand during greater than/less than lesson. Put hand down when another name was called.

9/15

"We're doing 382 − 2 and the answer is 380. I counted all this up 10, 20, 30, 40, 50, 60 through 190, um, 1,000,000? 191, 192, 193, 194 through 199, um?" I told her 200, she went 210, 220 through 290, 300, 310, through 380.

E X H I B I T   C

Overview of Kentucky Early Learning Profile (KELP)

Susan Brodie[1]

The Kentucky Early Learning Profile (KELP) is an instrument for primary school teachers to document individual student learning, development, and growth during the primary program. KELP was designed to help teachers monitor the progress of students in meeting the primary program objectives as established in the Kentucky Education Reform Act. KELP encourages teachers to communicate student progress to parents as well as facilitate staff development programs that focus on curriculum, instruction, and authentic assessment. The goal of KELP is to help teachers understand and document individual student development through observation and communication with parents so that curriculum and instruction can meet the needs of each student.

The Kentucky Early Learning Profile is an evolving document that begins when a student enters kindergarten or first grade and terminates at the end of third grade. During the primary years, teachers document the student's development through conversations with the student and parents, a diary of observations in the classroom, performances demonstrating knowledge, learning description summaries, and progress reports. When a student makes the transition into fourth grade, the student's KELP file is passed on to the fourth-grade teacher as an important resource on the child's development and achievements during the primary years.

---

[1]Susan Brodie teaches high school in Alton, Indiana.

E X H I B I T   D

Sample Lesson Plan—Fall

LEARNER GOAL

KELP Math Component: Number Concepts

MATERIALS

Various math manipulatives placed in a tub:

tile	money jars
bears	clocks
unfix cubes	calculators
base 10 pieces	cubes
fraction bars	story boxes

ACTIVITY

The children will meet together in their family group (multiage, multiability, p2–p4). The teacher writes the symbol for addition on a chart. The children and teacher engage in a discussion about vocabulary used for that symbol (addition, plus, sum, etc.). Children then share their previous knowledge of how you can "do" and "show" addition on the chart. Afterward, the students work in their journals to develop different ways to show addition.

GROUPING

Students may choose to work independently, with a partner, or in a small group.

ASSESSMENT

Anecdotal records on individuals' discoveries and quotes will be used to place the children into investigations (or skills) groups the following week. These skills may be on building the concept (or idea) of addition with one- or two-digit numbers, using manipulatives, or moving to symbolic addition up to four digits.

E X H I B I T   E

Excerpts from a Student's Notes

SAMANTHA

2/23

Question:	I wonder if it's true that people the same height jump the same distance?
Teacher:	What are you going to do?
Student:	See if they jump the same height, then publish the data.
Teacher:	How are you going to do it?
Student:	(1) Measure people, (2) have them jump.
Teacher:	What resources will you need?
Student:	Measurements, standing broad jump.

3/2

Research: I wonder if it's true that people the same height jump the same distance.

Summary of research by Samantha's group

Height Matches	Distance Jumped
Ben, Rob	Ben 5', Rob 5' 9"
Mallory, Powell	Mallory 4', Powell 4'
Ben, Billy	Ben 53", Billy 4' 8"
Laura, Alesha	Laura 4' 3", Alesha 4' 7"
Powell, Pamella	Powell 4', Pamella 4' 11"
Kristie, Laura	Kristie 3' 3", Laura 4' 3"

3/3

Samantha's Reflection

My question was if people the same height jump the same distance. I learned that people the same height don't jump the same distance. First, we planned out our data. Then we collected our data by measuring people in pairs that were the same height and had them jump and we found our hypothesis was wrong. We published in our math journals instead of a chart. Therefore, your height doesn't matter but it's how far you jump. Like in basketball, ice skating, ballet, track and swimming. So I learned your height doesn't matter.

DISCUSSION QUESTIONS

1. Describe the group of students Gretchyn and Harper teach. Is the group typical or atypical of most primary classrooms? Describe these teachers in terms of their teaching philosophy.

2. In what ways did Gretchyn and Harper exhibit bias in their classroom? Have you observed other types of gender bias in today's classrooms? What are some specific actions you could take to provide equal opportunities for both genders in the aspects of educational curricula?

3. Gretchyn and Harper have used two very different types of grouping patterns. Discuss the pros and cons of each.

4. Describe the physical setting of the classroom (see Exhibit A). Are underlying educational philosophies evident from the physical setting alone? Based on your educational philosophies, how do you envision your classroom setting?

5. The students in this classroom represent a range of ages, backgrounds, and abilities. The underlying philosophy is that all students can learn at high levels. Explain your position on this issue. If you had a class similar to Gretchyn's and Harper's, what kinds of instructional strategies would you consider to be most efficient?

6. The mothers of both Tommy and Robbie assertively expressed their concerns to Gretchyn and Harper about their sons' boredom in the Younger math group. The pressure that the teachers felt from these parents was an important factor in moving Robbie and Tommy to the Older math group. What positive and negative impacts does parental pressure have on teachers and students? What were alternative courses of action in how the teachers could have dealt with the involvement of parents, including Shellie's father?

7. Gretchyn and Harper believed that flexible grouping strategies enabled Math Workshop to become more developmentally appropriate. Can we automatically assume this? What are the issues? Describe the ways in which a workshop atmosphere may or may not meet the developmental needs of all individuals.

8. In this case you will find exhibits labeled "Sample Lesson Plan—Fall" (Exhibit D) and "Excerpts from a Student's Notes" (Exhibit E). These exhibits come directly from the Family Math portion of Gretchyn's and Harper's Math Workshop. Using the KELP rubrics and the student samples, divide the students into Beginning, Developing, and Independent math groups. Focus on what the students can do. Finally, develop a Beginning, Developing, and Independent math lesson for each of the groups to be used during Investigations.

9. Shellie is now part of a math program where she is given the opportunity to progress at her own rate. What evidence do we have that the new system of grouping is better than the previous one? What evidence is needed to make a clear determination?

10. Gretchyn and Harper orchestrated change in the classroom based on their own philosophies and practices. What are the core components of Gretchyn's and Harper's philosophy? What component stimulated the change? What are the main components to your teaching philosophy? What are the obstacles to your being more reflective? How can these be successfully overcome?

CASE 2

Discussion Question	Corresponding INTASC Principle
2,5	**3** The teacher understands how students differ in their approaches to learning and creates instructional opportunities that are adapted to diverse learners.
3	**4** The teacher understands and uses a variety of instructional strategies to encourage students' development of critical thinking, problem solving, and performance skills.
6	**10** The teacher fosters relationships with school colleagues, parents, and agencies in the larger community to support learning and well-being.
7, 8	**2** The teacher understands how children learn and develop, and can provide learning opportunities that support their intellectual, social, and personal development.
9	**8** The teacher understands and uses formal and informal assessment strategies to evaluate and ensure the continuous intellectual, social, and physical development of the learner.
10	**9** The teacher is a reflective practitioner who continually evaluates the effects of his/herchoices and actions on others (students, parents, and other professionals in the learning community) and who actively seeks out opportunities to grow professionally

Arts on the Line

"Are you really concerned about what happens at this school, Ms. Wosoba? Do you care enough about these kids to let them paint in the first grade?" Patsy Cox asked with her arms tightly folded, looking Carolyn Wosoba straight in the eye. It was an intensely muggy August, and Wosoba had barely arrived at Portland Elementary School as its new principal, eager to meet her teachers. She knew of Cox's reputation as an innovator and "master of the teachable moment" but had hardly expected such directness. Wiping the perspiration from her forehead, she managed a barely audible response: "Sounds fine to me."

Three weeks later, Wosoba decided it was time to see Cox in action. At first glance, the students in her classroom looked like a group of Casperlike miniature ghosts; each student was wearing a man's huge, white, long-sleeved shirt as a painter's smock—and there was paint everywhere. Cox's smile suggested she seemed genuinely glad for the visit as she gestured for the principal to come closer to the paint pots. "You see why I asked you about painting—the last principal was mad at me all the time." Wosoba's subsequent visits to the classroom showed how effectively Cox used art to promote student success in other areas, such as literacy. She was famous for making beautiful pop-up books in which characters in stories were so vivid they seemed to come alive. She allowed her students to take the books home, and for some children it was all they had to read with their parents. Would this dynamic teacher be even more than the new principal had hoped for in creating a school-wide commitment to long-term arts integration?

THE INTEGRATED CURRICULUM

Portland Elementary School, originally constructed in 1851, is on the outskirts of one of the oldest and least affluent sections of Louisville, Kentucky. The school motto is "Attitude is the mind's paintbrush. It can color any situation." Prominently displayed inside the main entrance is a student-produced paper quilt of symmetrical patches of red overlaid with yellow handprints. Such quilt making is emblematic of community involvement in the life of the school. On any given day, parent and grandparent volunteers, many skilled in quilt making and other local crafts, sit in quiet hall corners supporting and coaching individual students in their artistic endeavors.

Wosoba eagerly answers the often-posed question: How can a school be filled with outstanding student artwork without a full-time art teacher? "Our steady stream of visitors wants to know how we do it, and my answer is always the same," she said. "Our teachers are interested in and dedicated to making sure students learn in many different ways." With 93 percent of the student body on free or reduced lunches and a minority population of 20 percent, Wosoba explains the immense range of Portland's students' learning styles, abilities, and backgrounds. "It's important to me as a principal and to all of the teachers that we expose students to different ways of knowing each subject and multiple ways of learning essential skills and concepts." With Wosoba's arrival and her commitment to art as a prominent part of the curriculum, the challenge for the faculty was, "How can we effectively integrate art without a full-time art teacher and with limited funds?"

Building on the faculty's passion for art as a vital form of expression, Wosoba orchestrated the implementation of "Different Ways of Knowing" (DWoK), a constructivist-oriented, arts-infused curriculum that had to be used in conjunction with a multiyear program of professional development. Initially designed for elementary teachers, the curriculum has an interdisciplinary social studies focus. The basic conceptual framework is that key themes provide for integrated learning experiences, and the DWoK materials all support this integration. Activities in language arts, drama, history, math, and art collectively comprise the unit on American Families. For example, in the drama component, each group of students dramatizes a specific daily chore of families moving west in covered wagons, such as unhitching the horses or carrying water.

Although many Kentucky teachers had become understandably skeptical of trendy or new curricula that failed to meet students' needs, involvement in DWoK was supported by Portland teachers. The materials and accompanying professional development seemed to be quite consistent with insights based on their years of experience as well as with the goals of the state's mandated reforms (see Exhibit A).

One of the distinguishing characteristics of DWoK is its coherent approach to interdisciplinary teaching with a strong emphasis on the arts. Students can make vital connections while developing essential skills in each subject area. Given Kentucky's commitment to authentic assessment, DWoK's performance-based approach to student work was an acceptable fit. Wosoba noted, however, that "missing from the extensive training and materials was a *formal* structure for assessing student learning." On balance, Wosoba did not see this issue as an insurmountable one. The DWoK curriculum did represent a considerable investment, but it had developed a good track record for providing teachers a holistic way of thinking about teaching and the necessary supporting materials, minus some assessments, to make it happen. Given Cox's many years of experience integrating art in her teaching, she was an obvious choice to be one of six teachers who made a three-year commitment to Portland's first DWoK training.

PATSY COX

Red and yellow peonies, like the colors in a Jackson Pollock painting, adorn Cox's classroom. Flower bouquets from her English cutting garden is one more aesthetic detail that contributes to the gallerylike feeling of Portland. What she casually refers to as her lifelong passion for art does more than just infuse her teaching—it is how she lives. Her crocheting and cross-stitching could rival some of the best Appalachian crafts, yet Cox is never one to promote her own talents. Showing an earth-toned vest she recently made, she explains, "Yarns intrigue me—their character, feel, and color. I like to see how I can blend the colors and textures."

When Cox began teaching 16 years earlier, she was determined to make art a cornerstone of her teaching despite her lack of formal training—only one undergraduate art history course. "Anyone with dedication can teach art," she insists. Originally a special education teacher, she quickly noticed that her slower learners become more confident when expressing themselves through art. "Younger students are not so frustrated when they can draw a picture of a word they cannot spell or cut out a picture from a magazine to illustrate a word in a sentence. Because it worked so well with these students and helped develop their self-esteem, I was confident art could do the same with students of all ability levels."

Cox's multiage class consists of six-, seven-, and eight-year-olds of all abilities. Her 24 students regularly gather at five kidney-shaped tables, named Monday, Tuesday, and so on, up to Friday. This arrangement supports her extensive use of cooperative learning and art-based activities that are often combined. Moreover, it gives her easy access to each child, which is indispensable to her philosophy: "I believe it is my job to help children develop as individuals—to use every opportunity to bring out their unique abilities and skills. At the same time, they need engaging activities to promote their social skills now and for the future. Art projects really do both."

One of Cox's colleagues recalls an example of what she calls Cox's total spontaneity in seizing the teachable moment. "We'd combined our students for an integrated lesson where they were painting pictures based on a book we had just read. So here are 90-plus students all in their huge, white painters' smocks painting away. All of a sudden Cox stops everyone and focuses the whole room's attention to the work of seven-year-old Monique who had happened to mix blue and yellow. Immediately posting the picture on an easel, Cox asked her to describe exactly what she had done to get such a beautiful green. Then, totally unplanned, Cox launches into a discussion of primary and secondary colors, continuously referring to Monique's creation. The other two team members and I—we were just in awe of Cox's earnestness. Monique could have been another Georgia O'Keefe in the making."

Another one of the team members elaborates, "As our team leader, Cox inspires us to be creative, but she is a hard act to follow. She has this gift for reaching those kids who drove the rest of us nuts. As team leader she could have had the cream of the crop, but she always assigned herself to work with the slow readers and kids with problems. It's through art and her creativity that she is successful in reaching all

Patsy Cox spontaneously seizes a teachable moment to discuss primary and secondary colors by calling attention to a child's mixture of pigments.

types of students; sometimes I think that by just getting them painting they would listen to her."

Cox views her room as her canvas. Her full-time aide oversees the hands-on art center, located in the corner of the classroom, where children create and mix paints in beachcombing-size pails. The nearby east wall serves as backdrop for the current thematic unit, "Clothing for All Occasions," a topic in which children learn about geography and diversity while developing their art, language, and math skills. Life-size, cut-out clothing of every type and shape makes up the exhibit. Using construction paper for a frame, then stuffing it with crumpled paper from the recycling bin, students then paint the faceless mannequins. Once completed, students intently survey their products, quite pleased with their realistic three-dimensional clothing. After giving them feedback on their creations, Cox placed a price tag on each product in anticipation of a future math lesson for students to compare and contrast "good buys."

Having her own classroom is a recent development for Cox. For several years she and three other teachers team-taught in a pod-type classroom with between 80 to 95 students. When Wosoba assigned all teachers their own rooms, Cox's team elected to continue their collaboration and the regular sharing of ideas, materials, and problems. One team member remarked, "We never know what Cox might be cooking up, but it always keeps us fresh and on our toes." Cox, reflecting on the collaboration, says with a broad grin, "I think we're married." Although the team now does most activities individually, they continued to coordinate lessons for several projects, such as the 16-foot by 8-foot paper quilt hanging in the main hallway.

"I stay here because of the camaraderie and mutual support we have gained through working together for years," Cox said. "As soon as Wosoba arrived, she fostered team-building—she provides opportunities for all team members to attend workshops and meetings together. That's no easy task considering almost all of us commute from suburban communities."

An interior mural is framed by one of several rimmed archways that connect Portland's main areas.

THE SCHOOL

The interior structure of Portland comprises the oldest building in Kentucky known to be still in use. The downtown neighborhood surrounding the school, located on the Ohio River, suggests that in pre-Depression days this may have been a wealthy area, owing to the ornate post-Victorian facades on several homes and churches. Now, the area has a forlorn quality due to years of decay with little visual relief from the austerity of abandoned warehouses. Despite some deterioration surrounding the school, there is nothing forlorn about this vibrant school community. Renovated in the 1960s, Portland's exterior now consists of large curving "smokestacks" that flank the glass arched entrance doors, reminiscent of a river steamboat with portholes and paddle wheels (see Exhibit B).

Inside the two-story building, polished hallways bathed in natural light add to the gallerylike ambience. Folk art murals produced by local secondary students capture the history of nineteenth-century life in the Portland District. The largest (14-foot by 6-foot) mural is a scene of a crowded, bustling riverfront, depicting its commercial as well as social importance. Even Portland's passageways conjure up images of the past. Brick rimmed archways connect the school's main areas, all of which converge on the cafeteria. The striped awning that hangs over the lunch counters and the pastel-colored mural of a convivial street scene give the lunch room the air of a Paris café in a Renoir painting. The lunchroom is also used as the school's "town hall," reinforcing the implicit theme of community.

Working collaboratively, Portland teachers organize historic walking tours to develop students' community pride while they learn history, architecture, and science. Prominent on the tour are examples of designs in the "steamboat" style that were popular along the Ohio and Mississippi Rivers during the Mark Twain era. The walking tours are a permanent resource for teaching essential concepts in a natural environment. In one of Cox's combined math and art lessons, students discover the local architectural patterns by comparing and contrasting two "shotgun"-style[1] houses that were identical when originally built but are very different today (see Exhibit C). "By learning art concepts (like patterning) and making connections to math, science, history, and language arts as they walk through their neighborhood, students achieve a higher level of focus and remember what they have experienced," Cox explains. Many of the students' families have lived in the area for generations, and the tours give the children a new perspective on the value of their architectural legacy.

USING ART FOR MULTIPLE PATHS TO LEARNING

Patsy Cox is a leading proponent of the historic homes tour because, like other Kentucky primary teachers, she focuses on the concept of patterns in her teaching. The historic tour provides an ideal opportunity to extend and apply student's prior learning. She begins the year teaching patterns with commercial calendar activities such as the math kit Box It, Bag It.[2] As students select shapes from the bag, such as circles, squares, and triangles representing a different day of the week, they rely on their growing understanding of patterns to predict the next colored shape to emerge.

"I draw on children's natural curiosity to learn shape, color, and sequencing," explained Cox. "These art concepts support the development of the cognitive skills of inferencing and predicting. At first, students work to become comfortable guessing what colored shape will come next in a sequence. As they make more and more correct guesses, I ask them to explain their answers. When they can support their guess with an explanation, I know they are no longer guessing, but are reasoning—truly predicting—based on evidence. Students then apply this ability to identify and differentiate among patterns in a real-world setting during the walking tour. I had students take notes and make drawings of the patterns and shapes found in the architectural styles. Once back in the classroom, the students use the Portland

---

[1]A shotgun-style house is one in which all the rooms are in a direct line with each other, usually from front to back.

[2]Available from Math Learning Center, P.O. Box 3226, Salem, OR 97301; (503) 370-8130.

Museum Coloring Book to confirm their findings and learn some architectural terms. For example, they discovered that *fish scales* was a term that describes overlapping thin, flat layers of shingles. They have fun finding other examples from their learning outside the classroom."

With the DWoK curriculum, students test their new-found awareness of similarities and differences in local architecture. Adapting ideas from a social studies module on shelter, children in small cooperative groups designed and built shelters using newspapers, yarn, shingles, garbage bags, masking tape, sticks, and rope. Cox encouraged her student teacher, Donita, to facilitate the activity so that she could become familiar with DWoK materials. Impressed with Donita's organization and quality of student-produced shelters, Cox declared the entire process a success. Students were thoroughly absorbed in the task. Initially they focused on taping their desks and chairs together to produce strong foundations for their shelters. As the project progressed, students became more creative and identified important design features. The objectives of Donita's lesson included collaborating in small groups, producing a product demonstrating some essential aspects of shelter, and showing an understanding of related vocabulary.

Like Donita, other student teachers assigned to mentors involved in the DWoK process had a positive experience. Subsequently, Donita's professors at the University of Louisville received a grant to integrate DWoK into their early childhood master's program for beginning teacher certification. The philosophical rationale was straightforward: the DWoK materials were thematic, constructivist, and supported the concept that children learn in different ways. In addition, the professors knew their students needed just this type of integrated preparation. They required a portfolio entry in which student teachers showed evidence of using DWoK integration in their lesson planning and/or assessments.

ASSESSMENT

By February of her first year in DWoK, Cox's response to the curriculum and training program was tepid. "It has given me some useful ideas, but I was already using lots of art-based creative projects. I did not see any curriculum in DWoK that teachers could not develop themselves given enough time and opportunity for collaboration." Cox's curriculum revealed that it was hard to tell where her own activities and materials ended and DWoK began. Was there really anything new about DWoK? However, by the close of the school year, Cox's initial concerns had begun to dissipate—she did acknowledge that DWoK was expanding her thinking about assessment.

Early on, the Kentucky Assessment System (KIRIS)[3], a linchpin of the 1991 reform, had a concerted emphasis on performance assessment. Cox welcomed the new paradigm as a major step toward compatibility with the personalized learning essential to an arts-infused curriculum. Throughout her years of experience, she felt that the almost exclusive use of objective paper-and-pencil tests had deterred regular class-

---

[3]The Kentucky Instructional Results Information System was instituted in 1991 and replaced in 1998 by the Commonwealth Achievement Testing System (CATS).

room teachers from cultivating student creativity. DWoK offered some new, albeit informal, avenues for interpreting and appraising students' creative products.

Before her involvement with DWoK, Cox had used oral questions and some anec- dotal records to appraise what students learned through creative expression. Extending her own question-and-answer format for viewing student projects, she began using "gallery walks"—an idea she had picked up during DWoK training. In gallery walks, student-made sculptures, posters, and dioramas,[4] are carefully arranged to encourage whole-class and visitor viewing. At mid-year, Cox's students transformed their environment into a tropical paradise for a parent-attended gallery walk. Student research on Hawaii yielded gallery decorations such as clay sculptures of molten lava volcanoes and cascading waterfalls. Also on display were grass hula skirts made of newspaper and Hawaiian fruit made of papier-mâché.

Hand-in-hand, parents and students strolled through the tropical paradise, paus- ing in front of each student's creation, listening to the artist's brief report on the his- tory, culture, and economy of the 49th state. Cox used these oral reports and her stu- dents' answers to audience questions for the final assessment.

Cox explained, "This method proves useful in assessing reading comprehension and retention and is also applicable to any unit of study. When a student explains his or her creation, the depth of knowledge and understanding that prompts accu- rate and appropriate connections comes shining through." In the case of the Hawaiian gallery walk, each guest participated in a grand finale: A luau with sump- tuous Hawaiian food.

Portland parents, who frequently assist their children's research gathering, eagerly participate in the gallery walks. Cox discovered some surprising benefits from par- ent involvement in the art projects. "They serve as catalysts for students to spend quality time with their parents. I remember one little boy in my first year of DWoK, David, rarely received much attention at home because his mother was tired and felt overworked," Cox said. "His excitement and enthusiasm for school art projects ener- gized his mother, giving her the impetus to spend 'special' time with him."

Another DWoK-inspired gallery walk focuses on the hardships and sacrifices of pioneers in the 1800s. The pioneer theme is captured in *The Josefina Story Quilt* (Coerr 1986), one of the many books accompanying the DWoK curriculum. In choosing this story, Cox builds on students' prior knowledge of families as well as their under- standing of quilt making. As she makes her way through the gallery walk viewing cre- ations the story inspired, she asks students questions such as "What does this part of your quilt convey about pioneer life?" Their answers help Cox evaluate the depth of their understanding of the key themes in the book.

A NEW WAY OF THINKING ABOUT AND EXPANDING ASSESSMENT

Despite Cox's original lukewarm response to the DWoK curriculum, she ardently points out that her second year of participation in DWoK caused a change in her

---

[4]A diorama is a three-dimensional miniature scene with painted modeled figures and background.

thinking. Initially she had conceived art integration too narrowly, confining it only to social studies and science. By year two she was eager to experiment using art to enhance mathematical understanding as well. Inspired by activities about ethnic foods in the DWoK module on America's Family Stories, Cox's class conducted an ice cream survey, a hands-on project involving everyone at Portland. Her students canvassed the school, asking teachers, staff, and students if they preferred chocolate, strawberry, or vanilla ice cream. Students learned to graph the results and display them on a large sheet of construction paper tacked on the hallway wall adjacent to their class. Sections on the graph paper matched the color of flavors surveyed. Students created true-to-life paper ice cream cones representing the number of people choosing each flavor, using their understanding of color, form, and line to publicly present survey data. Since the graphs were essentially pictographs, they were assessed based on accuracy. Did students use the correct colors, accurate numbers, and shapes of the ice cream cones according to the graph key?

As the second year of her DWoK program continued, Cox further expanded her approaches to include appraising student work. Convinced of the importance of self-assessment, she wanted students to see for themselves the processes involved in their own thinking. Her newest approach was to have students work independently, or with a buddy, chronicling in their journals the specific steps taken in developing a project. Students eagerly scrutinized the journals during both self- and peer review.

"Kids are honest and are quite able to define similarities and differences between compositions, a key cognitive skill," Cox noted. "Journal writing and peer review, when matched with teacher assessment, provided checks and balances for emerging student insights." She also kept index cards for recording student progress concerning self-reflection in the following areas: collaboration with peers, approach to the artistic process, and the final product. She embraced this multidimensional strategy as a holistic method for detecting students' strengths and areas for improvement.

The DWoK program refers to the process of keeping anecdotal records as "kid-watching"—a procedure Cox uses while teaching the "clothing in literature" theme. After she reads her students the richly illustrated book A *New Coat for Anna* (Ziefert 1986), she leads them in a weaving project drawing on essential themes and weaving processes learned from the story. As Cox demonstrates how to fold and cut the paper, she has the students' rapt attention. "Why are the shops empty? How do Anna and her mother dye her coat red? What is the name for the yarns that go up and down on the loom?" Many hands go up, and Cox smiles broadly when she hears the correct answer, "weft." When Cox does not receive a particular answer she is looking for, she encourages them: "Think about the question while you work, and perhaps the answer will become clear." One student, Benjamin, pondered his weaving project. With only two strips of colored paper woven through, he knew something was wrong. He pulled the last blue strip out and tried to weave it back in the same way, but again, he saw that it was still wrong. Undaunted, Ben tried one more time, and success was obvious by the big grin on his face.

Through "kidwatching," Cox followed Ben through each attempt to rework his paper weaving and was pleased with this DWoK system as a major improvement over her index cards. She noted as part of her anecdotal records his perseverance,

Overview of Kid-Watching Forms (see Exhibit D for complete forms)

Name of Form	Objectives	Areas of Focus
The process of learning	Coming to know	—Engagement —Collaboration —Flexibility
The products of learning	Showing you know	—Understanding content —Conventions and forms —Presentations
Reflections	Knowing you know	—Where we've been —Where we go next

risk-taking, problem-solving, and revision strategies. At various times Cox used all three "kid-watching" forms developed by DWoK to collect and organize assessment information about her students.

By the end of her second year with DWoK, Cox was exhilarated with her expanded repertoire for student assessment. "Continuing kid-watching while adding strategies for student self-assessment is ideal for a multiage classroom—it helps me efficiently organize and plan lessons to meet the needs of all my students," stated Cox. "When I ask students how well they are meeting a particular goal, their responses show me not only what they think of their work but also what they were doing and why. They really had quite a bit to say. I've come a long way in my thinking about assessment. I know DWoK is in the process of developing specific assessment rubrics, and I am hopeful I can go even further in the future."

A PRINCIPAL LOOKS BACK

During what would have been Cox's third and final year in the DWoK training for Portland teachers, she surprised everyone when she announced she had accepted a position as an intern principal at another local elementary school. She explained that it was a goal she had been working toward for several years. Despite Wosoba's strong support for Cox's professional advancement, the principal could not hide her disappointment. Cox was not only an outstanding teacher, but as a DWoK team leader she was vital to the mission of arts infusion. If Cox accepted a full-time principalship the following year, what would happen with the DWoK team and the years of colleagueship? There are other issues facing the school as well. If Cox does not return, a new full-time teacher will be needed. If there are no applicants experienced with DWoK, will Portland have the financial resources to send the new teacher for training? Would she ever catch up? Could anyone? If not, how would a newcomer approach art integration and how would this affect Cox's former team?

EPILOGUE

Patsy Cox gazes out of the picture window of her remodeled and spacious wood-paneled office at Hartstern Elementary. "While still new to the role of principal, I am confident in my ability to support teacher innovation." Approving the agenda for an upcoming in-service day, Cox smiled as she displayed the list of several teachers who were signed up for training in the "Different Ways of Knowing" program. Her own successful experience propelled her enthusiasm for encouraging Hartstern teachers in the use of the DWoK curriculum. She believed the timing was vital since Kentucky had recently formalized a fine arts assessment for fifth, eighth, and eleventh grades. One nagging concern dampened her enthusiasm—the success of DWoK would require more than just a handful of enthusiastic teachers and her active involvement as principal. How would she foster the colleagueship she knew to be at the heart of systemic reform? Given her own success with Donita, she had counted on having some DWoK-trained student teachers from the University of Louisville to be part of her team-building approach. However, the university-based DWoK program requiring considerable resources had lapsed when the grant ran out.

Wistfully, Cox thought about her ten years as a primary teacher at Portland Elementary. The urban school, bordered by unending blocks of deserted warehouses, offered such a sharp contrast to the gentle landscape surrounding Hartstern, reminiscent of an Andrew Wyeth painting. What had kept her at Portland and made art integration such an exciting journey were the friendships—the intense sense of collegiality where "one for all and all for one" was axiomatic. How effective would she be in trying to recreate that experience for teachers at Hartstern, teachers who worked so successfully as individuals?

Cox's three former team members have continued to share and collaborate on occasional projects, but things are not the same at Portland. According to one teacher, "It's been some time now, and we have never had the fun and teamwork we had with Patsy Cox."

REFERENCES AND SELECTED BIBLIOGRAPHY

Buchbinder, J. (1999, November/December). The arts step out from the wings. *Harvard Education Letter*, 15(6), 14–20.

Coerr, E. (1986). *The Josephina story quilt*. New York: Harper Trophy Harper Collins.

Coeyman, M. (1999, February 2). Spelling—and art: History—and art. *Christian Science Monitor*, 4–5.

Gardner, H. (1999, November/December). Howard Gardner on the arts and multiple intelligences. *Harvard Education Letter*, 15(6), 8–13.

Giles, C., Andre, M., Dye, C., & Pfannenstril, V. (1998). Teaching about books: Constant connections through literature—using art, music, and drama. *Language Arts*, 76(1), 27–34.

Goodlad, J., & Anderson, R. (1987). *The nongraded elementary school* (Rev. ed.). New York: Teachers College Press.

Gordon, D. (1999, November/December). Making the case for arts in schools. *Harvard Education Letter*, 15(6), 31–34.

Katz, L. (1993). What can we learn from Reggio Emilia? In C. P. Edwards, G. Forman, & L. Gandiani (Eds.), *The hundred languages of children: The Reggio Emilia approach to early childhood education* (pp. 19–37). Norwood, NJ: Ablex.

Kellogg, R. (1970). *Analyzing children's art.* Palo Alto, CA: Mayfield.

Kellogg, R. (1970). *Children's drawings, children's minds.* New York: Avon.

Korzenik, D. (1973–74). Role-taking and children's drawings. *Studies in Art Education, 15*(3), 17–24.

Leeds, J. A. (1986). Teaching and the reasons for making. *Art Education, 39*(7), 17–21.

Newsom, B. Y., & Silver, A. Z. (1978). *The art museum as educator.* Berkeley: University of California Press.

Thompson, C. A. (1995). Transforming curriculum in the visual arts. In S. Bredekamp & T. Rosegrant (Eds.), *Reaching potentials: Transforming early childhood curriculum and assessment* (Vol. 2, pp. 88–98). Washington, DC: National Association for the Education of Young Children.

Wertsch, J. (1990). The voice of rationality in a sociocultural approach to mind. In L. Moll (Ed.), *Vygotsky and education: Instructional implications and applications of sociohistorical psychology* (pp. 114–126). New York: Cambridge University Press.

Ziefert, H. (1986). *A new coat for Anna.* New York: Alfred Knopf.

Overview of Different Ways of Knowing (DWoK)

The "Different Ways of Knowing" curriculum was developed by the Galef Institute.[1] As of 1999, it has been implemented in schools in 13 states: Alabama, Arizona, California, Florida, Hawaii, Kentucky, Michigan, Mississippi, Montana, New Jersey, Oregon, Texas, and Washington. The most extensive effort, however, has been in Kentucky, where it has expanded to include at least 40 percent of all elementary schools in two-thirds of the state's districts.

The Collaborative for Teaching and Learning, located in Louisville, Kentucky, supports classroom reform with the DWoK curriculum and accompanying professional development. The collaborative offers the three-year DWoK course of study to school teams of teachers and administrators. Professional development includes

- music, visual arts, drama, science, and mathematics;
- yearlong technical assistance and on-site coaching in the classroom;
- curriculum materials for teachers and students; and
- newsletters and access to an interactive Web site (DWoKNET).

An evaluation of DWoK in 24 Kentucky elementary schools (Hovda, R., & Kyle, D. [1997], *Different Ways of Knowing: Effects on teaching and learning practices*. Louisville, KY: University of Louisville) concluded that when the entire faculty participated in DWoK for at least two years

- DWoK changed teachers' knowledge, attitudes, and beliefs about how young children learn.
- DWoK changed teachers' instructional practices to accommodate differences in students' learning styles and strengths.
- Students in DWoK schools showed improvements in academic performance.
- Students in DWoK classrooms had better attitudes toward school and learning than students who did not participate in DWoK.
- DWoK helped increase collaboration among teachers, making school a more vibrant learning community.

---

[1]Contact Sue Beauregard or Amy Berfield. The Galef Institute, 11050 Sanat Monica Blvd., Third Floor, Los Angeles, CA 90025-3594; phone (310) 479-8883; E-mail, sue@galef.org or amy@galef.org.

For more about Different Ways of Knowing in Kentucky, contact

Dr. Linda Hargan, Executive Director
Collaborative for Teaching and Learning
3101 Breckinridge Lane, Suite 1B
Louisville, KY 40220
Phone: (502) 451-3131
E-mail: linda@ky-DWoK.org

Portland Elementary School

Shotgun Make-Over

Shotgun Make-Over
3518 and 3522 Northwestern Parkway

Many years ago, these two houses looked just alike. They were probably built by the same person. Today they are very different. How many things can you find that are similar? How many things are different?

E X H I B I T   D

DWoK Kid-watching Forms

STUDENT'S NAME Jessica

Coming To Know
The Process of Learning

DATE	LEARNING EVENT	ENGAGEMENT • pleasure and involvement • perseverance • risk-taking • responsibility	COLLABORATION • thoughts expressed • openness to feedback • use of input • group work	FLEXIBILITY • modalities used • problem-solving strategies • revision strategies
10/13	Wheel 2: Cluster 3 Exploring Forests (audiotape)	• Excited about new (unknown) project • Listened intently to audiotape • Made predictions	• Shared her predictions • Listened to other's predictions	• Changed some predictions after listening to others • Added details to sketches
3/18	Wheel 2: Cluster 5 Exploring Deserts (pointillism art)	• Read background information pointillism • Listened to others as they read • Looked at models	• Listened to other's comments/observations • Shared her observations • Worked with group to make collage	• Changed her piece of collage (revision) • Experimented with mixing points to create colors.

Kidwatching Form 1

Different Ways of Knowing. Copyright © 1994 The Galef Institute.

STUDENT'S NAME *Jessica*

Showing You Know
The Products of Learning

DATE	LEARNING EVENT	UNDERSTANDING CONTENT • verbal and nonverbal expressions of main idea	CONVENTIONS AND FORMS • first uses of conventions • practiced use of conventions	PRESENTATION • clarity • detail • focus • purpose • voice
10/13	Wheel 2: Cluster 3 Exploring Forests (forest bags)	• Is able to explain why she made the predictions/observations that she made • Drew pictures of content of bags	• Used both pictures and words to express thoughts • Lists items in the bags	• Explained predictions in a clear voice • Included details- focused on purpose
3/18	Wheel 2: Cluster 5 Exploring Deserts (pointillism)	• Quickly began placing points on paper • Was able to explain her thinking about the collage piece.	• Worked to make her part of the collage "perfect" • Tried to make her piece "fit" into collage	• Able to explain why she constructed her collage in the way she did • Collage piece is focused + detailed

Kidwatching Form 2

Different Ways of Knowing. Copyright © 1994 The Galef Institute.

STUDENT'S NAME   *Jessica*

Knowing You Know
Reflections

The essence of education may well be the ability to look back on the learning experience and evaluate what worked and why, and what didn't work and why. Self-reflection—thinking about learning—helps students discover what they have learned, how they learned it, and what they should do next to extend and refine their learning. Please duplicate the *Learning About My Learning* student self-reflection form (on the other side of this form) and use it whenever you feel it is appropriate. Your students' self-reflections will help you plan instruction and create curriculum that will best support them.

DATE	LEARNING EVENT	WHERE WE'VE BEEN • the learner's plan for learning • the learner's strengths	WHERE WE GO NEXT • the learner's needs
10/14	Wheel 2: Cluster 3 Exploring Forests	• Wants to study mangrove trees because she's never heard of them before. • Plans to use electronic encyclopedia and tree books for research	• Help her focus research on location and appearance.
3/19	Wheel 2: Cluster 5 Exploring Deserts	• Wants to know more about saguaro cactus • Interested in Seurat after learning about pointillism	• Help her find books on the saguaro cactus

Kidwatching Form 3

Different Ways of Knowing. Copyright © 1994 The Galef Institute.

DISCUSSION QUESTIONS

1. Describe the environment at Portland Elementary.
   - What is the school's general attitude toward education?
   - What is its relationship with the community?
   - What are some unique features of the teaching/learning environment?

2. Describe Patsy Cox as a teacher.
   - What is her teaching philosophy? Has it changed over time?
   - How has Cox's interest in the arts evolved?
   - Discuss her use of questioning and its value or lack of value for producing higher-order thinking.

3. Faced with the lack of a comprehensive art-integration program, Portland chose to purchase the DWoK program. Cox initially reports that with adequate time, the teachers could have developed similar activities on their own.
   - What are some other alternatives the school could have pursued to achieve art integration? With what consequences?
   - When a school lacks the resources to implement a program such as DWoK, can teachers successfully integrate art? If so, how?

4. When a school such as Portland invests money and training into a specific curriculum program, what issues need to be taken into consideration?
   - What issues arise when a new teacher with no DWoK training joins a faculty team that is using DWoK?
   - What is an individual teacher's responsibility to the team?
   - What are some possible outcomes for Portland's pending art program given Cox's decision to become an administrator?
   - What would you do in Cox's situation?

5. How does successful arts integration occur?
   - What is the role of the individual teacher? The school administrators?
   - Discuss the classroom teachers' responsibility to the arts with and without a full-time art teacher.

6. What are various ways of assessing student art? Discuss the pros and cons of each.
   - To what degree should assessment be based on anecdotal records and student self-assessment alone?
   - Discuss Cox's use of art or graphics to assess learning in various content areas. How viable is this information?

7. How did Cox's approach to assessment change over the time period captured in the case?

- How realistic was her ultimate approach to assessment?
- What would you do the same and what would you do differently? Why?

8. From Cox's viewpoint, a strong sense of collegiality is vital to the success of arts integration.
    - Do you agree or disagree? If you agree, discuss in detail specific kinds of collegiality that should occur.
    - How can teachers/administrators make this happen?

9. Although Portland did not have its own art teacher, it had three vital resources that did not involve additional funding: (1) a historic community, (2) high parent involvement, and (3) strong teacher teams.
    - Discuss the relative importance of each of these for art integration.
    - What other resources could facilitate the process?

10. Cox says, "Anyone with dedication can teach art."
    - Do you agree or disagree with this statement?
    - How might a trained art teacher respond?
    - What are the strengths and drawbacks of Cox's position?

11. What benefits are achieved through the use of art in Cox's classroom? Are there drawbacks?
    - For the teacher
    - For the student
    - For the parent

CASE 3

Discussion Question	Corresponding INTASC Principle
2	4 The teacher understands and uses a variety of instructional strategies to encourage students' development of critical thinking, problem solving, and performance skills.
6	8 The teacher understands and uses formal and informal assessment strategies to evaluate and ensure the continuous intellectual, social, and physical development of the learner.
7	9 The teacher is a reflective practitioner who continually evaluates the effects of his/her choices and actions on others (students, parents, and other professionals in the learning community) and who actively seeks out opportunities to grow professionally.
8, 9	10 The teacher fosters relationships with school colleagues, parents, and agencies in the larger community to support learning and well-being.
11	3 The teacher understands how students differ in their approaches to learning and creates instructional opportunities that are adapted to diverse learners.

Caroline Never Smiles

Cast of Characters

Mr. Cristoff	Special education teacher
Caroline Ellington	Special education student
Mrs. Ellington	Caroline's mother
Ms. Johns	Counselor
Ms. Shelton	Caroline's sixth-grade language arts teacher
Ms. Ward	Sixth-grade social studies teacher
Mr. Willey	Fifth-grade teacher

At the Belle Vista sixth-grade dance, heavy metal music pounded across the gym, reverberating out into the dimly lit stucco hallways. Adolescent boys milled on one side of the gym, hands in low-slung pockets and legs contorting in odd positions while the girls clustered in half circles, legs swaying casually amidst muffled giggles. Only rarely that evening did a courageous suitor venture alone across the wide, newly shined gym floor to ask a classmate to dance.

Like her female classmates, Caroline had devoted much time to preparing herself for the first dance of the year, a much-anticipated occasion. Her hair, elegantly braided with a grosgrain ribbon, seemed to sparkle under the fluorescent lighting. Her new, trendy lime-green outfit was the latest in preadolescent chic. Unlike the rest of her class, however, Caroline did not participate in the circle prelims. After her mother had dropped her off, Caroline entered the gym and eagerly watched her classmates, but only for a few minutes. Then, precariously perched on her prosthetic legs, she abruptly reversed her forward direction and walked out under the glaring orange exit sign. She moved slowly, winding her way down the empty hallway to the quiet isolation of the school cafeteria. She was glad to see her resource teacher, with whom she spent one period a day outside the regular classroom. After talking with him briefly, she moved to sit with a group of girls, where she remained until her mother arrived to take her home.

PHYSICALLY SPEAKING

"Why doesn't Caroline ever smile?" asked Ms. Ward, who taught the sixth-grade social studies class to which Caroline had been assigned. "You know, she seems like such an unhappy child."

The members of the Individualized Education Plan (IEP) team who were gathered to discuss Caroline Ellington's transition from elementary to middle school turned to Mrs. Ellington and awaited her response. The answer came loud and clear. "Caroline *can't* smile like you and me."

This simple explanation caught Ms. Ward and the other educators off guard. They glanced around at each other—each hoping someone else would be the first to speak. "I wanted to crawl under the table after I asked the question," Ms. Ward later reminisced. Although school had been in session more than a month, the teachers at Belle Vista Middle School were unaware of the full nature of Caroline's disabilities. Mrs. Ellington's explanation answered the teacher's question by identifying a defining characteristic of Caroline's disability. However, none of the teachers fully understood the parameters of the rare genetic disorder, Moebius syndrome.[1]

Moebius syndrome, identifiable at birth by a "masklike expression," is readily apparent, especially when the child laughs or cries. Facial weakness, muscle paralysis, or defective development of the jaw and tongue also causes difficulties in speech and swallowing. Other physical abnormalities often accompany the disorder and may include clubfeet, dislocated hips, and more or fewer than five digits on the hands and feet.

For Caroline, Moebius syndrome has impacted her ability to show facial expression and her ability to speak. Although her communication skills have far surpassed the expectations of medical and clinical experts, her partially paralyzed tongue has left her voice with little volume and has caused articulation problems. Consequently, her speech is difficult to understand, especially for those without prior knowledge who try to communicate with her for the first time.

In addition to the Moebius syndrome, Caroline was born with other physical abnormalities. Her left arm ends just below the elbow joint, and her legs terminate just above the knee. She uses prosthetic legs to move short distances and switches to an electric wheelchair for longer ones. When not wearing her artificial legs or traveling in her wheelchair, she ambulates her body by using her right arm in a crutch-like manner, lifting and swinging her body forward for each "step." She uses her foreshortened left arm to support and pivot her movements, a technique she taught herself during early childhood (see Exhibit A).

Surgery was used to ameliorate other physical problems such as creating an appropriate closure in her trachea. However, the stoma[2] still opens slightly when

---

[1]The Moebius syndrome Foundation provides information for families of affected individuals, the public or media, and professionals (for example, clinicians and teachers). The address is P.O. Box 993, Larchmont, NY 10538; phone (914) 834-6008.

[2]An incised opening in the throat maintained for drainage after removal of a trachea tube following a tracheotomy.

Caroline's masklike expression is caused by Moebius syndrome. Weak facial muscles prevent her from smiling.

Caroline coughs or clears her throat, causing air to enter the trachea. When there is cool weather or the wind is blowing, Caroline can't be outside because she feels as though she can't breathe.

Caroline has radiant translucent skin, a very slender build, fine features, and a chestnut brown ponytail. Sitting in her wheelchair, her right arm rests gracefully on the chair's arm. When she speaks, she often uses her arm to gesture and emphasize a point.

Caroline lives with her parents, Kendal and Katie Ellington, in a gated, exclusive community of upper socioeconomic families in a western state. Kendal is a vice president of a well-established insurance company, and Katie is a full-time home-maker. At 13, Caroline is the youngest of three children. Kelly, who attends college, is 21, and Matt is 16. "Caroline's independence and ability to keep up with everyone else is a tribute to her family who have 'done the right things,' " remarked Caroline's elementary school speech/language pathologist (see Exhibit B).

Friends and acquaintances would describe Katie Ellington as a positive thinker who raised Caroline to be her own best advocate—to take responsibility for her actions and to accept the consequences.

According to Katie, Caroline exhibits all the traits of youngest child syndrome. "She is funny and loves to play the role of the comedian and practical joker. She might even be considered a rascal at times." Very independent, Caroline refuses to identify herself as disabled, and accommodations at home provide her as much independence as possible. For example, breakfast items, snacks, and even treats for the dog are all placed within Caroline's reach either on lower shelves in the cupboards or on the bottom racks of the refrigerator.

Katie discusses her daughter's ability to understand people—how adept she is at reading facial expressions, body language, and emotions. Katie believes that Caroline's perceptiveness leads her to give people what she thinks they expect. For example, if teachers don't expect much from Caroline, she doesn't give them much in return.

Caroline reports being happy with and enjoying school. Like her peers, she engages in "complaining" about her teachers and has mood swings, particularly when it comes to relationships with parents, teachers, and other students. She experiences typical adolescent problems organizing school work, getting to class on time, maintaining good personal relationships, and wearing the "right" clothes. These normal developmental adjustments, however, are always compounded by the additional accommodations Caroline must make to cope with her disabilities. "I wish I looked like other people," she confided to a classroom aide.

THE SCHOOL DISTRICT

The Adams County School District is typical of many large, consolidated urban districts located in the western states. Encompassing the city and several urban-adjacent areas, it includes 46 elementary, 12 middle, and 6 high schools. A significant portion of families has low personal incomes: one-third, or 14,000 students, qualify for free or reduced meals. The 12 percent of students who qualify for special education services are comparable to the national average of 10 percent. Caroline's middle school, Belle Vista, reflects the demographics of the immediate neighborhood—a situation quite different from the district as a whole. The majority of the students come from families in the average to above-average socioeconomic strata, and only 9 percent qualify for free or reduced lunches.

During the 1980s and early 1990s, national focus on educational reform prompted administrators in the district to institute major changes. Once a junior high modeled on the open classroom pod concept of the 1960s, Belle Vista is now a burgeoning middle school with a 13 percent overload and several portable classrooms. The flat-roofed, chipped-cement building is distinguished by the lack of windows in most of the classrooms. Erecting walls in what were once the open spaces for "pod" classrooms has left many areas of the school with no natural lighting.

Like its regular education counterpart, the Adams County Special Education Department has been committed to reform. Special education administrators adopted a collaborative and inclusionary stand by placing students with special needs in regular classrooms across the entire school system. Special education teachers were encouraged to collaborate with regular education teachers by providing cooperative or auxiliary instruction for students with disabilities in the regular classroom.

Belle Vista, which includes grades six through eight, was committed to the middle school model early on and quickly moved from departmentalized instruction to a team-teaching model. Small groups of teachers work with approximately 150 students. Each team has four teachers, one for each of the basic academic classes: math, science, social studies, and reading and language arts. Using this team approach, teachers have developed an integrated and thematic curriculum. The core subjects are augmented by exploratory classes in technology, home economics, art, speech and drama, and three foreign languages.

Tensions, however, between "new practices" and old methods persist at Belle Vista. In spite of a districtwide policy committed to a middle school structure and a philosophy that emphasizes holistic, integrated teaching, many teachers continue to use lecture and recitation almost exclusively, with little emphasis on peer interaction. Using discipline-based texts almost exclusively, they present material in traditional lock-step fashion. There is little attempt to create cross-disciplinary problems to enhance student thinking despite the availability of team planning time. A statewide emphasis on student accountability has narrowed the focus of several Belle Vista teachers.

The school offers five special education programs. Two are resource settings for students with mild learning and behavioral problems. Three are self-contained programs: one each for students with severe behavioral disorders, learning disabilities, and physical disabilities. The middle school has a four-year record of success in educating students with physical disabilities. The special education teachers consider most regular educators to be cooperative and very helpful in the successful inclusion of students with physical disabilities into the regular classroom.

Caroline's full inclusion at Belle Vista is a continuation of the policy that began when she first enrolled in the school district. Starting with first grade, she always attended classes with students her own age in regular classrooms. But because of her pronounced physical disabilities, Caroline also received special education services based on an IEP.[3] In early grade school, the speech/language clinician worked closely with her, and during all her school years, teachers especially knowledgeable about physical disabilities were available to guide and support her. Although Caroline's family could well have afforded a private school, one especially designed to meet the needs of students with disabilities, they chose instead to enroll her in the Adams County School District because of its emphasis on inclusion.

ACADEMICALLY SPEAKING

"Caroline seems to have shut down this year," Katie Ellington sighed as she addressed the IEP team during the meeting she had requested. "I mean, she was not a straight A student in fourth and fifth grade, but she has never had D's and F's on her report cards before middle school" (see Exhibit C).

Katie's concerns about her daughter's academic and emotional progress in school were well founded, especially given the new types of demands Caroline

---

[3]According to the mandates of P.L. 94-142 (the Education of All Handicapped Children's Act) and P.L. 101-476 (Individuals with Disabilities Education Act), Caroline's main entitlements are defined as a series of rights to free and inclusive education.

faced in middle school. But the problems were beginning to develop long before Caroline reached Belle Vista. Caroline's eligibility for special education services had been determined by various assessments. The evaluations centered on speech-language tests, adaptive behavior scales, and achievement tests. These measures were used because her problems initially appeared to be totally physical. No IQ measure was ever administered to evaluate the possibility of cognitive delays or learning disabilities. In addition, no social-emotional evaluations were ever given.

Following speech and language assessments, Caroline received language therapy in the primary grades and benefited from these services. But they were discontinued later in grade school, because extensive school and medical tests indicated that she was surpassing expectations. Given the constraints imposed by Moebius Syndrome, Caroline's speech volume and enunciation were far better than leading experts predicted. Nonetheless, she was hard to understand by uninformed listeners and was unable to project her voice beyond her immediate vicinity. After becoming accustomed to Caroline's speech patterns, most teachers reported having little difficulty understanding her.

By law, students who qualify for special education must be reevaluated every three years. Among the tests used with students with physical disabilities are adaptive behavior scales, which measure the degree of personal independence and social responsibility achieved by an individual. A recently administered scale of adaptive behavior indicated that Caroline earned scores in the "adequate range" in the areas of communication, daily living skills, and socialization. Although all her scores were reported as "adequate," interpersonal skills stood out as her greatest strength.

A series of recent academic achievement tests indicated that Caroline's reading and written expression were average for her age and grade. Reading comprehension posed more difficulties for Caroline than word recognition. Moreover, she scored well below the average range on tests of mathematical achievement. Both her mathematics reasoning and mathematical computation fell significantly below the average levels of age-similar peers. Her resource teachers had not concerned themselves with this area of her development and, in fact, were unaware of the test scores. Consequently, no referrals or recommendations had been made to address the problem.

Throughout her public school career, Caroline had attended mainstreamed classes in all academic areas. Like most elementary students, she remained primarily in one classroom taught by one teacher in each grade. Mobility posed only minor problems. When Caroline needed to move from the main classroom to specialized ones offering art, music or computers, she used her wheelchair. During a typical school day, Caroline needed the physical assistance of an adult only to get on and off the bus and to use the bathroom.

During her first four years of elementary school, Caroline consistently received support from her peers. They helped her get materials from her backpack or desk many times throughout the day. When she needed help maneuvering her wheelchair in and out of the classroom or through the hallways, other students quickly came to her aid. According to Caroline's mother, students were eager to sign up for days and classes in which they could be Caroline's helpers. Clearly, the optimum strategies of inclusion were working well in this environment.

A radical change occurred, however, in the fifth grade when Caroline's peer-helper support system abruptly ended. The school administration, afraid of a potential lawsuit that had been threatened by parents of another student with disabilities, terminated the peer support policy for all students with disabilities. Caroline felt the change immediately. Mr. Willey, her fifth-grade teacher, adhering strictly to the district memorandum, suddenly discouraged students from helping Caroline. At the same time, he erroneously assumed that if Caroline needed help she would now ask him. However, instead of asking for help—something that Caroline was unaccustomed to—she began to withdraw and contribute less, even in her best subjects. Without the help of her classmates, it took Caroline longer to find needed materials, and she frequently dropped them. Soon she had more problems organizing her work and getting on task. Although Mr. Willey noticed that she interacted less with her classmates and spent more time alone, this issue was never discussed with Caroline's IEP team. Mr. Willey offered to help Caroline during and after school with her academic work, particularly mathematics, but she didn't take him up on it. Her parents found a private tutor to assist Caroline in mathematics.

The transition to sixth grade and the Belle Vista Middle School's structure compounded Caroline's problems. Still lacking peer support, Caroline now had to move hourly from classroom to classroom, adding to her organizational problems. She had difficulty maneuvering her wheelchair in the school's overcrowded classrooms and narrow hallways. These logistical issues meant that, for the first time in her life, Caroline was usually late for her classes.

Although she had only been at Belle Vista a short time, Caroline's burgeoning problems were cause for major concern on Katie Ellington's part. In addition to Caroline's increasing problems with mobility and organization, her academic grades had been on a gradual but steady decline. (For a list of Caroline's grades and medical history, see Exhibits A and C.) By midterm of her first year in middle school, her grades declined to D's in most subjects, and she failed both social studies and science.

By Halloween of the sixth grade, Caroline's falling grades became such a grave concern that Katie Ellington called a special meeting with the IEP team to consider the academic problems. The team consisted of Caroline's parents, her regular and special education teachers, and a school-based special education consultant. Caroline declined to attend; she claimed that she had work to finish and that the meeting was "probably unimportant anyway." Revising the full-inclusion plan of the previous spring, the IEP team now recommended that Caroline spend time daily in a resource room for students with physical disabilities. For the first time in her entire public school career, Caroline would spend time in a special education classroom. Seemingly embarrassed, Caroline referred to this as "my study hall time."

Initially, Mr. Cristoff, the physical disabilities resource teacher, reported that Caroline's special resource class was beneficial. She regularly sought help, asked questions, and worked industriously on her assignments. But as the school year progressed, she became withdrawn and stopped requesting any instruction or assistance. Although Cristoff frequently asked if she needed help, Caroline indicated she did not. She claimed everything was okay and that she understood her assignments. Cristoff did not check her work or connect with her regular classroom teachers but instead accepted her self-evaluation.

Another problem for Caroline was that her test-taking time was significantly slower than that of her peers. Because she consistently was unable to write the answers to open-ended test questions in the allotted time, her IEP team proposed another remedy. All of Caroline's answers to questions were to be scripted by a classroom assistant or teacher. But once again, Caroline refused help with the tests, preferring to tackle them on her own. She insisted on the independence, which she believed had been a key to achieving success during her first five grades.

Ms. Shelton, Caroline's sixth-grade language arts teacher, lent support to Caroline's quest for autonomy through a seemingly inadvertent remark. Caroline had unexpectedly shared with the class some background on her disability and how it might have come about (see Exhibit D). Ms. Shelton quickly responded, "Everyone has a disability, whether it is academic, physical, or social. People have to overcome their disabilities and do the best they can with what they have."

TECHNOLOGICALLY SPEAKING

One day, in the fall of Caroline's first year in middle school, after completing a language arts lesson, Ms. Shelton asked the class to begin work on a new reading assignment. Sitting at her desk, she answered individual students' questions that needed clarification or further explanation. All of a sudden, looking down, she saw Caroline on the floor beside her using her arm for balance, "How did you get here?" Ms. Shelton asked, stunned.

"I don't think she knew I was surprised. I tried not to act surprised, but I thought to myself, 'How did you get there?' I had never seen Caroline do that before [that is, move about without her wheelchair], and I didn't know she could."

Caroline did not appear by accident. She had pressed the remote control switch to lower her wheelchair using the electric lift. She traveled to Ms. Shelton's desk in the front of the room by using her right arm to lift and swing her body forward for each "step." After speaking to Ms. Shelton, Caroline returned to her wheelchair in the same way she had come to the front of the classroom. Using the wheelchair to raise herself back to the level of her desk, she transferred to her desk chair and continued with her assignment. "The rest of the class was not surprised that Caroline came across the floor," said Ms. Shelton. "I suspected Caroline had done this in other classes."

Indeed, from first through fifth grade, Caroline used her self-designed method to travel within the classroom. But, even though the teachers, parents, and other support personnel met at least once yearly to plan for Caroline's education, no one had taken the time to explain Caroline's various travel modes to Ms. Shelton.

For short distances, Caroline's self-propelled motor techniques had served her more efficiently in elementary school than her wheelchair. During grade school, she

Caroline surprised Ms. Shelton when she unexpectedly left her wheelchair and "scooted" up to retrieve a book.

"scooted" across the classroom floor to sharpen her pencil, get to the teacher's desk, and make presentations to the class. Because Caroline stayed in the same classroom most of the school day, this short-distance form of mobility presented few challenges. The multiple classrooms of middle school meant an abrupt change.

Caroline was fitted with prosthetic legs, but she seldom used them. They had obvious physical limitations. The artificial legs could not bend at the knee, and one leg could only be extended at nearly a right angle from her body while she was seated due to problems with hip alignment on this side. In addition, the legs were heavy and awkward and placed a considerable amount of physical pressure on her hips and upper thighs.

During her last year of grade school, Caroline was scheduled for flexible artificial leg replacements that hinged at the knee. According to Mr. Willey, Caroline was eager for the new legs to arrive. Unfortunately, they did not live up to Caroline's expectations. First, there was difficulty with proper fit, and she developed sores on her stumps, a common occurrence with prosthetic legs. Second, the knee hinges would suddenly collapse, and she fell frequently, unable to stand upright without assistance. The falls were embarrassing and compromised her independence. According to reports, Caroline received extensive support from her parents, teachers, and the school physical therapist, but the prosthetics just did not meet her needs. Not surprisingly, Caroline discarded the new legs by the end of the fifth grade.

Belle Vista Middle School and the sixth grade presented obstacle courses that challenged Caroline's mobility. The classrooms were small and crowded, the hallways were narrow and congested, and she now had to make frequent trips to her locker. Since Caroline had already stopped using her artificial legs and scooting was not possible for long distances, only her wheelchair remained. The wheelchair option was one she had used infrequently during elementary school, preferring instead the independence her scooting provided.

Middle school teachers tried to accommodate Caroline's wheelchair by placing it in the very back of the room. To give her extra time, she was excused early from classes so she could travel down less crowded hallways. While these modifications helped

Caroline's mobility, they increased her isolation, often leaving her alone and missing some of each class. She was no longer an integral part of any class.

The school district also made efforts to support Caroline's school progress by using technology. Toward the end of fourth grade, her IEP team met to plan her fifth-grade academic program. Because Caroline had functional fingers only on her right hand, they discussed her need for assistance in working with computers. The team was in agreement that a technological device or program might help her to use a computer more efficiently. The team requested an evaluation to determine if assistive technology would be appropriate for Caroline.

In spite of the law and the intent of Caroline's IEP team, nothing was done during the summer between fourth and fifth grade to pursue support through assistive technology. In October, the IEP team met again and made a formal request for a technological evaluation for Caroline. By June, an evaluation by an outside consultant was completed. Finally, in February of the following year, the IEP team met with an assistive technology specialist to discuss the evaluation report. The team was aware that in making decisions about the type of technology tools or supports a particular student might require, the recommended process is to start with the low-tech solutions and then work up the continuum to higher-tech solutions as needed. Although the specialist did offer a range of solutions, the team recommended that the district purchase a high-technology BAT keyboard for Caroline. Easily portable, the BAT is a very plain, four-by-four-inch, one-handed consolidated keyboard that replaces a traditional computer keyboard. Caroline received the BAT keyboard in the late spring, a full year after the team's first request for technological assistance. District personnel soon discovered that the BAT they had purchased was for the wrong computer platform (Macintosh- vs. IBM-compatible). The keyboard was exchanged, and one compatible with IBM computers finally arrived. Next, the keyboard had to be modified because it was too large for Caroline's hand; she could not access all the keys, so the BAT device was sent to a rehabilitative engineer. The engineer had to fabricate a whole new system that accommodated Caroline's hand. Although the district hired and paid an outside consultant to provide training, there is no evidence that Caroline or her teachers were trained to use the BAT keyboard, and no assistance was provided for family members. Still hopeful, Katie Ellington got permission for Caroline to take the keyboard home over the summer. However, when installing the BAT device caused inexplicable malfunctions to the family computer, it was put on the shelf. Caroline had always done quite well in her computer classes and had even won an award in one, so the Ellingtons did not pursue the usability of the customized keyboard.

When Caroline began Belle Vista, she left the BAT at home. Even though the computer class was her favorite, she made no mention of the device or that she had been told it would improve her speed. Prior to the beginning of the year, her special education teacher had been told of the keyboard but had not received training in its use and had not been reminded of its availability. Although use of the BAT keyboard was documented on her IEP, Caroline's teachers only remembered the BAT's existence when they were contacted by the public relations officer at the district office.

Concurrent with a new emphasis on assistive technology for students with disabilities, a film crew was scheduled to videotape Caroline using the BAT.

Meanwhile, the assistive technology specialist claimed that, all along, he had assumed Caroline was using the BAT regularly and proficiently but simply hadn't followed up once Caroline had taken the device home.

SOCIALLY SPEAKING

Caroline's social problems surfaced in the fifth grade. One day, in tears, Caroline arrived in Ms. Johns' office. Caroline told the counselor that some of the girls in her class were talking about her, making fun of her, and ignoring her. She demanded something be done about this. As Ms. Johns probed the situation, Caroline identified what she perceived as a clique and named the girls involved. Ms. Johns acknowledged that these particular girls were known to pick on other students who looked or acted different. At the same time, the counselor thought it was unusual that the problem arose in the fifth grade. As far as she knew, Caroline had always gotten along with her peers. Since Ms. Johns was currently working with the fifth graders on developing self-esteem, Caroline asked to be allowed to take part in one of the presentations to the class. Ms. Johns suggested that Caroline make a presentation to her classmates and share with them some of her feelings about being disabled and how people often treated her differently.

Excited about this opportunity as well as a bit nervous, Caroline asked her mother to be part of the presentation. "I can't do this," replied Mrs. Ellington. "You have to find your own words for this. I can't fight your battles."

As Caroline gave her well-rehearsed talk to the class, sharing how it felt to be excluded, she tactfully mentioned no names. But Ms. Johns noticed that some of the girls who were part of the clique seemed to lower their heads to hide their embarrassment. After Caroline finished talking to the class, she summarized her talk by playing the song *Healing* by Wynnona and Michael English:

> The chapter's been written
> It's all in the past
> I kept turning pages and
> I'm here at least
> I'm healing
>
> *Chorus*
> Healing: gonna take some time
> But I'm on the mend
> I'm healing
> Starting over at the end and feeling
> Stronger than I've ever been
> I'm healing

I can see me pulling through
Finding out I'm someone who
Is moving on and letting go
Picking up the pieces along the road[4]

When the song ended, she asked the class if they had any questions. No one raised a hand. Then, without prompting from Ms. Johns, the students applauded and raced to recess. Although Ms. Johns was originally apprehensive about Caroline's presentation, she felt the class reacted maturely to the lesson and that the intervention had proved to be a success.

That evening after supper, Caroline received a phone call from Sherri, one of the girls in the clique. Sherri said she was calling from a friend's house and wanted to apologize for her unkind behavior. Caroline later discussed her subsequent attempts to build a friendship with Sherri.

"I get home from school and this girl from my class calls. She says she wants to say she is sorry for treating me bad. I asked her if she wants to come over and play. She says 'no' because she is going to the ice cream store with some friends. I called her the next morning and the mom said she had left. That girl lied about not being able to come over. Nobody ever called me before, and I don't know how they got my number. They called for a trick."

Ms. Johns felt initially that personal relationships improved after the talk. But a few months later, the girls claimed that although they were now trying to build a friendship, Caroline wasn't. They accused her of seeking attention and reported that Caroline turned her back or did not answer them when they talked to her. They interpreted Caroline's behavior as anger toward them and decided simply to ignore her rather than risk more conflict.

By the time Caroline reached middle school, this fifth-grade social dilemma had developed into a pattern of exclusion and seclusion. Teachers reported that Caroline seldom talked with other students. She traveled alone in the hallways and sat at the back of every classroom. At the end of the school day, she was immediately helped onto the bus, excluding her from taking part in extracurricular activities. At noon, she invariably ate by herself. But no one referred Caroline for personal counseling, a school district service for which she was eligible.

Caroline did participate in class discussion when the topic broached her disabilities. After studying the book *Twenty-One Balloons* (DuBois, 1946/1986), members of Caroline's class raised questions about the results of repeated intermarriage among a limited number of families. Ms. Shelton explained the problems that sometimes resulted from these marriages, citing examples such as the genetic link between the royal families of Europe and hemophilia. She used the examples to explain state laws prohibiting the marriage of close relatives.

Caroline's hand shot up the second Ms. Shelton stopped talking. Caroline explained to the class that her father had traced their family history. As a result of

---

[4]From *Healing* by W. English and M. English, 1994, Zachery Creek Music, Inc.

his genealogical research, Caroline and her family surmised that a grandmother might be responsible for her disability. After a long pause in the discussion, Ms. Shelton asked Caroline if her grandmother felt guilty about passing on a disability. "No," responded Caroline. "Besides, I like me just the way I am."

EPILOGUE

Between Caroline's sixth and seventh grade, the Adams County School District embarked on a more focused effort to use assistive technology for children with disabilities. Newly available federal funding made this possible. During the summer, the district's assistive technology coordinator and Caroline's special education teacher worked individually with her in order to understand her needs more fully. This effort included several conversations with Katie Ellington.

At about the same time, Caroline's family initiated a redesign of the prosthetic legs that had been discarded a year earlier. As a seventh-grade student, she was now excited about her new legs. The legs were longer and fit better with specially added Velcro. Socks, neatly pulled over her stumps, served as a buffer to prevent pinching and to make the legs more comfortable. While the wheelchair remained parked in the school hallway for longer distances, Caroline now could maneuver into and around any classroom using her new prosthetic legs. "I enjoy walking in school now," said Caroline.

At the suggestion of the special education teacher and assistive technology coordinator, Caroline was assigned to a specific seventh-grade team—"The Tigers"— widely known as the "caring team." The team was composed of teachers who were enthusiastically committed to integrated thematic units in math, science, English, and social studies that encouraged and supported collateral learning.[5] They also made a special effort to include students with special needs in all team activities. This was accomplished by modifying schedules, by using a detailed team behavior policy, and by providing extra support for homework assignments. The group claimed its behavioral referral and failure rate was lower than that of other teams because of these strategies used in deliberate combination with instructional approaches that emphasized individual growth and accountability. In the "Tiger Team" classrooms, students are most often seen engaged in cooperative learning, peer conferencing, one-on-one instruction, and independent project work.

The teachers emphasize good communication such as talking regularly with parents via phone calls, notes, and parent-teacher conferences. Teachers send daily notes home, which itemize homework assignments and evaluate the student's academic and behavioral progress. "Caroline looks forward to going to school now," Katie Ellington commented, adding, "She seems to be getting her work completed and is earning higher grades than last year." While Caroline's grades in seventh grade have improved overall, recent assessments indicated that Caroline might have a learning disability in math.

---

[5] In *Experience & Education* (1938), John Dewey elaborates upon collateral learning.

Caroline's progress in the social area is mixed, and to date there has been no discussion about the possibility of counseling. After Thanksgiving, the Tigers went on a daylong field trip to a local science museum. At the insistence of her teachers, this was Caroline's first school trip without her mother. When the day finally arrived, she was excited about her independence but glad to have been assigned a buddy for the trip, Josh Madden. Caroline reflected on the connection with Josh. "He was like my best friend, or at least I thought he was. He talked to me a lot on the bus. But now he just says 'hi' in the cafeteria."

When asked who her best friend was by a newcomer to the school, Caroline identified her classmate, Sandy, a student with multiple disabilities (including cerebral palsy and cognitive delays). "We get to be together on the bus and during first period. And I got to go to her birthday party in June," exclaimed Caroline. "But we don't see each other outside of school, because my house doesn't have any wheelchair ramps, and Sandy can't leave her wheelchair."

Sensitive to Caroline's lack of friendships, her parents broached the subject of a facial operation with Caroline. This operation might allow Caroline to smile like other young adults her own age for the first time in her life. Based on the nationally publicized experience of Chelsea Thomas, another child with Moebius syndrome, Caroline's parents suggested that she might consider the same surgery. Chelsea's surgery had produced a beautiful smile. Quickly and vehemently, Caroline responded that she was not interested—that she had already been through too many operations. Caroline's family supported her decision. Mr. Cristoff struggles with the implications of Caroline's blunt and instantaneous decision and recalled the words of Chelsea's mother:

> Smiles are so important; they help us connect to other people, to communicate. They let people know that we're interested, that we're friendly. Being without that vital connection can be very isolating for a child. As her mother, I know Chelsea is interesting and friendly and bright. But [sic—before the operation] the rest of the world couldn't tell—at least, not at a glance. (Thomas & Stich, 1996, pp. 31–34)

A P P E N D I X   A

Special Education Mandates

A. Edward Blackhurst

Special education and related services for students are mandated by federal laws that have their roots in Public Law 94-142, which was passed by Congress in 1975. This law has been amended several times and is now known as IDEA, which is the acronym for the Individuals with Disabilities Act. IDEA guarantees the right of all children with disabilities to a free and appropriate education in the least restrictive environment. An individualized education plan (IEP) must be developed for all students who have been diagnosed as having a disability. As part of the IEP planning process, parents, teachers, and administrators are required to consider the technologies that may be useful in helping a child meet the objectives in the IEP.

When special education students reach adulthood, their rights to accessible employment will be protected by PL 99-506, which amended the Rehabilitation Act of 1973 by adding Section 508. Section 508 ensures access to computers and other electronic office equipment in places of federal employment. The guidelines ensure that users with disabilities can access and use the same computer equipment and programs as other users and that modifications will be made in the work environment to facilitate employment of people with disabilities.

Two other important laws affect the way schools, governmental agencies, and businesses provide access for people with disabilities. PL 101-336, the Americans with Disabilities Act (ADA), broadened the types of agencies and employers covered by Section 508 requirements and mandates additional protections, such as accessible public transportation systems, communication systems, and access to public buildings. These requirements are opening many avenues of employment for people with disabilities who were heretofore excluded from office work because of inaccessible equipment and work environments.

Public Law 100-407, the Technology-Related Assistance for Individuals with Disabilities Act, was signed into law in 1988. Under the auspices of that act, all states are developing systems for providing a variety of technology assistance to children and adults with disabilities and their parents and guardians. The purpose of PL 100-407 is to provide financial assistance to the states to enable them to conduct needs assessments, identify technology resources, provide assistive technology services, and conduct public awareness programs, among others. It also provided a definition of assistive technology devices and services, which was added to IDEA in one of its amendments.

When school personnel make decisions about the most appropriate educational program for students with disabilities, IDEA mandates that they must adhere to the following guarantees:

- The child's parents must be notified in writing when the child is to be tested for possible special education placement. They are assigned *due process rights* that ensure procedural safeguards in all matters related to the student's evaluation and educational placement.
- Each student with a disability is entitled to an education in the *least restrictive environment*. This means that, to the extent possible, they should receive education in educational settings designed for students without disabilities.
- Students who are to receive special education services are entitled to an IEP that specifies their strengths and weaknesses, educational goals, objectives, those that are responsible for their education, and dates for reassessment and revision of the IEP. Their parents must be involved in planning for the IEP, as should the student who will receive educational services, to the extent possible.
- The families of students with disabilities should expect *confidentiality and right to privacy* concerning records regarding their children, their school placement, and related activities.
- If the parents of a student with disabilities are unable to be involved in their education planning, they are entitled to the services of a *parent surrogate*.
- Students with disabilities are entitled to free and appropriate special education services until they are 21 years of age.

In addition to the IEPs that are developed for children of school age, preschool children with disabilities are entitled to the development of Individualized Family Service Plans (IFSPs), those who are completing their school careers are entitled to an Individualized Transition Plan (ITP), and those with disabilities who are receiving rehabilitation services are entitled to an Individualized Rehabilitation Plan (IRP). Similar procedures and guarantees are involved in designing and implementing each of those legal rights.

A P P E N D I X   B

A Functional Approach to Individual Differences

A. Edward Blackhurst

Most educators support the goal of responding to the individual differences exhibited by their students. Because of the logistics involved in dealing with large numbers of students, however, most teachers individualize instruction by grouping students with their peers who have similar characteristics. While such practices have produced successful results for most students over the years, teachers often have difficulty in responding to students who have unique characteristics that set them apart from "typical" students. A model that can be used to guide decision making and delivery of services for such students is presented in this appendix.

When decisions are being made about the provision of individualized services, a useful perspective is to focus on the problem the student has in functioning within his or her environment. For example, a preschooler with cerebral palsy may lack the fine muscle control that will permit her to fasten buttons so that she can get dressed independently. A boy with a visual impairment may be unable to use printed material that is being used for instruction in an English class. Another student, due to unknown cause, may be unable to solve math problems. Similarly, a child who has been in an automobile accident may have had a severe head injury that has impaired her ability to speak clearly.

In each of these cases, an environmental demand has been placed on the student to perform some function that he or she will find difficult to execute because of a set of unique circumstances or restriction in functional capability caused by the lack of personal resources. For example, the children mentioned lack the physical or mental capabilities to button, read, calculate, or speak clearly.

All of us face situations daily in which environmental demands are placed on us. Our goal is to understand the processes and relate them to the lives of students who face more complex and restrictive situations. There is the need to know many things, such as the nature of the demands that are being placed on the student from the environment and how those demands create the requirements to perform different human functions, such as learning, walking, talking, seeing, and hearing. It is important to know how such requirements are—or are not—being met by the student and how factors such as the student's perceptions and the availability of personal resources such as intelligence, sight, and mobility can affect the responses the student can make. In addition, it is important to understand how availability of external supports such as special education, different types of therapy, and technology can impact the student's ability to produce functional responses to the environmental demands.

Although each student will be unique, the common challenge is to identify and apply the best possible array of education and related services that will provide support, adjustment, or compensation for the student's functional needs or deficits. A variety of responses may be appropriate. For example, Velcro fasteners may be used to replace buttons on garments for the student having difficulty with buttoning. Braille or audio materials may be provided for the student who cannot read conventional print. The student who has difficulty calculating may require specialized, intense direct math instruction, while a computerized device that produces speech may enable the student who cannot speak clearly to communicate.

FUNCTIONAL AREAS

Students may exhibit individual differences in one or more of several areas of human function. Following are descriptions of some of the most common. Note how technology can be used and the roles that specialists can play in providing support services in each of the areas.

Existence.   Functions associated with existence are those responses that are needed to sustain life. These functions include feeding, elimination, bathing, dressing, grooming, and sleeping. Special education services, particularly those for preschool children and those with severe disabilities, may focus on teaching students to perform such functions. Special devices such as buttonhooks, weighted eating utensils, and combs with long handles may be provided to assist students in performing those functions. Assistance in using such devices also may be provided by occupational therapists.

Communication.   The reception, internalization, and expression of information are functions included in the category of communication. Communication aids, speech synthesizers, telephone amplifiers, hearing aids, and the services of speech-language pathologists and audiologists might be appropriate to support communication functions.

Body Support, Alignment, and Positioning.   Some students need assistance to maintain a stable position or to support portions of their body. A brace, support harnesses, slings, and body protectors are useful devices in this functional category, as would be the services of a physical therapist. Other medical personnel also may provide supporting services with functions in this category.

Travel and Mobility.   Functions in this category include the ability to move horizontally, vertically, or laterally. Wheelchairs, special lifts, canes, walkers, specially adapted tricycles, and crutches can be used to support these functions. Specialists, such as those who provide mobility training for children who are blind, may be called upon to provide services associated with this category.

Environmental Adaptation.   The environment can be adapted, or the person can adapt to the environment. This category includes functions associated with these adaptations as seen in the performance of many of the activities of daily living, both indoors and outdoors. Examples of functions include driving, food preparation, operation of appliances, and alteration of the living space.

It may be necessary to make a number of modifications to school facilities to accommodate functions in this category. For example, enlarged door knobs, special switches for controlling computers, grabbers to reach items on high shelves, chalkboards and desks that can be raised so that a student in a wheelchair can use them, and ramps to accommodate wheelchairs may be required. Often, assistive technology specialists are called upon to provide help with environmental adaptations.

Learning, Education, and Rehabilitation.   Functions in this category include those associated with school activities and various types of therapies and rehabilitation processes. Regular class teachers, special education teachers, speech-language therapists, rehabilitation counselors, psychologists, and others may be involved in providing direct services to students. In addition, numerous technologies also may be used within the context of schools. Included may be computer-assisted instruction, audio instructional tapes, print magnifiers, book holders, and other materials and equipment that can facilitate education.

Sports, Leisure, and Recreation.   Functions associated with group and individual sports and productive use of leisure time are included in this functional category. The services of a person trained in adapted physical education may provide a valuable resource in this area. In addition, there is a wide array of equipment and devices that can facilitate functions in this category, including balls that emit audible beeps so that children who are blind can hear them, specially designed skis for skiers with one leg, Braille playing cards, and wheelchairs for basketball players who cannot walk or run.

Many more examples of services and devices could be provided, but these should be sufficient to illustrate the importance of attending to human functions when planning and implementing education and related services. Also note that with this perspective it is more relevant to focus on the functions that a student can perform and those in which difficulty is experienced than to focus on a diagnostic label or disability category when planning special education services. Such an orientation enables teachers and those providing related services to more directly address a student's needs.

A UNIFYING FUNCTIONAL MODEL

The unifying functional model has been developed to illustrate the different elements of life associated with a functional approach to education and related services, including the provision of medical, instructional, and assistive technologies. The model is based on the work of Joseph F. Melichar (Blackhurst, 1997). When examining this model, note that the items in each box are meant to be illustrative and not all-inclusive.

Blackhurst's Unifying Functional Model
© A. Edward Blackhurst, 1993. Used with permission.

REFERENCES AND SELECTED BIBLIOGRAPHY

Alliance for Technology Access. (1996). *Computer resources for people with disabilities*. Alameda, CA: Hunter House.

Barry, J., & Wise, B. J. (1996). Fueling inclusion through technology. *School Administrator, 53*(4), 24–27.

Blackhurst, A. E. (1997). Perspectives on technology in special education. *Teaching Exceptional Children, 29*(5), 41–48.

Blackhurst, A. E., & Berdeine, W. H. (Eds.). (1993). *An introduction to special education* (3rd ed.). New York: HarperCollins.

Bryant, D. P., & Bryant, R. R. (1998). Using assistive technology adaptations to include students with learning disabilities in cooperative learning activities. *Journal of Learning Disabilities, 31*(1), 41–54.

Council for Exceptional Children. (1998). IDEA 1997: *Let's make it work*. Reston, VA: Author.

Dewey, John. (1938, 1998). *Experience and Education*. West Lafayette, IN: Kappa Delta Pi.

Downing, J. E. (1996). *Including students with severe and multiple disabilities in typical classrooms: Practical strategies for teachers*. Baltimore: Brookes.

DuBois, W. P. (1946/1986). *Twenty-one balloons*. New York: Puffin Books.

Hourcade, J. J., & Parette, J. P. (1997). Family and cultural alert! Considerations in assistive technology assessment. *Teaching Exceptional Children, 30*(4), 40–44.

Lewis, R. B. (1998). Assistive technology and learning disabilities: Today's realities and tomorrow's promises. *Journal of Learning Disabilities, 31*(1), 16–26.

Lindsey, J. (Ed.). (1999). *Technology and exceptional individuals* (3rd ed.). Austin, TX: Pro-Ed.

McGegor, G., & Pachuski, P. (1996). Assistive technology in schools: Are teachers ready, able and supported? *Journal of Special Education Technology, 13*(1), 4–15.

Scherer, M. J. (1993). *Living in the state of stuck: How technology impacts the lives of people with disabilities*. Cambridge: Brookline.

Thomas, L., & Stich, S. (1996, November). Our daughter couldn't smile. *Time, 71*(11), 31–34.

SOME USEFUL WEB SITES

AskERIC: http://ericir.syr.edu/

Adaptive Device Locator System: http://www.acsw.com/

Council for Exceptional Children: http://www.cec.sped.org/home.htm

Conduct on-line ERIC searches: http://ericae.net/scripts/ewiz/amain2.asp

Hyper-ABLEDATA: http://www.trace.wisc.edu/tcel/abledata/index/html

List of annotated links to numerous special education resources on a variety of topics: http://serc.gws.uky.edu/www/resources/resmenu.html

Note: For references regarding middle-level education, see case 5, *On the High Wire*.

Caroline's Medical History

Condition	Possible Cause	Treatment
Congenital triple amputee: no legs below the knees, no left arm	Mother experienced a stomach virus 30–35 days after conception—circulation between mother and Caroline was disrupted during this time. Development then continued.	Prosthetic legs and left arm, wheelchair with electric life, physical therapy for walking, surgeries on right hand (due to frequent use of right hand as a crutch)
Moebius syndrome: lifetime facial paralysis, causing difficulties in speaking and an inability to facially express emotion	This syndrome is thought to be genetically linked, possibly passed on to Caroline by a grandmother.	None. While experimental surgery to correct lack of ability to smile has been done on another child suffering from the same syndrome, Caroline has refused surgery for the present time.
Tracheotomy: an incision made in the trachea to allow for breathing when respiration is not possible otherwise	The surgery was performed when Caroline was two months old due to paralyzed vocal cords (most likely due to the Moebius syndrome)	Surgery was performed within the last nine months to close the tracheotomy. However, it was not possible to close it completely, and the surgery wound occasionally reopens when Caroline coughs and clears her throat.
Lack of body cooling system:	Due to the lack of limbs, Caroline's body cannot effectively regulate her body temperature	Caroline must drink continuously through the night to maintain her temperature, and outdoor activities are extremely limited. She must also avoid bright light due to the sensitivity of her eyes.

EXHIBIT B

Speech Pathologist's Report on Caroline

Testing revealed Caroline's language skills are within the range expected for a child of her age. Articulation errors were found to be minimal in single-word productions; conversational speech is more involved with difficulty due to the physical involvement of the oral structure. Improvement in sound production is noted over the three years since this same test was administered to Caroline. Difficulty with /k/ and voiceless /th/ continue to persist, however. Results of the voice worksheet would indicate a voice disorder to be severe in nature, however, given the nature of the physical involvement present and Caroline's exceptional ability expectations. This has been evidenced by her ability to overcome the hypernasality, which resulted in the removal of her tonsils.

Caroline is a remarkable young lady, who is well qualified to give us all lessons in spunk and attitude. She does not view herself as being less able than anyone else and is willing and determined to do and try anything. She has never been observed to take advantage of her handicap. Her independence and ability to keep up with everyone else is a tribute to her family who has "done all the right things" and raised her with the same expectations as the rest of the family. It is highly recommended that all individuals who work with Caroline take the time to read her medical history to fully understand all the obstacles that this exceptional individual and her family have endured and overcome.

EXHIBIT C

Caroline's Grade Record

Caroline's grade record shows the deterioration of progress in middle school.

Year in School	Grades
First grade	A—all subjects
Second grade	A/B—all other subjects
	C—math
Fourth grade	A/B—all other subjects
	C—math, reading, and social studies
Fifth grade: 1st & 2nd grading periods	A/B—all other subjects
	C—one subject (unknown)
Fifth grade: 3rd grading period	C—reading, language, and social studies
	D—math
Fifth grade: 4th grading period	C—reading, social studies, science/health
	D—math
	C—math
Sixth grade: 1st grading period	D—reading, social studies, science, and language arts
Sixth grade: 2nd grading period	D—math, reading, language arts
	F—social studies and science
Seventh grade: 1st grading period	Art: 91 (B)
	Home economics: 91 (B)
	Language arts: 88 (B)*
	Science: 83 (B)
	Math: 77 (C)
	Social Studies: 89 (B)

*Note: At the time of the writing of this case, all Caroline's grades had improved to A's and B's.

E X H I B I T   D

Caroline's Autobiographical Essay, Sixth Grade

On Saturday, April 30, 1983, I, Caroline Kaye Ellington, was born. I was four pounds and three ounces. I had one hand and no legs.

Before I was born and the doctors got their results, they showed them to my parents and said they thought that my mom needed to get an abortion, and my parents said "no." A few weeks after I was born the doctors told my parents that they thought my parents needed to have a mercy killing. A mercy killing is where you just let the baby die, by not feeding and neglecting it. My parents said "no."

The doctors gave my parents a list of things I couldn't, wouldn't do, and what I'd do to the family. The list included things like: couldn't walk, I'd be mute, deaf, retarded, blind, I'd break up the family, nobody would like me, and I'd be a burden to society. (This is 1996 and none of the above is true.)

One day when I was a few months old, Mom put me in a car seat and set me on the counter. There was a guy wallpapering the kitchen when I wiggled myself off the counter. My mom was at the other end of the kitchen cleaning out the pantry. I couldn't cry out loud because I had paralyzed vocal cords, but I was crying. The man was so scared! He went running to mom screaming. When Mom found me I was laying flat on my face. We all three cried.

My dog, Muffin, who died last April, helped teach me to sit up. I'd hold onto her ear and she'd get up and then I'd let go and sit there for a few seconds. Then I'd fall. She used to always knock me down the steps. Maybe she was telling me to hold on.

When I was two months old I got a tracheotomy. A tracheotomy is something you get when you can't breathe or can't breathe very well. The doctors said I had paralyzed vocal chords.

When I was one year old, I had surgery on my hand, heart, and hips. My heart is on the right side of the left side of my chest. They also had to take my teeth out.

Before I was two years old, I learned to walk on prosthesis. I was one of the youngest children to do that at the Shriner's Hospital. I even learned to roller skate when I was five.

DISCUSSION QUESTIONS

1. Describe Caroline in terms of her physical, social-emotional, and academic development.
   - In what ways are the developmental domains interdependent? Give specific examples from Caroline's case.
   - In what way is Caroline described as similar to typical adolescents?
   - In what way is Caroline described as dissimilar from typical adolescents?
   - Throughout the case, Caroline insists on being independent. How was this helpful to her? How was this problematic?

2. What are some underlying issues in this case?

3. How might the situation appear from the vantage point of the following characters?
   - Caroline
   - Mrs. Ellington
   - Mr. Cristoff, special education teacher
   - Mr. Willey, Caroline's fifth-grade teacher
   - Ms. Shelton, Caroline's sixth-grade teacher
   - Ms. Johns, counselor
   - Seventh-grade teaching team
   - Ms. Ward, Caroline's social studies teacher

4. Although Caroline's family could have afforded to enroll her in a private school especially designed to meet the needs of students with disabilities, they chose to place her in an inclusive setting. Evaluate this decision.
   - What are the possible benefits of inclusion? For children with special needs? For typically developing children?
   - What are the possible drawbacks? For children with special needs? For typically developing children?
   - Consider whether you think Mr. and Mrs. Ellington made the right decision for their daughter; explain why or why not.

5. Describe Belle Vista's approach to middle school education. Evaluate whether such an approach would be conducive to promoting inclusion of children with special needs in the regular program.
   - Explain your reasoning in theory.
   - Explain your reasoning in practice, as evidenced by Caroline's experiences in the sixth and seventh grades.

6. Describe the nature of the communication between various individuals and groups in this case. How effective was this communication? How might it have been made more effective to enhance Caroline's educational experiences? Consider the communication

   • between regular educators and special educators
   • among the specialists
   • between the teachers and Caroline's parents
   • between Caroline and her peers
   • between elementary school staff and middle school staff
   • between central office and school

7. On two occasions in her regular classes, Caroline speaks up about her disability. Compare and contrast the responses by Ms. Shelton and Ms. Johns.

   • What are some alternative responses and with what possible consequences?

8. Consider the quality of instruction in this case. What did the teachers do to adapt their instruction to meet Caroline's needs?

   • How might the teachers have better informed themselves of the nature of Caroline's physical and cognitive disabilities?

9. Caroline began to have social problems. What strategies might the teachers have used to help her develop social skills?

   • How effective were the teachers' strategies to promote Caroline's academic progress?

10. Consider the assistive technology that was used. What were the advantages? Disadvantages?

    • What might have been done differently?

11. Ms. Shelton, Caroline's sixth-grade language arts teacher, announced to Caroline's class, "Everyone has a disability, whether it is academic, physical, or social. People have to overcome their disabilities and do the best they can with what they have." What do you think Ms. Shelton meant by this statement?

    • Do you agree with it?
    • How might *disability* be defined?
    • Is this a useful way to help the other students to understand Caroline's disabilities? Why or why not? What other strategies might have been tried by Caroline's teachers?
    • Ms. Johns asked Caroline to make a presentation to her class to share her feelings about being disabled and how people often treated her differently. For what reasons might this have been a wise move? In what ways might it have backfired?

12. The Individuals with Disabilities Education Act (See Appendix A), a federal law, mandates that parents must be involved in making educational decisions for their children. Consider the role that Caroline's parents played in this case.

    • How effectively did Caroline's parents participate in the decision-making process for their daughter?

    • If you were Caroline's parents, what, if anything, would you have done differently?

    • When Ms. Johns asked Caroline to make her presentation, Caroline asked her mother to be part of the talk. "I can't do this," replied Mrs. Ellington. "You have to find your own words for this. I can't fight your battles." Why do you think her mother referred to this experience as a battle and not a learning opportunity? Determine whether you agree with Mrs. Ellington's comment, and explain why.

13. Discuss the various factors in Caroline's turnaround in seventh grade. Which do you consider most important and why?

14. Explore the possible ramifications of removing Caroline from her regular class to join the special education class for one hour a day.

    • How could the assistance she need have been provided without segregating her from the sixth-grade class?

    • What are the pros and cons of receiving support from the special education teacher and remaining with the sixth-grade class?

15. What options did her fifth-grade teacher have in providing student assistants to Caroline?

    • How could he have presented an alternate plan to the principal that did not entail students physically moving Caroline but still provided assistance for things such as getting books or materials?

    • Should these minor types of assistance have been continued, or did they undermine Caroline's independence?

16. Describe accommodations you could make for Caroline to assist her in school if she were in your class.

17. Consider the analysis of Caroline's need for technology. The decisions seemed to be based on a technology model of assessing need. Use the information in Appendix B to consider another model—a functional model—for understanding individualization.

    • Examine the information about a functional approach to individualization in Appendix B. This section includes specific activities and in-depth application questions for the Functional Model approach.

    • Using the functional model approach, evaluate the technology devices and services for Caroline. For example, consider the implementation of the BAT keyboard in terms of the functional approach. Would taking the functional approach have changed the decision? If so, how?

18. Should Caroline undergo the same operation as Chelsea? What are the pros and cons of this surgery? Who should make this decision?

Questions on Legal Aspects of Special Education

(Examine the special education legal mandates in Appendix A.)

1. Why do you think laws such as IDEA and ADA were enacted?

2. How do you think school personnel would have reacted to Caroline prior to the implementation of IDEA?

3. If you were a parent of a student without a disability, how would you react to the fact that Caroline receives an individualized plan for instruction, while your child does not?

4. What types of problems might arise in schools attempting to fulfill the legal mandates to educate students, such as Caroline, in the least restrictive environment? How do you think school personnel might cope with those problems?

5. What benefits have you noticed or heard about in places where the provisions of IDEA have been implemented?

6. What evidence have you seen to indicate that communities are complying with the provisions of ADA? If you have had no direct experience with either IDEA or ADA, what benefits would you anticipate in places where those laws have been implemented? What drawbacks?

CASE 4

Discussion Question	Corresponding INTASC Principle
1	2 The teacher understands how children learn and develop, and can provide learning opportunities that support their intellectual, social, and personal development.
6	6 The teacher uses knowledge of effective verbal, nonverbal, and media communication techniques to foster active inquiry, collaboration, and supportive instruction in the classroom.
6	10 The teacher fosters relationships with school colleagues, parents, and agencies in the larger community to support learning and well-being.
8	3 The teacher understands how students differ in their approaches to learning and creates instructional opportunities that are adapted to diverse learners.
12	5 The teacher uses an understanding of individual and group motivation and behavior to create a learning environment that encourages positive social interaction, active engagement in learning, and self-motivation.

CASE FIVE

On the High Wire

IN THE LOUNGE

"OK, let's talk," began Betsy Rogers, the team leader, as she looked around the table at the three members of her team. Ignoring the spring foliage and bright sunshine outside a nearby window, the three averted their eyes as Betsy continued. "We've never hesitated to tell each other how we feel before. You obviously don't seem altogether comfortable with this unit. Why?"

"I'll start," said David Campbell, a tenth-year teacher. "I have mixed feelings. You all know me. I'm used to being in front of the class more—even the kids ask when I'll start teaching again. I've become much more comfortable with cooperative learning during the past few years of reform, but my strength is in presenting material in an interesting and fun way—I think I've learned how to be effective doing that. With this unit, I stand around watching kids work. It's difficult not to control the decisions students make—but I admit they like it and are learning. The bottom line with this unit is that I feel like my teaching strengths have lost purpose."

Darlene Wood, in whom Betsy took a special interest because of her status as a new teacher, nodded in agreement. "I can relate to that. Even though I'm still learning what works best for me, I know I thrive on organization. Planning is one of my strong points, and during this unit I haven't been able to do much of that. I'm just not very comfortable in an unstructured environment, even though I felt better after we discussed strategies for facilitating student planning. Everything I've learned has encouraged me to be reform-minded, and I can't argue with what I've seen—fewer discipline problems and students effectively leading and participating in groups. Still, even with my limited experience, I think I have a better idea of quality learning experiences than most eleven-year-olds!"

"I have another concern," Nina Scott, a fourth-year science teacher, interjected as she shifted in her chair. "I'm concerned that we didn't generate enough grades this six weeks because of this unit. The fact that it is not graded has raised some eyebrows, and understandably so. I hope parents will understand that we will "assess" the unit without grading it. Also, some students are not contributing much to their

109

groups' efforts, and I don't think there is enough accountability to encourage them to make a serious contribution."

They all looked expectantly at Betsy. Because her team members were known for their flexibility and willingness to implement reform initiatives, she had felt certain they would welcome the opportunity to pilot a student-generated unit and that they would adjust quickly. Despite her continued enthusiasm for the concept, Betsy knew that her team's practical concerns would have to be addressed.

THE SCHOOL

Built in the late 1940s as the town high school, Wakefield Middle School was large and imposing. The interior was notable for its high ceilings and tall windows that framed the picturesque lawn surrounding the school. The halls were covered with worn gray carpet that suggested years of disrepair. A major renovation was taking place in planned increments. A few examples of student work adorned the interior of the school, but for the most part the wall remained an unrelenting off-white with one exception: a hand-painted stripe design in the school colors bordered the entrance stairwells.

The school was located at the center of Wakefield, a small town that served as a bedroom community for a large urban area nearby; recent and rapid economic expansion promoted new business opportunities and several housing developments in Wakefield. As a result of this growth, a majority of Wakefield students came from predominantly middle-class families.

The school had 35 faculty members in grades six, seven, and eight and an enrollment of approximately 700 students. Until recently, the school grouped students primarily through departmentalization and some tracking. With the passage of statewide reform and the arrival of a new principal, however, a number of innovations took place. The overall result at Wakefield was the establishment of a permanent team system. Each team consisted of four teachers, one from each of the following disciplines: math, science, language arts, and social studies. The sixth grade had two teams, and there was one team in both the seventh and eighth grades.

Living in a prosperous community close to a large city, Wakefield students had many cultural advantages children in more rural areas of the state did not. Through school field trips most students experienced award-winning theater, ballet, art, and other activities designed to promote their interest and knowledge in the humanities. Many of the students went on family vacations to coastal areas or other geographically and historically diverse locations and regularly attended area concerts. Activities such as intramural sports, dance classes, Scouts, and church activities kept many students involved and occupied after school. Rogers was confident that students' intellectual sophistication would add richness to the student-generated unit activities.

TEAM LEADER

Betsy Rogers was a dynamic, 39-year-old teacher who was recently named the state's Middle School Teacher of the Year. Her intense energy and insistence that students think for themselves were evident in all aspects of her teaching.

Rogers sought to put into practice the innovative concepts that she learned during her education and training at a small liberal arts college. "Open Classrooms," "student choice," and "learning centers" were still common catchwords when she graduated in the early 1980s. Moreover, her student teaching experience involved team-teaching second grade with another student teacher in an open classroom—a fairly unique assignment.

Rogers spent her first eight years teaching as the only fifth-grade teacher in a small mountain community. There, she frequently organized her teaching around student choice, emphasizing student contracts, learning centers, and the writing process. Meanwhile, she maintained a strong commitment to the substance of student learning and went through training in Junior Great Books discussions. Her success with effective and innovative teaching strategies attracted the attention of a local university; Betsy began teaching a reading and language arts methods course during the summer months and continued in this adjunct role for several years.

The importance of these early experiences to Betsy's professional development became a topic of conversations with Darlene Wood. Betsy took an active interest encouraging her younger colleague's involvement in innovative teaching strategies by reflecting on her own early successes and dilemmas and their relevance at Wakefield. As a language arts teacher at several grade levels, Betsy stayed current with research in middle school philosophy, reading and writing methods, and national reform.

TEAM TEACHERS

The other members of Betsy's interdisciplinary sixth-grade team brought varied experiences and perspectives to the collaboration. Scott, Campbell, and Rogers taught together for two years before being joined by Wood at the beginning of last year.

Having just completed a Master's degree, Nina Scott was knowledgeable in middle school concepts and philosophy. She had learned through her four years of experience how to keep students engaged but never at the expense of demonstrable learning. In her science classroom, she focused on concrete applications of principles and promoted the effective use of collaborative learning. For this reason, she placed great importance on her own demonstration lessons; she often gave open-note tests and quizzes to check for understanding. She occasionally required students to participate in small group performance tasks to demonstrate a science principle. Scott believed the ultimate test of her own teaching was whether students could articulate in writing the principles she taught. She incorporated all types of writing into her curriculum, including reports, essays, and poetry.

Darlene Wood was a first-year teacher with certification in social studies and math. Her sixth-grade social studies class focused on world geography, the title of the available textbook. Wood, however, rarely used the book, concentrating instead on group and individual projects and learning contracts. Prior to becoming a full-time teacher, she became familiar with the team system at Wakefield as a student teacher.

Team Members: Experience and Areas of Emphasis

Nina Scott—Science	**Darlene Wood—Social Studies**
• Experience: 4 years • Group/performance tasks • Open-note tests • Uses writing to assess learning	• Experience: 1st-year teacher • Individual/group projects • Learning contracts • Minimal use of textbook
David Campbell—Math	**Betsy Rogers—Language Arts**
• Experience: 10 years • Favors direct instruction • Some collaborative groups • Incorporates writing	• Experience: 17 years • Reading/writing portfolios • Reading/writing workshops • Direct instruction in skill areas

David Campbell, with ten years' experience, had an elementary 1–8 certification and a Master's degree in special education. He enjoyed working with middle school students, often telling jokes and funny stories to get his point across in math. Despite his consistent belief in the value of direct, teacher-led instruction, Campbell had changed his classroom style substantially over the past few years. Before Wakefield's implementation of the team concept, his students could be found seated in straight rows working diligently out of the textbook. With the implementation of teams, they sat at tables in collaborative groups and used many different types of materials to study and understand math concepts. Campbell also systematically incorporated writing into his daily lessons.

Betsy Rogers' language arts class emphasized developing fluency in reading and writing. In addition to conducting whole-group classroom instruction, she required students to reproduce extensive responses to independent reading assignments and to write for part of the assessment process. Rogers described her classroom as a reading/writing workshop supplemented by direct instruction in specific skill areas.

This sixth-grade team was well known for its emphasis on student-centered methods, but this prompted criticism from some colleagues. They contended that, because of the team's thematic and hands-on approach to teaching, students had a hard time adjusting to the instructional styles of more traditional teachers in later grades. The team was well aware that their collective reputation as innovators meant they were closely scrutinized.

THE UNIT

The idea of writing and field-testing a student-generated unit began with a request for grant proposals. The principal of Wakefield Middle School asked Rogers if she would be interested in applying for a state grant to write a model instructional unit. Rogers' proposal outlined a student-centered approach to learning that could be implemented as a unit within the existing team framework at Wakefield. When the proposal was funded, Rogers formed a planning committee for the unit consisting of herself, the seventh-grade team leader, the eighth-grade team leader, the principal, and a university professor who worked in a collaborative relationship with the school. All agreed that this unit, implemented across the three grade-level teams, should be designed to include learning experiences that would be developmentally appropriate for the learners involved. After discussing current middle school concepts and developmental theories, the faculty decided to base the unit on student-centered curricula using the philosophy and research of James Beane.

The committee endorsed Beane's notion that units should begin by asking young adolescents how they see themselves, what questions they have about themselves, and what questions they have about the larger world. In this approach, students look for patterns within their questions, and themes emerge. With teacher guidance, students decide what they want to know in relation to the questions, how they want to find out, and how and with whom they want to share their results. In theory, this allows students to develop various learning styles and their multiple intelligences in a context that recognizes different developmental levels, strengths, and abilities.

Planning committee members circulated a preliminary outline of instructional guidelines to participating teachers:

Instructional Guidelines

1. Tell students we will be using a new approach to learning. "In most of the past year, teachers have decided what you will learn, how you will learn it, and what you will do to demonstrate your learning. In the next three-week unit, you will have more to say about each of those three things." Explain the process (which follows).

2. Tell students we have decided to focus on the theme of "Transitions." (Write it on the board.) Ask them, "What do you think that word means?" They may want to speculate, some students may know, and others may want to look it up in various dictionaries. (*The American Heritage Student's Dictionary* defines "transition" as "the process or an example of changing or passing from one form, state, subject, or place to another.") See if, as a group, you can formulate a working definition, then ask students for examples of some transitions. This will allow you to see how well they understand the concept as well as provide concrete examples for others to consider.

3. Then tell students we have come up with an essential question that will help guide the overall learning of students at all grade levels. It is, "How have the transitions that children make from childhood to adulthood changed as the self, school, community, and the world have changed?" (Write this on the board also.) Ask students to think for one minute, then discuss with a partner near them, what they think that question means. Then invite them to share ideas about the meaning of the question (not possible answers to it) in the large group, calling on students randomly whether they have raised hands or not.

4. Tell them we will focus on transitions within a particular time period, with students at each grade level looking at a different time period. Sixth graders will look back at the transitions from childhood to adolescence, a more concrete activity in keeping with their developmental level. Seventh graders will look around at the transitions taking

place within adolescence. Eighth graders will look ahead at the changes and decisions taking place from adolescence to young adulthood, a more abstract challenge that is developmentally appropriate for these older students. (Write the time period for your grade level on the board.)

5. There are several ways to approach the next activity, which is helping the students relate to the Transitions theme and the essential question. We have listed them in the order most in keeping with Beane's approach to curriculum development, starting with a more open-ended approach. Recognizing that some groups of students may not know how to respond, we have provided three ways of approaching the same questions, each providing more structure (see Exhibit D for details of these strategies). We ask kids to be risk-takers in their writing and thinking, and this would be a good opportunity to model that behavior for them.

6. Another way to help students see how the world has changed and how that might affect the transitions they make from childhood to adulthood is to have students interview adults about their transitions. Talking with parents might be an easy starting place, though students should have the option of interviewing anyone more than 20 years older than themselves in case they are not comfortable interviewing their parents. Invite students to choose questions from the ones discussed previously in which they are most interested. Their goal is to find out about the kinds of transitions adults faced and to compare them with those of current middle school students. Students should write questions about the topics or areas of interest to them and the class but also should include some open-ended questions that allow the adult to mention transitions that current students may not face. For example, students might ask about options adults felt they had for careers and training after high school, if that topic is of interest to the students. An open-ended question about other concerns the adult had about life after high school might elicit comments about facing a military draft, a concern current students do not face. This is where you'll need to do a mini-lesson on interviewing, and you could make the lesson as extensive as time will allow. At the least, students need to check their questions for biased wording, completeness, and whether they will elicit comments on topics that students can't anticipate. They might want to practice interviewing peers and taking notes while listening to get experience. Discuss how they will record answers, and suggest that they might use a tape recorder, if one is available. That way they can go back afterward to add to the notes they took during the interview. Make it a homework assignment that they interview an adult and bring in the notes the next day.

7. Discuss results of the interviews. What aspects of school, community, and nation/world have changed? (Record on board or overhead.) How did those changes seem to affect the transitions of the people you interviewed compared to your transitions? (Example: "My mom didn't have to worry about being pressured to take drugs cause no one in school did that kind of stuff when she was in middle school, so she had less to worry about. On the other hand, she talked about the Cold War and being afraid we were going to get nuked by the Russians, and that's not something I ever think about.") Through this discussion, develop the idea that students' personal lives and concerns are impacted by what is going on in the school, community, and nation/world.

8. Here's where we start to get convergent and decide which questions (among the many that have been discussed) students would like to investigate further. Get students into groups of about four using preexisting groups, random assignment (number off, cards, birthdays, and so on), or your decision about groups that would provide diversity of opinion. Ask them to share the questions considered previously and see if the group can reach consensus on three to six questions they feel would be of interest to most group members. They can start with questions that appeared on several students' individual lists or on the board through various class discussions, and they can add others that arise as a result of their discussion in the group.

9. After the groups have had time to work, the teacher should then invite students to contribute questions to a class list, writing them on the overhead or blackboard. Collect the small-group lists to be sure to have a hard copy of all ideas. Invite students to see which questions or areas of interest the class seems to have in common. Agree on a list of questions that are of interest to many (but not necessarily all or even a majority of) class members.

10. Then invite students to think about how they might go about answering these questions. This would be a good time to repeat the procedure of thinking/writing individually for five minutes, then discussing with small groups, then sharing in large groups. Encourage them to think beyond traditional sources like textbooks, encyclopedias, and so on, since it is unlikely those sources will have the answers anyway. They might need suggestions about other ways to find out: interviews, look at documents or movies or news shows of the time period, call or write to agencies like substance abuse centers or police departments, design surveys, and so on.

11. Students then need to think about a final product and audience. Only then will you know what content and/or skills need to be taught, unless as a team you have predetermined some outcomes that your students need before testing. In that case, teachers need to guide students in that direction in the following discussion. After the discussion about personal and global concerns regarding transitions, have students brainstorm ideas for a sixth-, seventh-, or eighth-grade product. Ask them to explore and share their answers to the questions that have been chosen as well as how they might present these products to a real world audience. Guide them to consider different products they could produce, including those involving drama, technology, music, publishing, art, and so on.

12. Teachers should compare questions and ideas for products across groups of students within the team. You should then either take the most popular suggestion back to the students for discussion/consensus/vote or choose the questions and products that best meet the needs of students on the team.

13. Think about content and process skills in your discipline that would relate to students' questions and ways to answer their questions. Then think about general content/skills that would also be relevant and needed in order to carry out their investigation. Meet with your team to share lists and to discuss possibilities. This might also be a good time to go through the list of learner academic expectations from the state to choose two or three on which to focus. What skills, abilities, and concepts can you teach in order that kids create products high in quality with respect to both content and communicating effectively with their chosen audience?

TEAM DECISIONS

The committee decided to approach planning this unit with two modifications of Beane's theory. First, instead of allowing individual themes to emerge, all three grade levels agreed to implement the same theme—Transitions. Second, rather than having students generate the question, the teachers presented students with the essential question, "How have the transitions that children make from childhood to adulthood changed as they have changed and as their schools, communities, and the world have changed?" The teachers believed this would provide some structure while still assigning students primary responsibility for the substance and format of the unit.

The format of the unit plan also followed the state Department of Education curriculum framework[1] including the following elements:

- Establishing organizers
- Addressing academic expectations
- Formulating essential questions
- Planning a culminating performance
- Facilitating the culminating performance

The planning committee discussed and predicted possible outcomes for the unit. Due to the student-centered nature of the unit, however, teachers would be responsible for little prior planning once the unit began. Though the experimental unit would not be graded, assessment would take place based largely on a student-generated rubric; teachers, in turn, would use this rubric in their assessment of each group's product as well as of individual contributions. The unit would last approximately three weeks.

UNIT SNAPSHOT

Initially, sixth-grade students generated a list of possible questions and suggested ways in which each might be developed within the unit. Through the team-wide questioning process guided by the teachers, students determined that they were interested in finding out more about five topics: the transition to seventh grade in Wakefield Middle School, the transitions of twelve- and thirteen-year-olds throughout history, the transitions in society caused by medical and technological advances, environmental issues, and issues of crime and violence. Students were thinking on a more sophisticated and ambitious level than the planning committee had anticipated.

With their teachers acting as facilitators, the sixth graders subsequently discussed what form their culminating performances might take. This discussion raised some practical concerns for Rogers. Two cheerleaders had suggested a float for the

---

[1]Adapted from Kentucky Department of Education. (1995). *Transformations: Kentucky's curriculum framework* (Vol. 2). Frankfort: Author.

annual spring festival parade. According to their plan, the float would display facts about transitions in crime and violence, AIDS Statistics, statistics on rain forest depletion and its consequences, and historical perspectives on the transitions of twelve- and thirteen-year-olds. The two girls' enthusiasm was contagious, and the idea quickly spread throughout the sixth-grade team. More than a little concerned, the teachers were immediately worried about the appropriateness, logistics, and legality of the float idea and instead unilaterally chose to have students create a video magazine with segments done by different study groups on each of the above topics. This magazine would then be shared with other students in the school and district. Rogers' team breathed a collective sigh of relief.

Soon after, Rogers led the students in a brainstorming session to create an assessment rubric for the video magazine. Using a "Quality/Not Yet Quality" continuum, students identified properties of good and poor video productions (Exhibit B); Rogers kept a record of suggestions on an overhead projector. She made copies of the overhead for students to use as a guide for production and to use with the group evaluation tool at the end of the process (see Exhibits A–D). Though the team agreed that these categories could easily have been modified into an actual scoring rubric, the teachers agreed that grading would not yet be appropriate given the experimental nature of the unit.

For their contribution, Rogers' students decided, through intensive discussion, to create a video timeline of major historical transitions that twelve- and thirteen-year-olds had faced in American history. The class had previously discussed what they knew about timelines and American history. A library visit yielded varied topics to script the skits for the video timeline: Michael and Jimmy were writing a rap for the introduction to each segment of the video timeline; Nick, Tracy, and Adrienne practiced their slavery scene of the early 1800s; Maria and Cindy were painting a backdrop for their child labor scene of the early 1900s; and three other students continued to research the role of newly arriving immigrants. A small group of students worked on a school survey to complete their section on twelve- and thirteen-year-olds of the future.

When students asked questions, Rogers typically responded, "Did you consider all the possibilities? If so, this is your unit—you decide."

Rogers was impressed by how diligently and creatively the students approached their tasks without initial direct instruction. Michael, for example, was becoming quite a leader. It was his idea to introduce each segment of the timeline with a rap based on history, and he was keeping fellow students on track. Other students were displaying considerable creativity and resourcefulness.

STUDENT REACTIONS

Rogers sat alone at a table in her classroom reflecting on the Transitions unit that had just been completed. The team teachers had asked students to write their thoughts in journals using the following questions:

1. What did you like about the unit?
2. What did you dislike about it?

3. Did anything about the unit make you feel proud?
4. What is something that you learned by doing the unit?

Now she was anxious to read the responses. She placed the plastic container filled with dog-eared spiral notebooks next to her on the floor then randomly selected a small stack. She began to read.

> I liked how we got to choose the group we were in. I liked how we organized it all by ourselves. I like doing things with activities that I have to plan and work on. I have a better idea of things if I invent it. I disagreed with some of the things my class did. One was the commercial. One group from my class did it all. They didn't ask for suggestions or if anybody else wanted to be in it. My group had one leader for endangered animals. When she wasn't there everything went wrong—no leaders. Nothing made me feel proud. I learned about the very few rain forests. Many endangered animals are becoming extinct. I also learned that we have more responsibilities ahead of us for 2000.

> I liked having the freedom to choose the activities and work that we did. Also, the teachers made it fun, which I think is important. The video magazine was a lot of fun, but I learned a lot from it too! I think this was one of the better units we've done because we know what we like and it helps when we're doing something we like to do. I didn't like the fact that some of the group members goofed off the whole time while others put a lot of effort into it. It's not really fair, especially since they're getting the same grade. Other than that everything was great! I was kind of proud of myself and my group because this was challenging but we pulled through at the last minute! I learned that AIDS has become a war worldwide, and that a cure soon is doubtful. The percentage of people who have developed AIDS has increased a lot and is going to keep rising if something isn't done, especially in ages 15–25.

> What I liked about the Transitions unit is that we had a lot of control over what we did. I also liked doing the video because it helped us learn about how much goes into just ten minutes of video. What I didn't like about the unit was we didn't have enough time for the video. What I'm proud about is our whole tape. I think all of the groups worked hard. I learned a lot about how much time and effort goes into a video. I also learned a lot about video camera and editing and filming things.

> In the Transitions unit I liked that the kids got to decide how they wanted to work and do the video. It gave us a chance to use our creative minds, and we got the chance to show the teachers what we've learned. I disliked that some people didn't get into the groups they wanted. I had a good idea for the crime and violence group but it didn't get in. I liked the whole video because we made it. I learned that seventh grade is about the same as this year. The work is just a little harder and they have a little more to do.

> I liked filming ourselves. That way we know what we look like when other people are watching. I liked staying in one classroom most of the time. You get used to the teacher. I don't think we had enough time to film. Because there were so many groups we had to hurry and get it right the first time. I was proud that the students thought up a lot of the ideas. The teachers just pretty much motivated us. I learned a lot about filming and teamwork. I learned that a group has to work as a team to get anything done.

> I liked that we made the most of the decisions. Everything wasn't picked out or planned. We didn't have enough time to make improvements. I'm proud that we made a video that many people will watch. We weren't just doing it for a grade. It counted for something.

BACK TO THE LOUNGE

After each teacher had the opportunity to read the students' comments, Rogers called a meeting to address the team's concerns. "You have all said that students for the most part have been more motivated and better behaved, that all sorts of leadership and other talents have emerged, and that if we weren't crunched by the grant deadline, the products would be very high quality. Kids have incorporated into the unit all kinds of concepts like ecosystems, renewable resources, historical timelines, statistics, the impact of technology on society, health issues, the impact of violence on society, the developmental stages of early adolescents, and self-concept. All indicators are that, for students, this has been collectively our most successful unit."

"True, but how can we be sure that we couldn't do this better in a format we're more at ease with?" Campbell countered. "I can't help wondering whether Beane is just one more guru of the month we're following just because he's popular with the National Middle School Association people."

Wood seemed torn. "We talked about Beane's model in my university classes, and at the time it sure seemed consistent with everything else I had learned about early adolescent development. But David has a point. How do we know it's better than what we would otherwise do? More than that—with all the teaching strategies I was exposed to in school, I wonder about being "locked in" with this approach. Also, I hate to say it, but I have to worry about some more basic issues—my first-year evaluations and the fact that this kind of thing doesn't fit clearly within my internship accountability guidelines."

"I have to agree," Scott offered. "It puts us all as teachers in an awkward position. Beyond this experiment, there remains a question of accountability with the whole concept. How could we explain a student's grade with this kind of curriculum, where students decide what to study and generate their own rubrics for assessment? What happens when students accustomed to this kind of work have classes with more conventional teachers? If I taught this way on a more regular basis; would my students learn enough science concepts so I could feel I did my job?"

"I understand your concerns about the unit," Rogers responded. "The issues about accountability and content coverage have been less of a problem for me because language arts is so process oriented that I know kids can learn and use those skills studying most any content. But I have given some thought to this grade business also. Parents may see this as a waste of time, though we're clearly seeing high-quality learning taking place for many of the students. It is hard finding a match between this new approach to learning and the old system of accountability. And with the unpredictability of the questions on the statewide performance assessment tests, there's no guarantee our kids' learning will be reflected there either." The others nodded in agreement.

"I'm not really sure what I think yet," Rogers continued slowly. "On one hand, we have to admit that this approach is working for our students as far as motivation and self-concept are concerned. Content is certainly being integrated, and students are learning processes they need to know. On the other hand, I hear your concerns. And," she turned to face Wood, "I certainly wouldn't want to do anything to discourage you from experimenting further or to make you uneasy about your status. I'm sure we all appreciate that there is a certain amount of risk taking inherent in attempting something like this, especially on a more sustained basis."

Rogers paused, for the moment unsure how to continue. From her own observations of the implementation of the unit on three teams at sixth-, seventh-, and eighth-grade levels, she knew many of the positive student outcomes that the planning committee had predicted were taking place: increased student motivation, decreased discipline problems, ownership of learning, and creativity.

While Rogers understood the team's concerns, she remained confident in the philosophy of student-centered curricula. Moreover, she had hoped that implementing more units like this one would help refine the process. With the team's misgivings, however, it was uncertain whether this would take place.

"We can't afford to ignore how successful this has been for the students," she said. "On the other hand, I have the highest respect for all of you, both personally and professionally, and your concerns need to be considered. I guess the question we all need to think about is how to begin implementing reforms like this in a way that works for students and teachers alike."

EPILOGUE

After several follow-up discussions in the spring, participating teachers decided to retain aspects of the student-centered curriculum that had proven successful and to continue with varying degrees of interdisciplinary coordination.

The beginning of the next academic year, however, coincided with long overdue structural renovations at Wakefield. The physical constraints on flexible learning and teaching strategies quickly became evident; the unpredictable pace of renovation meant that classrooms had to be frequently evacuated—usually to the cafeteria so that teachers could be heard over the din of construction. The plans for continuing innovation were soon set aside in favor of what Rogers called "survival mode"—logistical chaos brought on by renovation. For Rogers there was one source of inspiration. Despite their earlier reservations, the teachers on her team expressed some regret over the delay in expanding upon their earlier successes. Rogers was particularly intrigued by Wood's newfound confidence in student-centered curriculum and her vocal concerns about "lost momentum."

For her own part, Rogers knew that if a student-centered approach was to reemerge successfully, it would have to come from other team members. "I must adopt a wait-and-see approach and put my own enthusiasm for moving ahead on the back burner."

REFERENCES AND SELECTED BIBLIOGRAPHY

Apple, M. W., & Beane, J. A. (Eds.). (1995). *Democratic schools*. Alexandria, VA: Association for Supervision and Curriculum Development.
Beane, J. (1990). *Middle school curriculum: From rhetoric to reality*. Columbus, OH: National Middle School Association.

Beane, J. (1997). *Curriculum integration: Designing the core of democratic education.* New York: Teachers College Press.

Brophy, J., & Alleman, J. (1991). Activities as instructional tools: A framework for analysis and evaluation. *Educational Researcher, 20*(4), 9–23.

Drake, S. (1998). *Creating integrated curriculum.* Thousand Oaks, CA: Corwin Press.

George, P., Stevenson, C., Thomason, J., & Beane, J. (1992). *The middle school and beyond.* Alexandria, VA: Association for Supervision and Curriculum Development.

Kohn, A. (1999). *The schools our children deserve.* New York: Houghton Mifflin.

LeTendre, G. (1999). *Getting answers to your questions: A middle-level educators guide to program evaluation.* Boston: Christopher Gordon.

Lipsitz, J., Mizell, M., Jackson, M., and Austin, L. (1999, March). Speaking with one voice—A mandate for middle school reform. *Phi Delta Kappan,* 533–540.

Manning, M. L. (1993). Developmentally appropriate middle level school. In H. Allen, F. Splittgerber, and M. L. Manning (Eds.), *Teaching and learning in the middle school* (pp. 87–93). New York: Maxwell Macmillan International.

McDonough, L. (1991). Middle level curriculum: The search for self and social meaning. *Middle School Journal, 23*(2), 29–35.

Shubert, W. H. (1994). Toward lives worth sharing: A basis for integrated curriculum. *Education Horizons, 73*(1), 25–30.

Spady, W. G. (1994). Choosing outcomes of significance. *Educational Leadership, 51*(6), 18–22.

Vars, G. F. (1991). Integrated curriculum in historical perspective. *Educational Leadership, 49*(2), 14–15.

Wheelock, A. (1998). *Safe to be smart: Building a culture for standards-based reform in the middle school.* Washington, DC: National Middle School Association.

Williamson, R., and Johnson, N. (1998). *Identifying talent and maximizing potential.* Washington, DC: Association of Secondary School Principals.

E X H I B I T   A

Questions Raised by Students Planning the "Transitions" Unit

The team worked through the question-generating process around the first question (What do we want to know?) and came up with the following types of questions:

When and how will I die?
Will there be a cure for AIDS?
Will my kids be exposed to the same violence and crime I am as a sixth grader?
How will technology in the future affect me?
Will there be any land left with the growth in the community?
Will there be any trees left?
Will the ozone layer hold?
Will potential racial/ethnic wars affect me as I get older?
Will (or how will) I be able to handle peer pressure?
Why are there guns in school?
Why do middle school and high school kids smoke, drink, and take drugs?
Who will be my future partner? And how will we live?
How will the school renovation affect me?

They synthesized the large list into seven team questions:

1. What will be important in the transition to seventh grade?
2. What impact will violence and crime have on my life?
3. How will diseases and medical advances affect me?
4. How will I use technology in the future?
5. What environmental issues will be important?
6. How will population growth affect my future?
7. How will transitions in governments affect my society?

The team decided that all these questions could fit under the guiding question: "What does the future hold for our class?" Students rank-ordered their choice of questions for work groups, and the last two questions were dropped due to little interest. However, the first question regarding transitions to seventh grade had enough interest for two subgroups.

Student-Generated Quality Continuum for Video Productions

Quality	Not Yet Quality
Informative	Not informative
Accurate	Inaccurate
Organized	Unorganized
Stays on topic	Gets off topic
Entertaining	Boring
Creative	Not original
Has an audience	Targets wrong people
Clarity of content (vocabulary)	Jumbled
Time limit (appropriate length)	Too short/long
Interconnections of groups	No communication
Good camera work	Audience can't understand video
Appearance (lends credibility)	Actors/interviewers dressed inappropriately
Nonoffensive	Racist/sexist/bad language

E X H I B I T   C

Description of Culminating Project for the "Transitions" Unit Video Magazine

Participating students brainstormed about a potential audience for the questions they were exploring. They decided that their audience would be other middle school students. They then brainstormed the format that would be needed to share their information. The students on the team made a list of suggestions then made a decision to create a team video magazine, which would have different segments for sharing their findings. This video magazine would be shared with the rest of the school through the school's closed-circuit TV systems, and they would also send copies of the videotape to the other middle schools in the country.

Each student chose the question that he or she was most interested in exploring, and those with the same choice formed a separate small work team to investigate the answers to their particular question and to plan their own segment of the video magazine. The question about seventh-grade transitions had enough interest for two class work teams. Segments on the video magazine included the following:

1. Introduction
2. Transitions of twelve- and thirteen-year-olds throughout American history
3. Transitions to seventh grade at Wakefield Middle School
4. Transitions to medical predictions and possible advances in the next 10 years
5. Transitions and possibilities in technology in the next 10 years
6. Transitions in violence and crime in America and its impact on kids
7. Transitions in the environment and its impact on kids
8. Closure

One student on the team acted as "host" of the video magazine to introduce segments and to provide some narration between segments. Each segment was planned, written, and filmed by the students involved in their own particular interest group.

The segment on the transitions of twelve- and thirteen-year-olds throughout American history was presented as a video timeline in which different eras of American history were researched and portrayed through the eyes of preadolescents of the time. The next segment on the transition to seventh grade in this particular school was handled though interviews and varied types of real-life reporting from the site. The grim statistics of teens with AIDS and its impact on society were revealed in a student-written and student-performed skit in the segment on the transitions in medicine. A student news broadcast, complete with commercials, reported the advancement of technology and its effect on the lives of today's students. The segments of the magazine dealing with environmental issues included several activities about pollution, recycling, and the depletion of the rain forest and what preadolescents can do to help.

The rubric, developed by student discussion about what would be quality and what would not be quality for the video magazine, was used to assess the final product.

EXHIBIT D

Strategies for Students to Personally Relate to Theme and Essential Question

STRATEGY 1

Ask students to think about questions they personally relate to in the overall theme and essential question. You might start with, "What kinds of questions do you have about change in yourself from (time period)?" If students seem unclear about the question, you might want to volunteer some of your experiences at the time period under consideration; for example, "When I was in junior high, none of my friends even thought about using drugs or drinking, though I suspect some kids (not my friends) did smoke cigarettes. I wondered why some kids did smoke, though." Give students about five minutes to think and write down several questions in which they are genuinely interested.

After this, give them another five minutes to think about questions they have on a more global scale. "What are some questions you have about changes in the world or country or our community and how that might affect you?" A personal example might be, "I lived in Miami at the time when lots of refugees were coming over from Cuba. I wondered how that might affect my life, if I would have to learn Spanish, and how they would fit into our school and city."

STRATEGY II

If your students seem to be in need of more structure, you might create these scenarios for them to consider.

Sixth Grade. "Think back to when you were in fourth and fifth grade. Remember what you looked like, what you liked to do after school, what you did in school, what was going on in the world, and so on. Jot down a few ideas you have." Give students three to four minutes to record ideas, circulating to ensure that all are participating. Invite them to share ideas in a class discussion. Now ask them to think about what they would have wanted to know about themselves as sixth graders. "If you had had a middle school student come visit with you in fourth grade, what questions would you have had for this guest about the changes that would take place in you and your world over the two years from fourth to sixth grade?"

Seventh Grade. "Think about the changes you are going through right now in middle school. It might help to think back to how you've changed just in the year and a half you have been here. Think about some eighth graders you know and how you might change even more between now and the end of eighth grade. Take four or five minutes to write some questions you have about the change you and your peers are going through during your three years in middle school, then we'll share ideas and see if we can come up with questions of interest to you."

Eighth Grade.   Think about the questions you have about the changes that will affect you over the next three to five years. Imagine that a high school senior or college sophomore, perhaps you several years into the future, can travel back in time to answer all of your questions. What would you want to know about how you will change? What about how your school will change? Your town? The country and world?"

STRATEGY III

List four categories on the board: self, school, community, nation/world. Ask students to think about changes they have experienced or can imagine within each category, jotting down ideas on a piece of paper. For example, the category of self might include physical changes in the body, dating, concrete to abstract thinking, what's fun to do recreationally, privileges and responsibilities at home, and so on. You could also pass out copies of the newspaper (world/nation and local sections) and ask students to look for world, national, or community issues. Take about five minutes for this, and circulate to be sure all students are recording ideas. Then, first as the small group, then as a large one or as a whole class, ask students to share their ideas as the group brainstorms possible areas of change within each category. Using this list of topics as a starting point, ask students to think about at least three questions related to transitions that she or he is personally interested in investigating. Keep in mind the time period on which your grade level is focusing. Personal examples might include: sixth grade, "Who will my friends be in middle school and how will I choose them?"; seventh grade, "What kind of decisions might I have to make in middle school about using alcohol, tobacco, or drugs?"; eighth grade, "What kind of career do I want to be involved in as an adult?"

To help students see how the topics listed under school, community, and nation/world might affect them, ask them to think about ones that might have changed from previous years. (Student example: "I saw an article about gangs and wonder if kids today are more concerned about violence than they used to be years ago.") Also, invite them to consider which world, national, or community changes might affect their own transitions. For example, changes in technology might affect the kind of education they get.

DISCUSSION QUESTIONS

1. Describe the situation from each of the following perspectives: the teachers on the sixth-grade team, Betsy Rogers, the students, the parents.

2. The planning team for this unit felt that a student-generated approach would help to meet their goal of using a variety of instructional strategies to encourage the development of critical thinking and performance skills. How well does Beane's approach, as implemented here, appear to meet the intent of this principle? What are the costs and benefits of such an approach? Among other considerations, include the following:

   • Scott's concerns with the thematic curricula center on her awareness of standard expectations for content coverage. What are the implications of having either students or teachers choose topic areas that do not converge with conventional or state-required content coverage of particular disciplines? How can teachers achieve convergence—is this a worthwhile goal?

   • Some educational reformers assert that "less is more" in terms of content coverage. How do you interpret this view, and does it accurately portray the situation at Wakefield? Do you agree or disagree?

   • Do some subjects lend themselves to a thematic approach (for example, Rogers states that language arts is process oriented and that students can learn the skills through most any content), whereas others need to be more tightly sequenced? Would your discipline lend itself to thematic teaching? Why or why not?

3. How important is a match between a teacher's natural teaching style and the format of instruction for successful learning to take place? Take into account the following:

   • Wood prefers much more structure and preplanning. To what degree should she sacrifice her teaching philosophy for team goals?

   • In the past, Campbell has effectively presented information and skills in a teacher-centered way, and he insists that at least some of his students seem to prefer his usual style. Should he change his teaching style if it has been effective for students? How can he be certain which style is the most effective way of teaching?

   • Are there ways teachers could modify the unit to meet their individual teaching styles and goals? Would these compromise the strengths of the unit and undermine its effectiveness?

4. Consider the advantages and disadvantages of cooperative learning as described in this case.

   • The state reform initiatives support a greater use of group work. Scott has noticed several students who do not seem to be contributing to the group projects on a consistent basis. In what ways might she ensure that all students participate equally? Discuss various methods for assessing individual contributions.

- Scott and the others also know that just working on a project does not mean that students understand the concepts being studied. In a method that uses group projects to demonstrate learning of concepts and skills, how can teachers distinguish and assess how much each individual has learned?

5. Consider the issue of assessment.

   - Scott wonders how to explain a student's report card grade to parents when she has only a few grades in her grade book. How should the team communicate to parents what students have learned and how they have shown their learning? Are there intermediate assessments that could be used to provide a yardstick of learning to both parents and students? What would you suggest?

   - Rogers and Scott raise the question of accountability, particularly in light of statewide assessment tests. Despite an increased emphasis on writing, the new tests remain very much discipline-based. Nina and Darlene wonder how well students will perform when their learning has been through interdisciplinary, thematic units. What are some options for handling this and the costs and benefits of each?

   - Assess Rogers' guiding questions for the students' journals. What additional information would you like to have, and how would you go about getting it? How would you use the information?

   - The end-of-unit student evaluations as well as teachers' observations provide data for determining the effectiveness of the unit. Based on this information, explain whether you agree or disagree with Rogers' claim of student success.

6. The members of the teaching team feel the burden of their collective reputation as the innovators in the school. Perhaps some teachers are waiting for them to give up. In contrast, other teachers may be interested in trying out similar units if the team is successful. How might these pressures affect the team's reaction to the unit?

   - What do you see as the advantages/disadvantages for a beginning teacher to be part of a teaching team? How would you feel about being part of this experimental program?

   - Some colleagues believe that students have a hard time adjusting to the more traditional approach of teachers in subsequent grades. If you were a teacher attempting this type of reform, how would you explain this to parents who express concern that their children may not be prepared in later grades?

7. Campbell wonders aloud whether Beane's approach is truly effective or if his method is simply another fashionable approach embraced by theorists.

   - How would you suggest that teachers assess new instructional ideas for which there is scant research on their effectiveness for learning? What should be the basis for teachers' decisions to embark on voluntary innovations? List specific criteria.

   - Each of the team members is at a different level of experience. How might this affect their responses to change?

8. Review questions 1–7 in Exhibit A.

   - Which questions were addressed by students in the unit? How likely is it that students will develop an in-depth understanding of all the concepts in a three-week period? Consider whether this unit sacrificed breadth and depth of content to student motivation and interest? As a teacher, how would you prioritize the most important concepts?

   - To what extent should curriculum be designed around a balance of cognitive and affective goals? To what extent should developmental level be the determining factor?

9. Assume you are part of the interdisciplinary team for the third year. The renovations are completed, and the group has decided to try the interdisciplinary approach again, but with major refinements.

   - What refinements would you suggest and why? If there are elements of the unit that should be kept, identify which ones and explain why. How will you determine the unit's effectiveness the next time it is taught?

CASE 5

Discussion Question	Corresponding INTASC Principle
2	**1** The teacher understands the concepts, tools of inquiry, and structures of the discipline(s) he or she teaches and can create learning experiences that make these aspects of subject matter meaningful for students.
5	**8** The teacher understands and uses formal and informal assessment strategies to evaluate and ensure the continuous intellectual, social, and physical development of the learner.
6	**10** The teacher fosters relationships with school colleagues, parents, and agencies in the larger community to support learning and well-being.
7	**9** The teacher is a reflective practitioner who continually evaluates the effects of his/her choices and actions on others (students, parents, and other professionals in the learning community) and who actively seeks out opportunities to grow professionally.
8	**5** The teacher uses an understanding of individual and group motivation and behavior to create a learning environment that encourages positive social interaction, active engagement in learning, and self-motivation.
8	**7** The teacher plans instruction based upon knowledge of subject matter, students, the community, and curriculum goals.

"I Don't Think I Can Teach This Again"

"I just don't know if I'm prepared to teach *Huck Finn* again. This book has caused so much dissension and heartache," Leslie Jenkins confided to her good friend and colleague, Helen Benroe. Despite the fact that both were veteran teachers and had taught the book before, Benroe nodded sympathetically.

Jenkins and Benroe were attending a weeklong summer conference at The Mark Twain House, a museum in Hartford, Connecticut, dedicated to the study and celebration of the life and works of Samuel Clemens. More than 30 teachers from around the country had gathered to talk and think about how to teach *Adventures of Huckleberry Finn* in the 1990s.

The scholars at The Mark Twain House did not want this classic text, the most frequently taught novel in American schools (Carey-Webb, 1993), to become a victim of cultural conflicts. Instead they felt *Huck Finn* was a valuable tool in fighting racism. Jenkins' goal was to sort out some of the issues in the novel that had caused such controversy in a nearby district. She hardly wanted a repeat of that situation, but she also did not want to give up teaching this classic.

One of the most banned books in America since its publication in 1884, *Huck Finn* was not new to controversy. It was first banned as coarse and immoral "trash" in 1885 in Concord, Massachusetts (Champion, 1991). In the more recent past, there had been efforts to remove the book from school curricula in such disparate places as Virginia, Texas, and Washington, DC.

Closer to home, the issue of whether to teach *Huck Finn* had exploded a few months earlier at a middle school in Sandbury, a racially diverse Connecticut city only an hour's drive from The Mark Twain House. The parent of an African American student raised objections when an eighth-grade English teacher was teaching the novel in that school for the eighth time. Although the teacher and school principal tried to explain their educational rationale for teaching *Huck Finn*, concern grew. African American parents objected in particular to the use of the word "nigger" over 200 times in the novel. After all, many questioned, how would Jews react if their children had to read a book in which "kike" appeared over and over? Would Italian American parents tolerate it if their children were required to read a book that used the term "wop" over 200 times? Parents of diverse backgrounds were sympathetic to this point of view. Several believed that Twain's novel negatively stereotyped African Americans as superstitious, uneducated, passive, and childlike, and they felt that this portrayal threatened to undermine the self-esteem of Black youths. One African American parent complained that her son had been upset when he overheard White classmates mimicking the dialect of Jim, a slave (see Exhibit A).

Parents expressed other opinions as well. Instead of condemning the novel, many praised it for exposing the evils of racism. They perceived Jim as the most noble and sympathetic character in the story. Others maintained that, while the book might be an important literary work, eighth graders were not intellectually mature enough to understand Twain's sophisticated satire. Some parents complained of being bull-dozed; they felt it had been impossible for parents to discuss openly the pros and cons of teaching the novel for fear of being labeled racist. And yet another group of parents was flatly opposed to censorship (see Exhibit B for opposing positions).

Two middle school parents aired their criticisms on a local radio station; soon, the wire services had picked up the story, which appeared in national newspapers and on national television. Interest in the novel seemed to peak around this time, when *The New Yorker* (Bradley, 1996) published a newly discovered episode of *Huck Finn* as well as commentaries by several novelists and critics about Twain and his novel.

Halfway through teaching *Huck Finn*, the English teacher at the Sandbury Middle School was ordered to stop until the school system could determine how to respond to parents' concerns. Finally, the superintendent made a decision to remove *Huck Finn* from the eighth-grade curriculum, contending that it was tearing the school apart along racial lines. Since students would still be able to borrow the book from their school library, the superintendent averred that this was a curriculum issue and not a case of censorship.

A few months later, Jenkins and Benroe were attending the conference at The Mark Twain House, listening to David Bradley, an African American professor of English from Temple University, discuss the controversy that had swirled around *Huck Finn* since its publication and argue that the work served to remind Americans of the racism in our society—then and now. He quoted Ernest Hemingway, who claimed that all American literature came from *Huck Finn*. Discussing the use of the word "nigger," Bradley asked, "Isn't the classroom the safest place for a child to encounter a potentially harmful word—and in the hands of a skilled teacher, instead of on the playground?" (Schuster, 1995, p. A3).

Bradley, nonetheless, readily admitted the difficulties in teaching *Huck Finn*. Teachers knowledgeable about Twain, *Huck Finn*, and its historical period had to teach students how to read carefully. The context was unfamiliar, the dialects diffi-cult, the satire complex, and the various points of view confusing. This was not a book for beginning readers and could aggravate problems in a class or school already experiencing racial tensions.

Jenkins was both intrigued and worried as she listened to the speaker. Would she be up to teaching this controversial novel to her class of "average" eighth graders in her suburban town? Although she understood the concerns of those who considered the book racist, her stance was that it was not.

LESLIE JENKINS

"From the time I was young, I knew I wanted to be a teacher," commented Jenkins. At college, her student teaching experience was a disaster, however. Her master teacher, a 70-year-old veteran, had decided not to retire and had difficulty relinquishing control. "When she felt I was doing something wrong," Jenkins explained, "she would jump up and say, 'No, no, sit down and watch me do it.' I lost credibility with the students and felt incompetent. My college supervisor was supportive and promised to pass me as long as I tried, but that's not the way I ever wanted to do anything—just getting by."

After that experience, Jenkins took a break from the classroom. A year later, she was hired to teach English and reading to middle schoolers in a small private school. There, colleagues took her under their wings, and she thrived. At the same time, she completed her Master's degree in teaching, gaining new tools to practice in her classroom.

After three years, Jenkins and her husband, Robert, decided to start a family. She taught part-time when her two children were young. Jenkins had now been teaching full-time at Webster Middle School for four years.

THE SCHOOL AND COMMUNITY

Webster Middle School was nestled into the gently rolling countryside of Hillsdale, a town of approximately 15,000. Once a cluster of farms, this upper-middle-class community was dotted with homes resembling Colonial mansions. In most of the two-parent families, both parents worked as professionals—doctors, lawyers, and insurance executives. In a corner of the town, there was a small development of subsidized apartments for low-income families.

Many Hillsdale residents worked in Oldtown, a city of 130,000 located 30 minutes away. A stark contrast to Hillsdale, Oldtown reflected the fate of many major northeastern cities as it struggled with decaying factories, aging schools, a high level of poverty, and a fleeing middle class. Still, its many cultural institutions, excellent restaurants, and lively nightlife continued to draw citizens from around the state.

While approximately 90 percent of the public school population in Oldtown was minority, suburban Hillsdale was almost completely White. There were only a few African American children at Webster Middle School and some children from Asian backgrounds. There was one synagogue in town; most families belonged to mainstream Christian denominations.

Webster Middle School was a modern structure accented by circular windows and interior communal spaces with conferencing tables for students and teachers to meet in small groups. It had about 180 students per grade level, with classes typically of 18 to 20 students. Webster was proud of its fine academic reputation.

THE CLASS

Jenkins taught three sections of eighth-grade English. The school was on a six-day schedule. Half the periods were 45 minutes, and half were 90-minute sections. Jenkins valued the longer sessions because they gave time to focus in greater depth on a topic; however, it was sometimes hard for eighth graders to sustain their attention.

Although her preparations were seemingly identical, the three sections were tracked and moved at different paces. Jenkins preferred working with the middle-level students. "I like the 'average' kids because it's a challenge to try to reach them," she said. "The diversity of ability levels and learning styles keeps me on my toes, thinking of new and creative ways to reach them." Her favorite group this year, the lively fourth-period class, had 21 students. Two-thirds of the class worked just at the mastery level and one-third at slightly below mastery level in reading and writing. There were six students who had been identified as having attention deficit disorder (ADD), two who were learning disabled (LD), and one who was identified as having behavior disorders. Many of the children had stepparents, and three were from single-parent families. All of the children were White except Sandra, an African American.

Jenkins called this highly animated, social group her "runaway train." Jenkins felt a great responsibility to spur their enthusiasm and not to harness them by working too hard to "keep them in line." But the class met right before lunch, when the six students with ADD had just about run through their medication. Jenkins found that she constantly had to change their seats to try to keep them focused. When she succeeded in keeping them involved, they followed through and often challenged her intellectually. "I think several of these students are very bright and stimulate the others. Even the less capable students come up with wonderful thoughts."

JENKINS' REASONS FOR TEACHING *HUCK FINN*

Jenkins explained why she had chosen to teach *Huck Finn*. "A few years ago, the eighth-grade teachers and the language arts coordinator decided that it was a key text that should be taught. Now our students read it after studying *To Kill a Mockingbird* to continue the themes of growth, maturity, and discrimination. During the year, they also read Steinbeck's *Of Mice and Men* and several short stories. Although *Huck Finn* is a requirement, I could avoid it if I wished. Some teachers say they don't have enough time, since it's taught at the end of the year. But I feel that *Huck Finn* is an important book. I always try to make connections so students see a book's relevance to their own lives. I've admitted to the kids that I feel some apprehension because of its controversial aspects. It's a stretch for me, but we're going to be learning together. If the students are really turned on, they'll gain new insights that I never thought of and that I can bring to future students."

After taking the summer seminar at The Mark Twain House, Jenkins was enthusiastic about teaching *Huck Finn* again. Although Jenkins had taught *Huck Finn* twice before, she felt she needed a better connection to the novel to teach it well. She was familiar with the names of the scholars who were speaking at the conference and was eager to hear them.

She also was motivated by concern. She had read newspaper accounts about the Sandbury middle school controversy and wanted to find out more about the issues and possible objections to the novel. After she attended the conference, if parents expressed concerns about *Huck Finn* at Webster, she would be better able to address these.

In the past, Webster parents had seemed pleased by the idea that their middle schoolers were reading a text frequently taught at the high school and college levels. Jenkins speculated that they saw this as a sign of their children's ability. But now that the Sandbury incident was known all over the state, she wondered how the parents would respond.

PREPARING STUDENTS TO READ THE NOVEL

After attending the conference, Jenkins approached the novel differently. Previously, she had focused primarily on plot (see Exhibit C for plot summary). Although she had spent some time discussing the themes of the text, she now decided to explore these much more fully and to help her students understand Twain's literary techniques, including his satire and irony.

Holding up a new copy of *Huck Finn*, Jenkins introduced the novel by discussing how controversial it had always been. Sharing quotes from the scholars at the conference, she asked students to read them carefully and try to paraphrase the scholars' concerns in their own words. She wanted students to consider seriously whether they were likely to be upset or offended by the book and whether they might not want to read it. She explained that she was still learning about the novel and was offended by certain aspects of it, like the use of the word "nigger." Then she posed a challenge: "Some people don't think middle schoolers are ready to read this book. There's offensive language in it, the dialect is hard, and the satire is difficult. It's obvious that the district thinks you're up to it, but what do you think?" she asks her students.

The combination of their teacher's challenge and the new books sparked the students' interest. The student with a behavior disorder, an avid reader, suggested passing out the book before the upcoming spring vacation for those students who wanted to get a head start. Twelve out of the twenty-one students ran to the desk to pick up their copies. Although Jenkins originally had intended to provide more historical background information before the students began reading, she decided to let them follow their own interests.

To introduce the theme of racism in *Huck Finn* after spring break, Jenkins had the students read a short story by Angelica Gibbs titled "The Test." In the story, a young Black woman is treated in a demeaning fashion by the White man giving her a driver's test. When she loses her composure and confronts him, he fails her on the test. Through group discussion, Jenkins' students readily understood his abuse of power and the racist intent of his comments.

She thought that students would understand the novel better if they were knowledgeable about Clemens' background. For fun, she asked them to collect and share 10 interesting facts about the author. Students dug up information about Clemens' work as a newspaper reporter and riverboat pilot.

To prepare students to understand the author's voice in *Huck Finn*, she shared primary materials she had received at the conference supporting the position that Clemens was not a racist. These included a letter from Clemens to the Yale Law School offering to pay the tuition of Warner T. McGuinn, a Black student. Students also read a story Clemens wrote that satirically condemned the stoning of Chinese men in San Francisco. They discussed how Clemens capitalized on the power of satire to express his outrage at the mistreatment of others. To introduce the character of Huck, Jenkins gave students chapter 6 of the *Adventures of Tom Sawyer* in which Twain first presents Huck in his writings. They read about Huck as the juvenile pariah of the town.

Jenkins related *Huck Finn* to an interdisciplinary unit on the study of a local river. She and the science teacher collaborated and supervised the students' building of seaworthy, biodegradable model rafts and then took them to the river to test the rafts.

STARTING THE NOVEL

Once students began reading the book, they used their journals to document their observations (Exhibit D). Jenkins asked them to start making observations about the characters. They discussed the distinction between Huck's voice as the narrator and Twain's point of view. Through this process, students began to understand that Huck does not always understand what he is reporting.

Jenkins worked to help students understand the characters' dialects. "It's almost like learning a foreign language. By reading passages aloud, students got a sense of cadence. When they began to understand the meaning of the language, they loved it and felt a real sense of accomplishment," she said.

To facilitate students' understanding of the context of the story, they discussed the characters' superstitions. They recognized that many of these were grounded in common sense and revealed the characters' closeness to nature. The class compared ancient and modern superstitions and created posters representing them.

One of Jenkins' main goals was to make connections between her students' lives and Huck's life, so that the story would have personal meaning for them. The students compared Pap Finn's expectations of Huck to their parents' expectations of them. They questioned a town's responsibility to intervene if a parent is neglectful, comparing Huck's situation to examples of present-day child abuse and neglect.

TEACHING PERSUASIVE WRITING

For the eighth-grade state mastery test, students had to be able to write a persuasive essay. Jenkins decided to integrate the teaching of this skill with the teaching of *Huck Finn*. She asked students to write a persuasive essay to convince a jury who should be Huck's guardian—Pap, the Widow Douglas, the judge, or Huck himself.

After writing their essays, the students presented them as speeches in class. Students took notes during each speech and then provided verbal feedback to the speaker, analyzing the persuasive strategies used (Exhibit E). In a variety of ways, each speaker exhorted the jury to protect Huck from his father's abuse.

Then, Jenkins concluded the lesson. "I'm very proud of you. You used the persuasive techniques that a great debater would use—rhetorical questions, cause and effect, good comparisons, and evidence and examples from the book. And you certainly got people's attention with lively images, like 'Pap Finn sleeps with the pigs and the only time he comes to church is to steal the wine.' "

Driving home that afternoon, Jenkins mused that the topic of child neglect and abuse seemed to engage and challenge her students, whereas racism, the issue that had fired the Sandbury controversy, hardly raised a stir. "I'm not sure that's good," she thought to herself.

Moreover, there had been no concerned calls from parents. Jenkins speculated that, since parents in their primarily White community considered themselves open-minded, as a group they would not be likely to feel offended by the novel. Were the responses of students and parents in Hillsdale and Sandbury different because of the racial makeup of the two communities, she wondered, or did it have more to do with the way she was teaching the novel?

OTHER STRATEGIES

Students engaged in several kinds of writing to help them understand the novel better. To help students understand the irony in *Huck Finn*, Jenkins asked them to list examples of irony from the text in their journals and share these in class (Exhibit D). She also gave them a list of ironical quotes to analyze in their journals. Jenkins followed a similar procedure with other literary techniques, such as satire.

She required students to write an essay by choosing a theme, showing how Twain develops it throughout the book, and drawing a conclusion about the author's purpose. First, the class brainstormed possible themes. Then Jenkins read them a sample essay that she had written on the theme of education in *Huck Finn*. She asked them to evaluate the essay and find any shortcomings. The students thought the essay was great, but Jenkins said she'd only give it a B, explaining that she needed to expand it by providing more specific details. Their task was to edit her essay to show where she needed to elaborate. Jenkins felt that it had been only fair for her to write her own essay first. "If I'm asking the students to do it, I should realize how hard the assignment actually is. Then, when it comes time for the students to write, they chuckle, 'Well, she's already done it, so I guess I can.' "

"Sometimes they get frustrated with the time it takes for me to return their papers. I explain that they've spent considerable time composing their essays; it wouldn't be fair of me not to read them carefully. After reading them all once, I reread each paper. I return their quizzes the next day, but this takes about a week," Jenkins explained.

For a culminating activity, Jenkins wanted something special. Her only stipulation was that their projects creatively demonstrate their learning from the novel. They first had to write a proposal for her to review.

MODIFICATIONS FOR STUDENTS WITH SPECIAL NEEDS

For the students with special needs, Jenkins tried several strategies. Often, these students needed written explanations as a complement or follow-up to oral discussions. She asked for volunteer scribes to summarize key ideas generated from group discussions and to show them on the overhead projector. To ensure that students had accurate descriptions of their assignments, she handed out written directions or wrote the assignments on the chalkboard for students to copy.

When forming small groups, she divided the students with special needs among the groups. Then, if one had a hard time understanding something, a peer was available to explain. "When they're having difficulty, they seem to do better when peers give them an explanation than when I do," she said.

For help developing essays, four students received additional assistance either from the special education teacher or the teacher staffing the writing lab. In addition, Jenkins often paired students for peer editing. They had to outline their partner's paper, using a graphic organizer to identify gaps. She found that if students worked with another person on the same theme, both developed new insights. Also, if students having difficulty with writing worked with a better writer, they had a model from which to learn.

WHAT'S THE CONTROVERSY?

Since its banning at the Sandbury middle school and the ensuing conference at The Mark Twain House, *Huck Finn* continued to be prominently featured in the local and national news. Public radio hosted a talk show about teaching *Huck Finn*. Jane Smiley (1996), a Pulitzer Prize–winning novelist, published an article in *Harper's Magazine* accusing the novel of being racist, arguing that neither ". . . Huck nor Twain takes Jim's desire for freedom at all seriously . . ." (p. 63) and challenging the putative "greatness" of the novel's literary style. Twain biographer Justin Kaplan (1996) mounted a counterargument in *The New York Times Book Review*. It was perhaps no coincidence that a new edition of the novel, which included previously unpublished passages, was advertised in a special edition, "Black in America," in *The New Yorker* (Bradley, 1996).

Given the controversy, Jenkins kept waiting for the other shoe to drop as she was teaching the novel. So far, very few of the concerns raised at the conference had surfaced in her classroom.

She had not seen signs of racism. She found the students occasionally making fun of the dialect, but they seemed to view these passages as southern dialect, not Black dialect.

Generally, they did not react to the word "nigger." Jenkins had given them David Bradley's (1996) short article from *The New Yorker* in which he discussed the critical difference between the way Huck uses the word and the way Tom uses it.[1] When the class read the novel aloud, Jenkins permitted students to skip over the word "nigger" if they chose to. In most cases, they read it without seeming to pay much attention to it. Jenkins presumed this resulted from their discussion of Bradley's article. One student substituted the word "Negro." Two other students seemed to skim ahead as they were reading and never volunteered to read a passage in which "nigger" appeared.

---

[1] Bradley points out that Huck uses "nigger" to mean "Negro," without negative connotations, whereas Tom uses it disparagingly. From reading *Huck Finn* as a child, Bradley began to learn the difference between connotation and denotation and to evaluate people's intent based on their actions, not their words.

Jenkins discussed the students' perceptions of Jim. "The students have some trouble understanding Jim's dialect. They tend to view Jim like Huck in many ways. For example, they're both seeking their freedom, and they're both superstitious. I don't think the students see Jim as ignorant because he's Black. We've compared Jim to Pap Finn and pointed out that Jim is a loving, truly concerned father figure. But they miss the idea that Jim is being treated unfairly by Huck. They think once Huck has stopped tricking Jim, Huck sees him as an equal. Perhaps we just haven't discussed this enough. I've been hesitant to discuss nineteenth-century racial theories of the inferiority of African Americans, for fear that I'd heighten misconceptions and offend, rather than clarifying the historical framework for my students. Maybe we haven't talked enough about the entire society being racist; I've tended to focus more broadly on human beings' inhumanity to each other. By the end, I want to show the growth in the way Huck sees Jim. Sometimes they gloss right over it. They're still literal-minded. They're not looking deeply into the fact that one of the major ways Huck changes is in how he perceives his friend. I also want them to see how courageous Jim is."

Sandra, the one African American student, was always in the back of Jenkins' mind. "I don't want to offend any of the kids. I certainly don't want to single Sandra out, yet I wonder whether she'll be upset by anything I say, such as my interpretation or way of explaining the racist attitudes in the novel. I want to be sure that I'm sensitive," Jenkins said.

"Sandra tends not to want to share," Jenkins continued. "When I asked the students a question about a racist episode in *To Kill a Mockingbird*, Sandra said, 'I don't know.' On the other hand, other kids gave the same response. I want Sandra's perspective to be that of just a child. I don't want her to feel she has to be the only spokesperson for the African American community. Though she's one of the three or four African American kids in the school, I don't think the kids treat her any differently. Today, I found myself glancing at her when I said, 'Finally, *Huck Finn* is seeing Jim as a person. What was the problem before?' We related this to *To Kill a Mockingbird* in which Bob Ewell assumes that because he's White, he's a better person than Tom Robinson, the Black man accused of rape. I was proud of the kids when they pointed out the irony that Bob's skin was probably just as dark as Tom's since he didn't wash. This is the one time I heard the kids refer to the fact that Sandra is darker. A student who had just come back from a Florida vacation said to her, 'I've got darker skin than you.' 'No way,' said Sandra. I'll always be darker.' "

Summing up the class's responses, Jenkins said, "The issue that people would assume would be most volatile—racism—hasn't been, perhaps because there's not much of a racial mix of students at the school. In retrospect, I might have used the journals to encourage more of a personal response, but that can be touchy, too."

Then she reflected further. "Making the book powerfully relevant to my students has had more to do with coming-of-age issues and concerns about child abuse and neglect than with racism, given the school community. I have to admit that I'm not as comfortable discussing racism as I had hoped I would be, and I'm only relieved that there hasn't been more controversy in the classroom or any criticism from parents. I've certainly tried to open the students' eyes to the problem of racism in the book, but should I have forced the issue? Does the responsible teacher *create* a controversy when teaching this book? I want to teach the book conscientiously, but I don't want to end up on page one of the newspapers like the teacher in Sandbury did."

OTHER CONCERNS

Jenkins found that student boredom was her greatest concern. The class was not moving through the book as quickly as expected. One reason was that she had fallen behind in the rereading she needed to do to keep on top of the details. She slowed the class's pace so she could keep abreast of the reading.

Also, as she stated, "I get caught up in all the things I want to share, yet I don't want to overteach. We've been working on this book for six weeks, and maybe we've beaten it to death. The hardest thing is dragging the kids through the reading. It's just tedious for them. Like the ebb and flow of the river, they speed up when the book gets exciting and slow down when it's less intriguing to them. It's ironic; when Huck and Jim are relaxing on the raft, they take a break themselves—during the more philosophical dialogues. I don't like to have to use the threat of a quiz to make them do the reading, but sometimes I have to."

To give students enough time to read, she provided digressions. For example, they made a chart comparing the social ills of the 1830s to the social ills of the 1990s. Then they discussed what an author's responsibility is to influence social issues and whether he or she can really effect change. "They just looked at me like I'd just grown a second head," she said. Then, to try to relate this to their lives, she asked if they had ever read a book or seen a movie or TV show that had changed their thinking, "What kind of a reaction was Mark Twain trying to get from his readers?" she questioned her students. "We didn't get far, but it may have sparked some thought," she later commented. "I want to pull them into the text, to see how this relates to them, and I'm buying time to let them catch up on reading. They protest when I tell them too much of the story, but they're falling behind."

Sometimes, the kids themselves provided the digressions, seemingly to enliven the class. Jenkins felt a constant tension between letting the students take charge of the discussion and drawing them back to the text. "Sometimes I feel they're more interested in the connections to real life than the novel. After a discussion of the Duke and King's scams, they regaled each other with stories about con artists. Yet I don't know if that's wrong. If the intention of literature is to mirror life, isn't it important to connect the book to what they've seen? Don't I want them to come away with a new understanding of what's fair and what needs to be reformed in their own lives?"

FINISHING THE NOVEL

To quicken the pace, Jenkins decided to skip the last chapters, from chapter 34 to the end, where Tom and Huck conspire to free Jim from the Phelps plantation. This was a first for her, but she felt it was necessary now. She summarized the remaining plot, and the class read aloud and discussed the ironic intent of key passages. Although it was not required, many students read the chapters on their own.

Jenkins decided to shorten the final test because of the many assignments on *Huck Finn* the students had completed already:

- four essays
- seven quizzes
- several short projects
- culminating project

In addition to the test, Jenkins gave the students Langston Hughes' poem "I Dream a World" and asked students to write a take-home essay comparing it to *Huck Finn* in terms of tone, theme, and the two authors' background and historical times. She also asked students to consider whether we, as a society, have moved forward in terms of eliminating racist attitudes and whether we still have a long way to go. After grading the tests, she was pleased with the results. There were some simple comparisons, such as that Hughes was African American and Twain was White, but also some more sophisticated responses. Several students thought that Hughes was more optimistic and foresaw the end of racism, whereas Twain was misanthropic and had far less confidence in the goodness of humankind.

The students presented their culminating projects after taking the test. Among them were four board games, model rafts, skits, several children's books based on scenes from the novel, and a gigantic papier-mâché model of the river. Jenkins felt that the projects were valuable in reinforcing certain ideas, such as what life on a raft might be like, and in providing an opportunity for those students who had difficulty comprehending the text to use their creativity.

FINAL REFLECTIONS

Summing up her feelings about the experience of teaching *Huck Finn*, Jenkins said, "It was pretty successful. For the most part, students enjoyed reading the book, and there are signs of continuing interest. Last week, we had a book fair, and I was delighted to see that at least 10 kids bought copies of *Tom Sawyer* for summer reading."

I don't think middle school is the only time *Huck Finn* could be taught or necessarily the best time. They'll take from it what they can and hopefully come back to it someday. A good novel is meant to be reread. There are always some unanswered questions."

"Every time I teach it, I do it differently because I think there's something I forgot before or something that's more important that needs to be considered. Next time, I'd be better organized and try to stick to my time frame. I kept revising and adding things. I got really excited about the book and tried to do too much."

"For the very last activity, I gave the students a Twain quote, 'Travel is fatal to prejudice, bigotry, and narrow-mindedness,' and asked them to answer the following questions in their journals:

1. How does this relate to what you know about Samuel Clemens?
2. How does this relate to *Huck Finn*?
3. How does this relate to your life and life in general?"

"We had a lively discussion about the quote. One student said, 'If we're still traveling through life, at fourteen we haven't lost all our prejudices and ignorance. We need time to work our way through and to have more experiences to help us lose our prejudices. The more experiences you have, the more prejudiced you might become. My parents are more prejudiced than I am.' "

"I don't think the theme of racism really hit them. They haven't had to deal with it personally. They were as upset or more by the way Pap Finn treated Huck and left him with little supervision. They could identify more with that."

"Their limited understanding is partially because of what they bring to the novel. Middle schoolers have had just so many experiences; hopefully, we'll take them a little beyond those."

Then, Jenkins paused. "It wouldn't matter whether I were teaching middle schoolers or not, I think this book would be much more challenging to teach in a racially diverse school district where kids have more direct experience with racism. I'd have to think about whether this might change the way I teach the book. How would I teach it if I were teaching in the city half an hour away?"

She paused again, recalling the stories she had heard of the Sandbury incident, as well as what she had read in the papers—how bitterly angry and pained for their children the African American parents were and how unfairly attacked the White teacher felt. "Or would I even teach it?" Jenkins asked. "I wouldn't want to abandon teaching this book—I feel it has such merit. Yet would I willingly face that maelstrom?"

REFERENCES AND SELECTED BIBLIOGRAPHY

Bradley, D. (1996, June 26). That word. *The New Yorker*, p. 133.

Chadwick-Joshua, J. (1991). Mark Twain and the fires of controversy: Teaching racially-sensitive literature: Or, "Say that 'N' word and out you go!" In L. Champion (Ed.), *The critical response to Mark Twain's Huckleberry Finn* (pp. 228–237). Westport, CT: Greenwood.

Chadwick-Joshua, J. (1996, August 17). Pro & con: Should schools keep *Huck Finn* off the reading lists? No. Great books make us uncomfortable. *The Hartford Courant*, p. A–10.

Carey-Webb, A. (1993). Racism and Huckleberry Finn: Censorship, dialogue, and change. *English Journal*, 82(7), 22–34.

Champion, L. (1991). *The critical response to Mark Twain's Huckleberry Finn*. Westport, CT: Greenwood.

Fishkin, S. F. (1993). *Was Huck Black? Mark Twain and African American voices*. New York: Oxford University Press.

Hughes, L. (1963). I Dream a World. In A. Bontemps (Ed.), *American Negro poetry* (pp. 71–72). New York: Hill & Wang. (Originally published 1926)

Kaplan, J. (1996, March 10). Selling *Huck Finn* down the river. *The New York Times Book Review*, p. 27.

Leonard, J. S., Tenney, T. A., & Davis, T. M. (Eds.). (1992). *Satire or evasion? Black perspectives on Huckleberry Finn*. Durham, NC: Duke University Press.

Lew, A. (1993). Teaching *Huck Finn* in a multiethnic classroom. *English Journal*, 82(7), 16–21.

Pierce, R. N. (1996, August 17). Pro & con: Should schools keep *Huck Finn* off the reading lists? Yes. The book is too sophisticated for teens. *The Hartford Courant*, p. A–10.

Schuster, K. (1995, July 25). Teachers examine 'Huck Finn.' *New Haven Register*, pp. A3, A5.

Smiley, J. (1996, January). Say it ain't so, Huck. *Harper's Magazine*, pp. 61–67.

The Mark Twain House helps teachers teach *Adventures of Huckleberry Finn*. (1995, Fall). *Mark Twain News, 3*, 3–4.

Wallace, J. H. (1992). The case against *Huck Finn*. In J. S. Leonard, T. A. Tenney, & T. M. Davis (Eds.), *Satire or evasion? Black perspectives on Huckleberry Finn* (pp. 16–24). Durham, NC: Duke University Press.

Note: For references on integrated curriculum and middle school teaching see case 5, *On the High Wire*.

E X H I B I T   A

The Case Against *Huck Finn*[1]

John H. Wallace

THE ISSUE

The *Adventures of Huckleberry Finn*, by Mark Twain, is the most grotesque example of racist trash ever written. During the 1981–82 school year, the media carried reports that it was challenged in Davenport, Iowa; Houston, Texas; Buck County, Pennsylvania; and, of all places, Mark Twain Intermediate School in Fairfax County, Virginia. Parents in Waukegan, Illinois, in 1983 and in Springfield, Illinois, in 1984 asked that the book be removed from the classroom—and there are many challenges to this book that go unnoticed by the press. All of these are coming from black parents and teachers after complaints from their children or students, and frequently they are supported by white teachers, as in the case of Mark Twain Intermediate School.

For the past forty years, black families have trekked to schools in numerous districts throughout the country to say, "This book is not good for our children," only to be turned away by insensitive and often unwittingly racist teachers and administrators who respond, "This book is a classic." Classic or not, it should not be allowed to continue to cause our children embarrassment about their heritage.

Louisa May Alcott, the Concord Public Library, and others condemned the book as trash when it was published in 1885. The NAACP and the National Urban League successfully collaborated to have *Huckleberry Finn* removed from the classrooms of the public schools of New York City in 1957 because it uses the term "nigger." In 1969 Miami-Dade Junior College removed the book from its classrooms because the administration believed that the book creates an emotional block for black students that inhibits learning. It was excluded from the classrooms of the New Trier High School in Winnetka, Illinois, and removed from the required reading list in the state of Illinois in 1976.

My own research indicates that the assignment and reading aloud of *Huckleberry Finn* in our classrooms is humiliating and insulting to black students. It contributes to their feelings of low self-esteem and to the white students' disrespect for black people. It constitutes mental cruelty, harassment, and outright racial intimidation to force black students to sit in the classroom with their white peers and read *Huckleberry Finn*. The attitudes developed by the reading of such literature can lead to tensions, discontent, and even fighting. If this book is removed from the required

[1]From *Satire or Evasion? Black Perspectives on Huckleberry Finn* (pp. 16–24) by James S. Leonard, Thomas A. Tenney, and Thadious M. Davis (Eds.). Copyright 1992, Duke University Press. Reprinted with permission.

reading lists of our schools, there should be improved student-to-student, student-to-teacher, and teacher-to-teacher relationships.

"NIGGER"

According to *Webster's Dictionary*, the word "nigger" means a Negro or a member of any dark-skinned race of people and is *offensive*. Black people have never accepted "nigger" as a proper term—not in George Washington's time, Mark Twain's time, or William Faulkner's time. A few white authors, thriving on making blacks objects of ridicule and scorn by having blacks use this word as they, the white authors, were writing and speaking for blacks in a dialect they perceived to be peculiar to black people may have given the impression that blacks accepted the term. Nothing could be further from the truth.

Some black authors have used "nigger," but not in literature to be consumed by children in the classroom. Black authors know as well as whites that there is money to be made selling books that ridicule black people. As a matter of fact, the white child learns early in life that his or her black peer makes a good butt for a joke. Much of what goes on in the classroom reinforces this behavior. Often the last word uttered before a fight is "nigger." Educators must discourage the ridicule of "different" children.

IN THE CLASSROOM

Russell Baker, of the *New York Times* (14 April 1982), has said (and Jonathan Yardley, of the *Washington Post* [10 May 1982], concurred):

> Kids are often exposed to books long before they are ready for them or exposed to them in a manner that seems almost calculated to evaporate whatever enthusiasm the students may bring to them. . . . Very few youngsters of high school age are ready for *Huckleberry Finn*. Leaving aside its subtle depiction of racial attitudes and its complex view of American society, the book is written in a language that will seem baroque, obscure and antiquated to many young people today. The vastly sunnier *Tom Sawyer* is a book for kids, but *Huckleberry Finn most emphatically is not*.

The milieu of the classroom is highly charged with emotions. There are twenty to thirty unique personalities with hundreds of needs to be met simultaneously. Each student wants to be accepted and to be like the white, middle-class child whom he perceives to be favored by the teacher. Since students do not want their differences highlighted, it is best to accentuate their similarities; but the reading of *Huck Finn* in class accentuates the one difference that is always apparent—color.

My research suggests that the black child is offended by the use of the word "nigger" anywhere, no matter what rationale the teacher may use to justify it. If the teacher permits its use, the black child tends to reject the teacher because the student is confident that the teacher is prejudiced. Communications are effectively severed, thwarting the child's education. Pejorative terms should not be granted any legitimacy by their use in the classroom under the guise of teaching books of great literary merit, nor for any other reason.

EQUAL PROTECTION AND OPPORTUNITY IN THE CLASSROOM

To paraphrase Irwin Katz, the use of the word "nigger" by a prestigious adult like a teacher poses a strong *social* threat to the black child. Any expression by a white or black teacher of dislike or devaluation, whether through harsh, indifferent, or patronizing behavior, would tend to have an unfavorable effect on the performance of black children in their school work. This is so because *various psychological theories suggest that the black students' covert reactions to the social threat would constitute an important source of intellectual impairment.*

Dorothy Gilliam, writing in the *Washington Post* (12 April 1982), said, "First amendment rights are crucial to a healthy society. No less crucial is the Fourteenth Amendment and its guarantee of equal protection under the law." The use of the word "nigger" in the classroom does not provide black students with equal protection and is in violation of their constitutional rights. Without equal protections, they have neither equal access nor equal opportunity for an education.

One group of citizens deeply committed to effecting change and to retaining certain religious beliefs sacred to themselves are members of the Jewish religion. In a publication issued by the Jewish Community Council (November 1981), the following guidelines were enunciated regarding the role of religious practices in public schools: "In no event should any student, teacher, or public school staff member feel that his or her own beliefs or practices are being questioned, infringed upon, or compromised by programs taking place in or sponsored by the public school." Further, "schools should avoid practices which operate to single out and isolate 'different' pupils and thereby [cause] embarrassment."

I endorse these statements without reservation, for I believe the rationale of the Jewish Community Council is consistent with my position. I find it incongruent to contend that it is fitting and proper to shelter children from isolation, embarrassment, and ridicule due to their religious beliefs and then deny the same protection to other children because of the color of their skin. The basic issue is the same. It is our purpose to spare children from scorn, to increase personal pride, and to foster the American belief of acceptance on merit, not color, sex, religion, or origin.

THE TEACHER

Many "authorities" say *Huckleberry Finn* can be used in our intermediate and high school classrooms. They consistently put stipulations on its use like the following: It must be used with appropriate planning. It is the responsibility of the teacher to assist students in the understanding of the historical setting of the novel, the characters being depicted, the social context, including prejudice, which existed at the time depicted in the book. Balanced judgment on the part of the classroom teacher must be used prior to making a decision to utilize this book in an intermediate or high school program. Such judgment would include taking into account the age and maturity of the students, their ability to comprehend abstract concepts, and the methodology of presentation.

Any material that requires such conditions could be dangerous racist propaganda in the hands of even our best teachers. And "some, not all, teachers are hostile, racist, vindictive, inept, or even neurotic," though "many are compassionate and skillful." Teacher attitudes are important to students. Some teachers are marginal at best, yet many school administrators are willing to trust them with a book that maligns blacks. *Huckleberry Finn* would have been out of the classroom ages ago if it used "dago," "wop," or "spic."

When "authorities" mention the "historical setting" of *Huckleberry Finn*, they suggest that it is an accurate, factual portrayal of the way things were in slavery days. In fact, the book is the outgrowth of Mark Twain's memory and imagination, written twenty years after the end of slavery. Of the two main characters depicted, one is a thief, a liar, a sacrilegious corn-cob-pipe-smoking truant; the other is a self-deprecating slave. No one would want his children to emulate this pair. Yet some "authorities" speak of Huck as a boyhood hero. Twain warns us in the beginning of *Huckleberry Finn*, "Persons attempting to find a motive in this narrative will be prosecuted; persons attempting to find a moral in it will be banished; persons attempting to find a plot in it will be shot." I think we ought to listen to Twain and stop feeding this trash to our children. It does absolutely nothing to enhance racial harmony. The prejudice that existed then is still very much apparent today. Racism against blacks is deeply rooted in the American culture and is continually reinforced by the schools, by concern for socioeconomic gain, and by the vicarious ego enhancement it brings to those who manifest it.

Huckleberry Finn is racist, whether its author intended it to be or not. The book implies that black people are not honest. For example, Huck says about Jim: "It most froze me to hear such talk. He wouldn't ever dared to talk such talk in his life before. Just see what a difference it made in him the minute he judged he was about free. It was according to the old saying, 'give a nigger an inch and he'll take an yard.' Thinks I, this is what comes of my not thinking" (chap. 16). And in another section of the book, the Duke, in reply to a question from the King, says: "Mary Jane'll be in mourning from this out; and the first you know the nigger that does up the rooms will get an order to box these duds up and put 'em away; and do you reckon a nigger can run across money and not borrow some of it?" (chap. 26).

Huckleberry Finn also insinuates that black people are less intelligent than whites. In a passage where Huck and Tom are trying to get the chains off Jim, Tom says: "They couldn't get the chain off, so they just cut their hand off and shoved. And a leg would be better still. But we got to let that go. There ain't necessity enough in this case; and, besides, Jim's a nigger, and wouldn't understand the reason for it" (chap. 35). On another occasion, when Tom and Huck are making plans to get Jim out of the barn where he is held captive, Huck says: "He told him everything. Jim, he couldn't see no sense in most of it, but he allowed we was white folks and knowed better than him; so he was satisfied, and said he would do it all just as Tom said" (chap. 36).

Twain said in *Huckleberry Finn*, more than 100 years ago, what Dr. W. B. Shockley and A. R. Jensen are trying to prove through empirical study today. This tells us something about the power of the printed word when it is taught to children by a formidable institution such as the school.

Huckleberry Finn even suggests that blacks are not human beings. When Huck arrives at Aunt Sally's, she asks him why he is late:

"We blowed a cylinder head."
"Good gracious! anybody hurt?"
"No'm. Killed a nigger."
"Well, it's lucky; because sometimes people do get hurt." (chap. 32)

There are indications that the racist views and attitudes implicit in the preceding quotations are as prevalent in America today as they were more than 100 years ago. *Huckleberry Finn* has not been successful in fighting race hate and prejudice, as its proponents maintain, but has helped to retain the status quo.

THE BLACK STUDENT

In 1963 John Fisher, former president of Columbia Teachers College, stated:

> The black American youngster happens to be member of a large and distinctive group that for a very long time has been the object of special political, legal, and social action. . . To act as though any child is separable from his history is indefensible. In terms of educational planning, it is *irresponsible*.
>
> Every black child is the victim of history of his race in this country. On the day he enters kindergarten, he carries a burden *no white child* can ever know, no matter what other handicaps or disabilities he may suffer.

The primary school child learns, almost the minute he enters school, that black is associated with dirtiness, ugliness, and wickedness. Much of what teachers and students think of the black child is color based. As a result, the black pupil knows his pigmentation is an impediment to his progress.

As early as the fifth grade, the black student studies American history and must accept his ancestors in the role of slaves. This frustrating and painful experience leaves scars that very few educators, writers, and especially English teachers can understand. We compound these problems for black children when we force them to read aloud the message of *Huckleberry Finn*. It is so devastatingly traumatic that the student may never recover. How much pain must a black child endure to secure an education? No other child is asked to suffer so much embarrassment, humiliation, and racial intimidation at the hands of so powerful an institution as the school. The vast majority of black students have no tolerance for either "ironic" or "satirical" reminders of the insults and degradation heaped upon their ancestors in slavery and postslavery times.

Dorothy Gilliam (*Washington Post*, 12 April 1982) makes a good case for protecting the rights of students when she says, "Where rights conflict, one must sometimes supersede the other. Freedom of speech does not, for example, allow words to be deliberately used in a way that would cause someone to suffer a heart attack. By the same token, the use of words in ways that cause psychological and emotional damage is an unacceptable exercise of free speech."

RACISM

If indeed, as *Huckleberry Finn*'s proponents claim, the book gives a positive view of blacks and has an antislavery, antiracist message, then the Nazi party, the Ku Klux Klan, and the White Citizens Council must see something different. Most of the hate mail received when a school in northern Virginia restricted the use of the book was from these groups.

It is difficult to believe that Samuel Clemens would write a book against the institution of slavery; he did, after all, join a Confederate army bent on preserving that peculiar institution. Also, he could not allow Huck to help Jim to his freedom. It seems he was a hodgepodge of contradictions.

Huckleberry Finn is an American classic for no other reason than that it ridicules blacks to a greater extent than any other book given our children to read. The book and racism feed on each other and have withstood the test of time because many Americans insist on preserving our racist heritage.

Marguerite Barnett (1982) points out:

> By ridiculing blacks, exaggerating their facial features, and denying their humanity, the popular art of the Post-Civil-War period represented the political culture's attempt to deny blacks the equal status and rights awarded them in the Emancipation Proclamation. By making blacks inhuman, American whites could destroy their claim to equal treatment. Blacks as slaves posed no problem because they were under complete domination, but blacks as free men created political problems. The popular culture of the day supplied the answer by dehumanizing blacks and picturing them as childlike and inferior.

In this day of enlightenment, teachers should not rely on a book that teaches the subtle sickness of racism to our young and causes so much psychological damage to a large segment of our population. We are a multicultural, pluralistic nation. We must teach our young to respect all races, ethnic groups, and religious groups in the most positive terms conceivable.

RECOMMENDATIONS

This book should not be used with children. It is permissible to use the original *Huckleberry Finn* with students in graduate courses of history, English, and social science if one wants to study the perpetration and perpetuation of racism. The caustic, abrasive language is less likely to offend students of that age group because they tend to be mature enough to understand and discuss issues without feeling intimidated by the instructor, fellow students, or racism.

EXHIBIT B

Pro & Con: Should Schools Keep *Huck Finn* Off Reading Lists?[2]

No. Great Books Make Us Uncomfortable

Jocelyn Chadwick-Joshua[3]

Mark Twain's *Adventures of Huckleberry Finn* represents more than just a canonical space-holder for the late 19th century. It represents a realistic rather than romantic rendering of the antebellum American South and the ambivalent post-Reconstruction North.

Is such a work comfortable reading? Most decidedly not, but then are *The Iliad, Othello, The Merchant of Venice*? Are any of these works ever taught without careful guidance and preparation by the teacher? I sincerely hope not. I have yet to meet the student who needs no guidance for any piece of literature.

Twain's use of "nigger" and "poor white trash" are uncomfortable terms used deliberately to allow the reader to experience what characters Jim, Huck, plantation slaves, and others in the book feel. Nineteenth-century African-American writers who chose the American South as their focal point often used the same terminology to make their points. Do we ban them, too?

Adventures of Huckleberry Finn is not racist. What Twain accomplishes in this novel is to immerse the Northern and Southern audience into the (re)thinking and (re)imagining of the African American in this country. Who better for such a task than one who was reared in the slave-holding South, whose family had slaves and who came to the issue with one idea firmly established and then changes that idea when the facts do not match with what he had previously learned?

We observe Huck Finn in this identical dilemma: An adolescent boy who believes what he has been told by "trustworthy" people is put in a traumatic and disillusioning position when he is confronted by a different truth.

So why is this novel consistently on the list of banned books across this country? It seeks to agitate and succeeds in agitating. Huck and Jim invade the comfort of our private spaces and compel us to listen to and observe what is being said and who is saying it; what is being done and who is doing it. It takes the modern reader into the life of a slave of the South and, more important, into the mind and motivation of a slave.

---

[2]From *The Hartford Courant:* (Saturday Commentary) Saturday, August 17, 1996, p. A–10. Reprinted by permission.

[3]Jocelyn Chadwick-Joshua is associate director of the Teachers Academy at the Dallas Institute of Humanities & Cultures.

So, do we ban this book? I ask, do we ban the Confederate flag? Do we ban the Bible or the Koran or the Pentateuch? Literature provides for the mind a safe window from which we can observe how other people who resemble ourselves respond to situations and problems and truths.

Through this literature we begin to understand more clearly Huck Finn's evolving understanding of Jim and his race as equal, human individuals. Huck's recognition is one that because of what he has been taught all of his life somehow "don't seem natural, but I reckon it's so"—that Southern slaves have feelings and emotional and filial relationships just as their white Southern counterparts.

Banning *Adventures of Huckleberry Finn* from school curriculums is submerging texts that can aid us in never forgetting from where we have all come, how we came to be here, and where we go from here.

Yes. The Book is Too Sophisticated for Teens

Richard N. Pierce[4]

Although I have given my honors-level 12th-graders the option of reading "Adventures of Huckleberry Finn," I don't think the novel is appropriate for general use in grades 7 through 12. The very fact that "one of the greatest anti-racist works of fiction ever written," as Twain scholar Shelley Fisher Fishkin called it, has been accused of racism suggests that there's more to the work than might appear on the surface.

First of all, the novel is subtly satirical in its nature. Satire, relying on irony to expose human foolishness and corruption, is easily misunderstood. The ability to recognize irony is said to be one of the surest tests of intelligence and sophistication, for the reader has to understand that the intended meaning is the opposite of the expressed meaning.

When, for example, in Chapter 19 Huck and Jim hear the Duke's story about how far he's fallen in life, Huck says, "Jim pitied him ever so much, and so did I." By this time, however, we readers, if we are discerning, feel no pity because we realize the Duke is a fraud, a fact not clear to Huck for a long time.

It is the satirical tone of the work that takes the edge off the word "nigger," which is offensive to many. Since the whole novel ridicules a society that cleaves to racist institutions, "nigger," every time it's used, punctuates the story with critical barbs against racism. The height of the struggle comes in Chapter 31 with Huck's exclamation, as he decides to help Jim go free: "All right then, I'll *go* to hell."

Huck's very conscience has been constituted by a society in which religion and law conspired to enslave human beings. He may not understand that his decision is right and noble, but we readers, if we are discerning, surely do.

And if the subtle satire isn't enough to thwart young readers' understanding of Twain's novel, there is also the fact that it stands at the juncture between two major

---

[4]Richard N. Pierce retired from Hartford's Weaver High School English faculty in 1994. He teaches writing at the University of Hartford's College of Arts and Sciences.

Schools of American literature—romanticism and realism, which themselves add a depth of meaning to the story.

Romanticism, which was fading fast after the Civil War, emphasized imagination and heroic adventure. Realism, by contrast, was obsessed with the everyday life of the average person. The two ideologies face off during the last quarter of the novel. In Chapter 33, when Huck meets Tom on the road to Aunt Sally's, he confides in Tom that he is trying to steal Jim out of slavery. Tom almost blurts out the news that Jim has already been freed by Miss Watson's will, but he first stops and thinks. Then "his eye lit up" and he said, "I'll *help* you steal him!" In Chapter 42, when asked why he did it, Tom says, "I wanted the *adventure* of it." For Huck, the realist, stealing Jim had been a wrenching decision and desperate struggle; but to Tom, the romanticist, it was all a make-believe adventure.

Adventures of Huckleberry Finn is appropriate for older teens and adults, but most younger people haven't attained the intellectual maturity needed to interpret the satire or to understand Twain's espousal of realism. Let's be fair and teach the novel to those who can best understand it.

E X H I B I T   C

Adventures of Huckleberry Finn Plot Summary

In the *Adventures of Huckleberry Finn*, Huck, an adolescent growing up along the Mississippi River in the 1840s, tells his own story. The son of the town drunkard, he has been abandoned by his father and virtually adopted by the Widow Douglas and her sister, Miss Watson; Huck is prone to drinking and swearing. Huck resists their restrictions and resents being sent to school to learn to read and write. He slowly begins to adjust when his abusive father returns to claim him and, not coincidentally, a fortune recently found by Huck and his friend, Tom Sawyer. Anticipating his father's greedy motive, Huck signs the fortune over to a local judge to prevent his father from acquiring it.

Nevertheless, Huck's father takes his son from the Widow Douglas to a cabin in the woods, where he keeps the boy prisoner and brutally beats him. Desperate to get away, Huck escapes, faking his own death to avoid being recaptured. While hiding on a nearby island, Huck discovers Jim, Miss Watson's slave. Jim had run away, fearing that he would be sold to a new owner.

Huck and Jim decide to flee downriver on a raft. Among their many adventures, they encounter two con artists, the Duke and the King, with whom they travel for some time. Stricken by his conscience, Huck ultimately exposes the two as frauds. The Duke and the King escape, however, and rejoin Huck and Jim. Later, the Duke sells Jim to Silas Phelps for ransom money. Huck feels torn between what he feels is an obligation to return a slave to his original owner, Miss Watson, and his feelings of loyalty and love for Jim. He decides he is willing to "go to hell" for Jim and decides to help him escape from the Phelps' plantation.

At the Phelps' plantation, Huck is mistaken for Tom Sawyer, the Phelps' nephew. When Tom himself arrives, he assumes a different identity and plays along with Huck's ruse. To Huck's surprise, Tom agrees to help set Jim free—but only if they stage an elaborate escape, like an adventure story. Jim continues to suffer while Tom carries out his ridiculous scheme. When Jim finally escapes, Tom is shot in the leg during the ensuing chase. Despite his mistreatment, Jim sacrifices his opportunity for freedom to nurse Tom while Huck goes for the doctor. Later, Tom reveals that Miss Watson had died two months earlier and in her will had set Jim free already. Soon, Tom's Aunt Polly arrives and exposes the true identities of the two boys. When Jim reveals that he had seen Huck's father dead floating down the river, Huck decides to head for new territory to avoid being adopted and "sivilized" by Aunt Sally.

EXHIBIT D

Journal Activities

QUESTIONS

Respond to (one of) these questions in your binder. Please date your entry (entries).

1. What is your initial response to the reading?
2. What did you like or dislike about the reading?
3. Formulate a question based on the text. Answer that question.
4. While you were reading, what surprised you, made you think, or upset you?
5. Name two details in the text which you consider important. Explain their importance.
6. List any new learning or appreciation that occurred during the reading of the text.
7. What about the text would you like to know or talk more about?
8. Does anything in your reading (character, setting, plot. . .) remind you of another piece of literature, movie, opera, TV show, etc.?

IRONY ASSIGNMENT

All of the following quotations illustrate Mark Twain's masterful use of irony.
Directions
In your journal, answer the following questions for each quotation:

- Who is speaking?
- What has just happened or is now happening at this point in the novel?
- Why is this quotation an example of irony?

1. Persons attempting to find a motive in this narrative will be prosecuted; persons attempting to find a moral in it will be banished; persons attempting to find a plot in it will be shot. (p. 10)
2. I did wish Tom Sawyer was there; I knowed he would take an interest in this kind of business, and throw in the fancy touches. (p. 41)
3. If they'd 'a' had some bullets in, I reckon they'd 'a' got the corpse they was after (p. 46)
4. Yes: en I's rich now, come to look at it. I owns myself en I's wuth eight hund'd dollars. (p. 54)
5. I'm unfavorable to killin' a man as long as you can git aroun' it; it ain't good sense, it ain't good morals. (p. 74)
6. It was fifteen minutes before I could work myself up to go and humble myself to a nigger; but I done it, and I warn't ever sorry for it afterward, neither. (p. 99)

7. Dah you goes, de ole true Huck; de on'y white gentleman dat ever kep' his promise to ole Jim. (p. 92)

8. . . . what's the use you learning to do right when it's troublesome to do right and ain't no trouble to do wrong, and the wages is just the same? . . . after this always do which ever comes handiest at the time. (pp. 94–95)

9. I was powerful glad to get away from the feuds . . . there warn't no home like a raft . . . other places do seem so cramped up and smothery, but a raft don't. You feel mighty free and easy and comfortable on a raft. (p. 117)

10. . . . here am I, forlorn, torn from my high estate, hunted of men . . . degraded to the companionship of felons on a raft. (p. 123)

11. Set down, my boy; I wouldn't strain myself if I was you. I reckon you ain't used to lyin, it don't seem to come handy; what you want is practice. You do it pretty awkward. (p. 193)

12. All right, then I'll *go* to hell. (p. 207)

E X H I B I T   E

Persuasive Speech Activity

For the student presentations, Jenkins had written note-taking guidelines on the chalkboard:

- Orator:
- Quotes and/or comments:

After reviewing her guidelines, she asked for a volunteer to begin the speeches. She advised the other students, "Invoke your great listening skills and practice your note-taking. Within Jamie's first paragraph, you should be able to determine right away what she proposes." Jamie delivered a long, eloquent speech, full of vivid details from the novel.

When she finished, the class broke into spontaneous applause. With her usual supportive tone, Jenkins asked, "How about some comments?" After several student responses, Jenkins summarized, "Jamie did a fine job of considering the social, educational, and psychological aspects of Huck being with each of the possible guardians. She elaborated on each, using good examples from the book. Remember when we read *To Kill a Mockingbird*? Jamie was our child psychologist then. She shows the same concerns about Huck."

Next, Nathan gave his speech, emphasizing the importance of Huck receiving adequate physical care, psychological support, and educational opportunities. He concluded, "Don't let biological ties waver your instincts," and then rushed to get out of the limelight. "Stay right here," Jenkins cajoled. Turing to the class, she asked, "What persuasive techniques did Nathan use?" They pointed out his strong conclusion and appeal to emotions. Jenkins added that he had asked rhetorical questions, such as, "Don't we want to break the cycle of abuse?"

Then it was Jesse's turn. After his rousing speech, the students gave feedback and Jenkins summarized. "Jesse used a couple of great strategies. 'If Huck stays with his father, he'll become his father,' he said. Showing cause and effect is an excellent persuasive tool."

Melissa began her speech by asking, "Gentlemen, how many of you think that education is important? Well, I certainly do. *Huck Finn* has the opportunity to get an education at the Widow Douglas's house." She concluded by stating, "The Widow Douglas wants a child to love and care for while Mr. Finn just wants another drink." Jenkins's class pointed out that Melissa had effectively used the technique of comparison and contrast, highlighting the differences between the Widow Douglas and Huck's father.

DISCUSSION QUESTIONS

1. How did attending the conference at The Mark Twain House affect Jenkins' teaching of *Huck Finn*?

2. Identify and evaluate Jenkins' teaching strategies.
   - How effectively does Jenkins promote critical thinking?
   - How effectively does she encourage the development of writing skills?
   - How effectively does she create instructional opportunities that are adapted to diverse learners?
   - How effectively do the activities and projects foster students' deep understanding of the novel?

3. What other teaching materials or strategies might Jenkins have used?
   - Do you agree with Jenkins' decision to skip the last chapters? Why or why not?
   - After reviewing Exhibit E, what kind of preliminary activity or pre-teaching would you do for the persuasive speech activity?

4. Curriculum integration is a major goal in most middle schools. If the novel were to be part of a thematic, interdisciplinary unit, what might the themes be and what would be the content in other subjects? Are there benefits to teaching it as part of a thematic unit in this or higher grades?

5. Jenkins comments that the "the intention of literature is to mirror life" and tries to make the novel relevant to her students' lives. Do we overemphasize "relevance" in schools? Why not approach the novel historically and use it to help students understand people and places unconnected to them?
   - Jenkins skipped providing more of an historical background to the novel because students were eager to begin reading. Was it wise to let students follow their interests? Why or why not?
   - How can students ever appreciate the concept of history if they spend all of their time bringing everything back to themselves? Can they understand literature that is set in a certain historical period if they do not have knowledge of that period? For example, *Huck Finn* is set in the 1840s, before the Civil War, when fugitive slave laws were in effect. Runaway slaves who were caught were subject to brutal punishment, such as whipping and maiming. Those who aided a slave's escape were penalized. Twain wrote *Huck Finn* during the 1870s and 1880s, when Jim Crow laws made racial segregation legal in many parts of the South. Do students need this type of background knowledge to determine the motivations of the main characters as well as Twain's intent in writing the novel? Or should "great" literature stand on its own, independent of context?
   - How might an American Studies teacher approach teaching *Huck Finn*?

6. Although Jenkins referred to the controversial aspects of *Huck Finn*, she adopted the stance that the novel is not racist. What do you think about that?

- From a pedagogical point of view: Are middle schoolers capable of evaluating the opposing positions?

- From an ethical point of view: The information Jenkins chose to share from the summer conference documented only one side of this controversial issue. Was that appropriate?

- If you were teaching the novel, would you share, for example, John Wallace's article (Exhibit A), which condemns the book as racist? Why or why not?

7. Consider further the issues in teaching racially-sensitive literature.

- Do you think it is possible that Jenkins has misread Sandra's responses to *Huck Finn*?

- Was Jenkins singling out Sandra by bending over backwards not to single her out?

- Should Jenkins have asked Sandra more directly for her contributions? Might both Sandra and the other students have benefited from hearing and discussing Sandra's perspectives on *Huck Finn* and racism?

- The superintendent of the Sandbury middle school decided to ban *Huck Finn* from the middle school curriculum. Considering the arguments that were presented in this case, do you agree with his decision?

- Consider how Jenkins handles the use of the word "nigger." What are other options?

- Consider the question Jenkins asks herself at the end of the case: should she teach the book any differently if she were teaching in a racially diverse school? Why or why not? If so, how?

- If Jenkins were teaching *Huck Finn* in a racially diverse school, what might be possible parental concerns, and how should she address these?

8. In a field such as English, where experts might compose a canon, or list of "must reads," how do responsible professionals determine what should be on the list?

- What criteria should be used to identify which "classics" should stay on the list and which should go?

9. Do you think middle schoolers in general are intellectually and emotionally mature enough to read *Huck Finn*?

- Is it developmentally appropriate? Give evidence from the case to support your position. What were Jenkins' successes in teaching the novel? Problems?

10. Discuss how similar controversies could occur in other disciplines, and give specific examples. (This question may be explored in greater depth by having students break into groups by subject matter areas.)

CASE 6

Discussion Question	Corresponding INTASC Principle
1, 2	9 The teacher is a reflective practitioner who continually evaluates the effects of his/her choices and actions on others (students, parents, and other professionals in the learning community) and who actively seeks out opportunities to grow professionally.
2	7 The teacher plans instruction based upon knowledge of subject matter, students, the community, and curriculum goals.
3	3 The teacher understands how students differ in their approaches to learning and creates instructional opportunities that are adapted to diverse learners.
3	6 The teacher uses knowledge of effective verbal, nonverbal, and media communication techniques to foster active inquiry, collaboration, and supportive instruction in the classroom.
5, 9	2 The teacher understands how children learn and develop, and can provide learning opportunities that support their intellectual, social, and personal development.
6	4 The teacher understands and uses a variety of instructional strategies to encourage students' development of critical thinking, problem solving, and performance skills.
10	1 The teacher understands the concepts, tools of inquiry, and structures of the discipline(s) he or she teaches and can create learning experiences that make these aspects of subject matter meaningful for students.

Compromise and Defeat: A Power Struggle at Watermill

Will Watermill Middle School see major changes in class scheduling for its three grades? These changes hinge on the actions of a 12-member school council scheduled to meet today at 4 P.M., one month before the summer recess. The pending vote may conclude a lengthy debate on the changes.

The School-Based Decision Making (SBDM) Council has been struggling for months to reach a decision by "consensus" according to its own bylaws. However, some observers think true consensus may be one of the casualties in a battle of opinions arising from three specific camps: a determined administrator, dedicated teachers, and concerned parents.

Contemplating today's 4 P.M. meeting, Jane Brinkman, middle school teacher and council member, wonders whether the working parents on the council will be able to attend, given the short notice of the meeting. She also thinks the last-minute notice may heighten the parents' level of mistrust of the principal, Jack Carnes.

THE CONFLICT

This debate on the future of the middle school all began when a last-minute agenda item surfaced at a regularly scheduled council meeting in February. Principal Carnes added a proposal to change the existing class design to an interdisciplinary, heterogeneous, nongraded middle school structure.

This new approach would ignore student age as the criterion for class assignments. Students would be grouped and regrouped based on their developmental level for various subjects within a teaching team. In effect, they would be with the same group of teachers for three years with some of the students (the eighth graders) leaving and new ones (sixth graders) entering each year.

A number of parents, both council members and nonmembers, were quite concerned that Carnes did not provide adequate support for his proposal. Where was the research to support this new approach to middle school structure? Carnes adamantly argued it was the core strategy necessary to achieve higher student performance, but he mentioned only briefly research that linked this approach to higher student achievement. The only documentation he provided was a one-sheet handout with eight points about how positive it was to mix the grade levels.

Parent complaints revealed they perceived Carnes' action as arrogant. "It might be related to his reputation as an expert and the fact he has been invited to speak elsewhere on reform matters," a teacher attempted to explain.

Parents were generally opposed to the nongraded concept from the beginning and expressed fears about mixing sixth graders with eighth graders. They were worried that the younger students might face intimidation from the older ones. They were also concerned that Carnes' plan represented a dramatic change from the existing class schedule and structure at Watermill.

Although teacher reactions to Carnes' idea were mixed, many were seized by his enthusiasm and immediately threw their support behind the proposal. Jane Brinkman, a middle school math teacher with a widespread reputation as an excellent instructor, was one of the dissenters. She could see some advantages to the team idea but feared students would miss out by not being exposed to all of the teachers in the school during their three years at Watermill.

"Carnes' proposal for a continuing team concept was supposed to be a very positive thing, to build relationships between teachers and children—more like a family atmosphere," Brinkman said. "But from personal experience that goes back many years, I also see a lot of negatives with this concept. There are many teachers who don't work well with certain kids. And there are many kids who like certain adults. They wouldn't have a chance to experience other teachers. Plus, there are some very effective teachers in our eighth grade to whom these children would never be exposed. In addition, a teacher who specifically likes seventh-grade material would now have to change gears and prepare for grades six and eight."

THE SCHOOL AND THE SBDM COUNCIL

Watermill Middle School first opened its doors to sixth, seventh, and eighth graders in the late 1980s. Initially, the middle school concept, a clear departure from the traditional elementary and junior high school approaches, received negative community reaction. Frequent discipline problems drew unfavorable press coverage. The original principal was encouraged to leave when teachers developed mistrust, prompting them to request expansion of the SBDM Council from 6 to 12 members. Because Carnes had been a successful high school principal in the same district, with a reputation as a strict disciplinarian, he was selected for the Watermill position. The district gave him a mandate to improve all aspects of education at the school.

Carnes attacked the challenge with zeal and enthusiasm, holding tight to the belief that the students had been given a "bad rap." He believed his middle school youngsters were capable of reaching high levels of excellence in every subject area. In his opinion, high student achievement was accomplished through proper discipline and a faculty deeply devoted to students.

When Carnes came on board, the SBDM Council had been functioning for one year. During his first year, the faculty voted to expand the council to 12 members—

twice the membership recommended by state law. The council consisted of six teacher representatives, elected by faculty colleagues; four parents, elected by the parent organization; the principal; and another administrator. All parents on the council received extensive training.

Following established hiring procedures that were under the jurisdiction of the council, Carnes conducted searches to fill several teaching vacancies in the wake of recent retirements. The process proved contentious when some council members complained that Carnes had intentionally limited the list of viable candidates he presented to them.

"It was a not-so-neat experience, putting in all those hours, and then he picks who he wants," complained one of the teacher representatives. "But, on the other hand, principals have to make tough decisions that others may not understand. It's one of those plus-minus kind of things."

Others were not as sanguine about the results of the selection process. "We really didn't have much of a choice and were forced to choose the candidates he wanted despite our supposed power," fumed a parent representative. These complaints about the process had little impact; positions were eventually filled by new faculty members who apparently met Carnes' criteria for continuing his crusade for school reform.

Well before his proposed new structure, the principal applied for a state grant and received sufficient funding to move Watermill toward major instructional changes. "Education reform" became the buzzword throughout the school. Frequent meetings became an integral part of the school routine. Faculty spent time developing what for them were new teaching methods and participating in long-term planning sessions. Paperwork increased significantly for all faculty members. Meanwhile, student scores climbed while discipline problems showed a marked decrease.

THE PRINCIPAL

Jack Carnes came to the school district from out of state with what many considered a preconceived agenda for change. His 20 years in education included 13 years of experience in the classroom and 7 more as an administrator.

Not only did he arrive with high expectations for Watermill students, but he also held lofty goals for teachers. He continually declared that the best teachers "cared about kids." His operational definition of "caring" included spending considerable time and effort attending instructional planning meetings, teaching classes, and assessing students' work—without complaining and sometimes without extra pay. Carnes felt this extra effort on everyone's part was the key to improving student performance.

The new principal set a demanding pace to implement reform. Within three years of his arrival at Watermill, his successes securing higher student achievement and good publicity for the school gave rise to his reputation as an expert in education reform. Other principals frequently requested that he speak at state and local conferences. Carnes accepted all invitations, indicating he enjoyed his growing acclaim as a highly effective change agent.

THE PARENT

Holly Smith was flattered by her election as one of four parent representatives on the SBDM Council. She had three children, with her oldest just starting the sixth grade at Watermill. Although she had been extremely active as a tutor/volunteer at the elementary school, Watermill's previous history of discipline problems made her apprehensive about her new role as a council member. However, the chance to work with a new principal gave her hope, and she felt her role on the SBDM Council was to ensure a sound educational experience at the school for her children.

"I decided this was a good way to keep up with what was going on at school since my kids were entering that critical stage that determines the path they will walk in life," Smith said about the challenge of her new council position. "I was not currently working at a job and decided that my time could best be spent as a member of the SBDM Council. I was honored to be given the opportunity to affect my own children's education as well as the education of other students at Watermill."

THE TEACHER

Jane Brinkman had been teaching in the district for more than a decade and was well respected by students, teachers, and parents. Her selection as a teacher representative to the council was considered by most to be a well-deserved honor, reflected by her three successful reelection bids.

Brinkman expressed reservations about the new size and structure of the SBDM Council. Her primary concern was the amount of time needed for twelve people to exchange views and develop a sense of competence and fairness in making collective decisions.

"We need to remember that the council is something new," she said. "We are not used to being in positions of making even the smallest decision. We are used to having them made for us."

Because of its large membership, the council created a policy restricting open discussion at its meetings. Guests were allowed to speak at the beginning of meetings, but subsequent discussion was limited to council members, who could address only predetermined agenda items.

THE COMPROMISE

Time passed, and the tension about restructuring classes at Watermill grew. It continued through two more council meetings with heated debate but without resolution.

As the year drew on, Carnes was convinced the battle lines had been decided. The longer the discussion continued, the more confrontational the situation became. At the fourth council meeting to discuss the new middle school proposal, Carnes lost patience and announced what he termed a "compromise."

"OK, this is it. I'm willing to place only the seventh and eighth graders in the nongraded structure, but that's as far as I'm willing to compromise," he said. "In fact, if you don't accept this compromise, then I'll tell you what I'm going to do with the sixth graders. I'll totally self-contain them, just like they were in elementary school again with no departmental subject matter and no changing classes or regrouping with other sixth graders. They will have the same teacher and classmates all day long, every day."

Jane Brinkman felt her stomach tighten in response to the principal's declaration. She folded her hands in her lap and thought, "This was what comes from having 12 people trying to reach a consensus." She was extremely aware of the fact many parents felt their voices were falling on deaf ears, even at SBDM Council meetings.

On the other hand, her fellow teachers on the council had been urging Brinkman to give Carnes' plan her vote of support. For the past two months, they had said, "All consensus means is that you think you can live with this idea. You don't have to be entirely for or against it, but if you can live with the decision, go along." Most teachers at Watermill favored the proposal.

By contrast, the parent representative, Holly Smith, couldn't believe her ears as she listened to Carnes. His solution was an ultimatum; why was he calling it a compromise?

"Fine," she stated emphatically. "Let the minutes show that I am only agreeing to this because I feel under threat that if I don't, kids will suffer from being in self-contained classrooms."

Despite her agreement, Smith remained confused. "I don't know what to do," she told herself. "After all, I have to work with this principal and these teachers over the next four years with my other children."

In a hushed conversation following Carnes' compromise announcement, Smith whispered to a community observer, "We couldn't find any parents who were really ready to accept that proposal. There were many parents who had begun coming to the meetings to express their opposition. They thought the older kids would negatively influence or intimidate the sixth graders."

"But this point of view didn't get heard," Smith continued. "When additional people were at the meetings, Mr. Carnes got nervous. He couldn't control the numbers. He doesn't like feeling out of control."

She continued to quietly share her concerns with the interested observer.

"When the proposal first came up, I said no to this idea," she whispered. "At that time, a split occurred between the parents and teachers. Originally, the teachers had mostly sided with us, then suddenly they were going against the parents. Immediately, we felt uneasy around them. We have been taking this stand by ourselves, except for Mrs. Brinkman, who agreed with us."

Smith glanced around the meeting room and continued. "When we left meetings, Mrs. Brinkman would talk to us and agree with us. But once she would see another teacher or Mr. Carnes coming, she would say, 'Oh, I have got to go! I can't be seen talking to you!' I don't think she realized how that made us parents feel."

Jane Brinkman acknowledged the support she and another teacher representative felt for the parents' point of view. She said she was reluctant to restrict students to one set of teachers, but the other teachers on the council kept urging her to just give Carnes' approach a try.

"You know, as tough as this is, I try hard to be tactful when I disagree," Brinkman said. "But I don't hesitate to do it." She also offered some insight into the relationship between parent representatives on the SBDM Council and Carnes.

"I think parents thought the principal was intimidating, but I think parents generally feel this way about any principal," Brinkman said. "This is especially true of parents who are women, which all our parent council members are. They seemed to feel Mr. Carnes didn't think they knew what they were talking about or that their opinions were valid." Brinkman continued with her assessment of the tension between the principal and the parents.

"He really does respect what they think," she said. "He has to look at them differently than he looks at educators because we come from different backgrounds. We all have one thing in common, and that's the kids. I am sure he respects the parents, but they just don't believe that. One parent told me she always felt like one of the male teachers talked down to her. I can see where parents might be a little intimidated. They have to work with all these people who are supposed to be 'authorities,' whatever that means."

Despite the requirement for consensus in the council's by-laws, Carnes felt the need for immediate action when he demanded passage of the "compromise" at the previous meeting. Carnes' compromise and the apparent administrative approval of it stunned parents and teachers alike. Jane Brinkman and Holly Smith each had to rethink her position. Smith felt certain the "compromise" proposal involved a behind-the-scenes arrangement between Carnes and the superintendent but had no evidence to support her conjecture. The superintendent had remained silent even though he was well aware of the parents' concerns about both the proposal and the questionable process by which it was introduced as a last-minute agenda item in violation of council by-laws. Smith was convinced this implied the superintendent's blessing.

THE VOTE

The only potential obstacle to Carnes' compromise could be today's council vote. As the sweeping hands of the clock on the wall of the council meeting room approached 4 P.M., Carnes reflected on the calls he had received from nearly all parent representatives protesting the time of the meeting. He recalled his conversation with the superintendent who had suggested rescheduling the meeting, but Carnes had refused to change the timing of his announcement of moving ahead with the new structure. He had received the council's reluctant go-ahead at the last meeting, and implementation of the compromise plan needed to begin immediately before more objections could be raised. He must have this final vote.

The four parent representatives on the council filtered into the meeting room along with the superintendent. Carnes took the floor quickly, explaining that the new structure would mix only seventh and eighth grades, and next year's seventh graders would remain with the same team for two years. There were no new surprises. Both Brinkman and Smith were among the council members who voted for the principal's compromise. Brinkman decided there was little harm in experimenting with the new grouping arrangement. She felt it could be reevaluated and changed if it failed to succeed. Smith felt compelled to go along with the idea because she feared her children might suffer repercussions from Carnes if she voted against him.

Carnes' compromise passed.

EPILOGUE

Ironically, the principal saw the results of his plan for only the first year of implementation. Before the second year began, Carnes accepted a prestigious state education position to design and present workshops on educational leadership. His assistant principal, Mike Gohran, became acting principal responsible for the nongraded schedule. Within one year and concurrent with his full-time appointment to the principalship, Gohran pushed for the elimination of the nongraded plan, which had kept seventh graders on the same team for two years. The council approved the recommendation. Watermill returned to the old, pre-Carnes structure. "I believe the teachers who had the seventh graders two years in a row did not want to have that happen again," Gohran explained. "They had a very challenging group of students."

A Parent's Reflection

Holly Smith felt locked in a no-win situation when the scheduling plan was pushed by Carnes. She was convinced that Carnes' compromise proposal could result in kids getting stuck with a "bad" teacher for their last two years at the middle school. She wished the principal and teachers favoring the change had produced research that demonstrated this scheduling approach would help improve student learning. However, she had failed to do any homework of her own involving research. Could she have found documented research to support her reservations?

Moreover, Smith was uncomfortable with the notion that Watermill had to be "first" to make changes. Why did Watermill have to lead education reform? The principal and teachers on the council assumed what they were doing was in the best interests of the children. She felt they dismissed any insights or expertise parents had to offer about their children. As a parent, Smith was convinced she also knew what was good for kids despite the seeming indifference toward her suggestions.

Smith's volunteer efforts at school all but disappeared the next year. Carnes' "controlling disposition" turned her away from volunteer activities at Watermill. She wasn't alone. All four parent representatives who had served during the compromise debate would not seek another term.

Privately, these parents said they did not want to waste their time in meetings in which they felt their views were not respected, but publicly they remained low-key about their reasons for not running again. All confided that they were worried about making their viewpoints too visible and their children vulnerable.

Smith was the last parent representative to reach the decision to leave the council. She said she didn't want to let Carnes "kick her out." In defiance, she completed her term just to prove she would not be "bullied." In all other school functions, she deliberately kept a low profile because she said she needed to "protect" her children.

A Teacher's Perspective

Jane Brinkman remained optimistic about the entire experience. She said she believed his series of sometimes painful events was necessary for the council, as a whole, to define the term *consensus*. To her, *consensus* meant reaching an agreement to "try it out for a while."

Brinkman knew the question of the two-year program for seventh and eighth graders remained unresolved, even though Carnes' compromise was accepted. She suspected that although the program became accepted, it would be questioned again by the faculty in the future, and she was proven correct. "That's the beauty of the SBDM Council," she explained. "The decisions we make are not written in stone. We can always take another look at the situation and change our minds."

Following the restructuring incident, the Watermill teachers voted almost unanimously to downsize the council back to six members. The return to a smaller council reinforced Brinkman's belief that achieving consensus was less difficult with fewer members.

She admitted, however, that parents were still limited in the expression of opinions in council meetings. She favored changing the restricted time policy to allow parents the freedom to discuss issues of interest whenever they surfaced at council meetings. But strong parental support for this change in policy never materialized.

One major change, in addition to the size of the council, took place. Approval of policy changes no longer required a complete consensus. Former parent member Holly Smith explained the change this way: "The by-laws have been changed with regard to policies. The council does not require complete consensus. They can do a majority vote. However, they need at least one parent to vote yes to change or make a new policy."

As a parent with children still in school, Brinkman knew that Smith was keeping tabs on council actions and said she felt comfortable with this new policy. But Smith's feelings about Carnes were reinforced by his departure to take a prominent state job. "Mr. Carnes just wanted to stand out and be on the cutting edge," she said.

REFERENCES AND SELECTED BIBLIOGRAPHY

Berger, E. H. (2000). *Parents as partners in education* (5th ed.). Upper Saddle River, NJ: Merrill/Prentice Hall.

Canady, R. L., & Rettig, M. D. (1995). *Block scheduling: A catalyst for change in high schools.* Princeton, NJ: Eye on Education.

Conway, A., & Calzi, F. (1996). The dark side of shared decision making. *Educational Leadership,* 53(4), 45–49.

Fullan, M. (1993). *Change forces: Probing the depths of educational reform.* London: Falmer.

Lindle, J. C. (1994). *Surviving school micropolitics: Strategies for administrators.* Lancaster, PA: Techtronics.

National Education Commission on Time and Learning. (1994). *Prisoners of time.* Report of the National Education Commission on Time and Learning. Washington, DC: U.S. Government Printing Office.

Productive use of time and space. (1995, November). *Educational Leadership,* 53(3), 3–46 (entire issue).

Schneider, B., & Coleman, J. S. (1993). *Parents, their children and schools.* Boulder, CO: Westview.

Sizer, T. R. (1986). Rebuilding: First steps by the coalition of essential schools. *Phi Delta Kappan,* 68, 38–42.

Sizer, T. R. (1990). *Horace's school: Redesigning the American high school.* Boston: Houghton Mifflin.

Steinberg, L. (1996). *Beyond the classroom: Why education reform efforts have failed.* New York: Simon & Schuster.

DISCUSSION QUESTIONS

1. How did this situation of disagreement develop? What are some underlying issues in this case?

2. What is consensus?
   - Define the terms *consensus, compromise,* and *majority rule.*
   - How did each of the following people view consensus: Mr. Carnes? Jane Brinkman? Holly Smith?

3. Evaluate Carnes' leadership style.
   - What qualities seem to make him effective?
   - What qualities seem to cause problems?
   - Discuss other courses of action Carnes might have taken.

4. Consider the effects of the following factors on communication: council size, proportion of teacher to parent representatives, and degree of communication of representatives with their constituencies.
   - What processes might be set up to improve communication in this case?
   - What are the teachers' responsibilities regarding communication in the situation depicted in the case?

5. If micropolitics are the daily acts of influence, negotiation, and participation in the way things get done in school, what is micropolitical about this case?
   - What power issues are there? How much power does the council really have?
   - How are claims for legitimacy made and supported? What apparent exchanges or bargains are made?

6. If you had been a teacher representative on the council, what would you have done? Explain your position.

7. In discussing the role of parents on the council, Jane Brinkman states that Carnes "has to look at them (parents) differently than he looks at educators."
   - Identify what parents can bring to school governance.
   - Identify what teachers can bring.
   - Should parents have a significant role in school governance? Why or why not?
   - Do you agree with Brinkman's position on parental involvement? Elaborate on your response.
   - What, if anything, did the school lose when those parents (and possibly others) "gave up"?

8. INTASC Principal 5 calls for the teacher to use "an understanding of individual and group motivation and behavior to create a learning environment that encourages positive social interaction, active engagement in learning, and social motivation." How might nongraded grouping affect a teacher's achievement of this principle?

- What are possible negative effects? Evaluate, for example, the parents' concern that older students would negatively influence or intimidate sixth graders.
- What are possible positive effects? Consider, for example, a student's opportunity to progress according to her interests and abilities rather than her chronological age.

9. Consider Jane Brinkman's role in this experience.
   - What else might she have done to influence the results before the compromise was reached?
   - Once a compromise was reached, would it have been appropriate for her to reach out to the parents to help them find some "good" in the new structure? Why or why not?
   - If so, how might she have reached out to the parents?

10. Do you agree with Brinkman's definition that consensus means to agree to "try something for a while?" Is this a workable definition? Why or why not?
    - Once institutional change is effected, how easy is it to change again?
    - How long should an educational reform be tried out before it can be fairly assessed? What are some factors to consider?

11. Do you think Carnes' departure from the school impacted the life of this reform attempt? How and why?

CASE 7

Discussion Question	Corresponding INTASC Principle
4	**6** The teacher uses knowledge of effective verbal, nonverbal, and media communication techniques to foster active inquiry, collaboration, and supportive instruction in the classroom.
5, 7, 9	**10** The teacher fosters relationships with school colleagues, parents, and agencies in the larger community to support learning and well-being.
8	**5** The teacher uses an understanding of individual and group motivation and behavior to create a learning environment that encourages positive social interaction, active engagement in learning, and self-motivation.

Staying the Course:

Professional Development and Managing Change

MORTON COUNTY HIGH SCHOOL: THE DILEMMA BEGINS

With shaking shoulders and tears in her eyes, Christy Sullivan, a fourth-year English teacher, blurted to other teachers in the cramped faculty lounge. "Wait until you hear this! I just got out of the principal's office, and I don't believe what he told me!"

Ann Powers, the English Department Chair, immediately set aside the papers she was grading and pulled her chair close to Sullivan. "What is it, Christy? What did Lloyd just say to you?"

With a troubled look, Christy Sullivan began talking. "You all know how busy we get before the end of every nine-week grading period. I was swamped with papers from earlier this quarter, and the only way I could picture myself conquering that stockpile of papers was to spend the entire weekend grading. Well, yesterday in class I told my students their grades, and one of the girls in the class, Pam, was absolutely shocked when she found out hers had dropped from a C at mid-quarter to an F."

Having captured the rapt attention of all the teachers in the now overcrowded faculty room, Sullivan continued to explain her dilemma. Her frustration, however, was based on more than just the problem she had encountered in her classroom. "Pam's mother called me this morning, and she was furious that I hadn't notified her sooner that her daughter was failing. I tried to explain that by not handing in two out of four writing assignments during the last half of the grading period, Pam caused the failing grade, but it didn't seem to matter. She wouldn't hear of any possible explanation for why this occurred, and I got off the phone feeling more anger than I have ever experienced with a parent. Nothing I said made any difference, and she immediately called the principal."

Due to the requirements of education reform in her state, Sullivan had been motivated to reexamine how she taught English. During the summer, she had made major changes in her approach to the teaching of writing. The incident with Pam's mother revealed Sullivan's mounting frustrations with the demands involved in teaching writing well and with what she perceived as a lack of administrative support for the innovations she had made. Later, she reflected, "The most infuriating part of the entire situation was the principal's response. I've taken the initiative to develop as a writing teacher, but now he wants me to teach less writing so I'll have more time to communicate with parents. That might help in avoiding this kind of parental flare-up, but how is it going to help my students become better writers?"

THE COMMUNITY AND THE SCHOOL

Morton County High School (MCHS) was located in a rural farming town of 5,000 people. The school and its immediate surroundings were situated on the main street of town, exactly in the center of this tightly knit community. The expansive grass playing fields were well kept, and like the tennis courts, were visible from Main Street. A few blocks from the school were two local hangouts, Arby's and Wal-Mart, where parking lot cruising was the norm any weekend night.

Immediately inside Morton's oversized oak doors was a meandering display of burgundy and blue school colors. This was an "all-American" high school with endless rows of blue student lockers and varying renditions of a burgundy cougar (the school mascot) on every wall. Occasional lockers bore "Good Luck" signs—one of the many status symbols associated with being a Morton County athlete.

The strong sense of community and school spirit belied considerable status differences within the 1,000-member student body, which was drawn from the entire county. While some students lived barely above the poverty level in adjacent rural areas, for others home was a sprawling and profitable farm. The school had very little ethnic diversity, and the disparity in economic backgrounds was reflected in the school culture. Many of the less well-off students, often labeled as "vocational," spent their mornings at vocational school and afternoons in the general level or lowest track classes. The school "preps," on the other hand, consisted of the athletes and intellectuals, who distinguished themselves by their trendy clothes.

The community surrounding Morton County High School.

They were the college-bound group who populated the honors and advanced placement course.

Close to two-thirds of graduating seniors planned to attend college, usually a local college 40 miles from Morton County. The main concern of most other seniors was to graduate from high school and begin steady work. For these students, there was strong parental pressure to remain within Morton County and continue the tradition of single-family farming. Their potential departure was considered a threat to the fragile economic base of the area.

Located in what is considered the Bible Belt of the country, the community surrounding MCHS was a model of stability with a definite religious influence. It was not possible to travel more than a few blocks without encountering one of over fifteen churches in town. Frequent church attendance and strict moral codes of behavior were prevalent among the student body. Many students attended church regularly on both Wednesdays and Sundays, and others were consistently active in church choirs, youth groups, or Bible study groups. Since Morton was a dry county, alcohol could not be bought or sold in town. Although the high school had its fair number of "partiers," the majority of students, when asked, would respond that they did not drink.

MORTON COUNTY STAFF

Like most students, adults at the high school had firmly planted roots. Over half of the 49 faculty had spent most of their careers in Morton County. Both the principal, Lloyd Carter, and the vice principal began teaching at MCHS in the 1970s.

For Carter, the early years of statewide reform were a time of both soul-searching and nostalgia. A former science teacher, he had long been committed to inquiry- and performance-based learning, with the goal of making learning directly relevant to adolescents' lives. He easily embraced the philosophy of reform, but like many of his teachers, he began to feel the stress of conflicting demands.

"When I started here as principal 22 years ago, things were different. I felt like I knew each and every one of my students, and I was able to spend much more time observing and helping my teachers. Now, with everything I am asked to do with reform, the most I can hope for is to stay caught up with all of my work. I guess I feel like I'm being pulled in so many different directions that I can't do anything well anymore. There are many aspects of the new reform guidelines that I like. But if ultimately it means I'll no longer know my students or my faculty, I just don't know if it's worth what we're being asked to do."

Under Carter's leadership, the Morton faculty attempted to understand and respond to the multifaceted requirements of systemic reform as mandated by state legislation. Change did not come easily—especially to a school where most of the faculty and student body had grown accustomed to the security of a stable environment. For example, the school was one of the last in the region to initiate a school-based decision-making council, which by law gave parents and teachers decision-making power in many areas of school life. Other changes, however, came about more quickly. To help with the increased responsibilities of reform, Carter appointed department chairs for the first time in the school's history. According to one very involved teacher, the department chairs were a driving force in getting Carter to support teacher-led initiatives.

By frequently working with members of other departments, Sullivan was gaining a reputation for leadership in change efforts. The statewide emphasis on writing portfolios required teachers from all disciplines to provide students with appropriate writing assignments, and Sullivan willingly assisted teachers across disciplines; in the spring, she helped a history teacher, Mr. Williams, design a student research project on Martin Luther King (see Exhibit A). "Mr. Williams knew exactly what he wanted his students to write about, but he wasn't sure how to frame the question their papers should answer. By working together, we came up with a question that the students understood, and the final pieces of writing were some of the best either one of us had ever seen," Sullivan recalled.

Sullivan believed the new emphasis on team teaching had students far more involved and interested in learning. Collaborative efforts between the English, drama, and history departments produced a Constitution Day and the school's first Renaissance Fair. According to Sullivan, "The efforts of teachers to collaborate has been very productive. These all-school events provide cohesion and connecting themes for students—it's getting to the heart of what systemic reform is all about."

THE UNRESOLVED DILEMMA

Several days after the outburst in the teachers' lounge, Sullivan still felt shaken by recent events. She did not understand how she could continue to put so much time and energy into her students' writing, especially without clear support from the principal. "I met with Lloyd," she explained, "to try to convince him that the only real way to deal with the problem is to reduce class size. He recognized that classes should be smaller, but his major concern was that I make the time to send regular progress reports home as a way to keep parents informed. He recommended that I meet with Pam's parents as soon as possible."

"I phoned Pam's parents and arranged for a conference during my planning period the following morning. Their major complaint was that they had not been notified of the drastic change in their daughter's grade within the past four weeks. Although they admitted that Pam was partially to blame, the father basically told me it was my responsibility to keep up with my paperwork since it was the profession I chose. He demanded to know why I hadn't let Pam know she was behind two assignments rather than giving her an F."

"I couldn't believe the way the parents handled the situation, and I'm still so frustrated by Lloyd's lack of support. He just didn't seem to understand why I waited until so late in the quarter to grade those papers. He said the students need constant feedback on their standing in the class, and waiting until the ninth week to collect and grade assignments makes it impossible to keep parents and students informed. There is just no possible way I could have gotten to those two assignments any earlier. By the time I collected them, I was totally backlogged with papers from my other four classes. We're just being asked to do too much with too little time."

For Sullivan, the only comfort in the following weeks came from her department chair. Powers said she knew that Sullivan was working as hard as she could and that keeping each parent informed at every moment throughout the semester was not the teacher's responsibility. Moreover, she suggested that the parents should have taken the initiative if they were concerned about their daughter's grade.

CHRISTY SULLIVAN: HER TEACHING PHILOSOPHY

Sullivan tried to maintain a balance between the demands of school life and those of her family, and she looked for ways to make creative use of any unscheduled time. During her 55-mile commute to work each morning, she reviewed her lesson plans and made mental lists of the stories she planned to read to her children that evening.

Sullivan attributed her calling as a teacher to a love of both reading and writing that began in first grade, when her aunt began to read to her on a daily basis. Some years later, her aunt gave her *Little Women*, a favorite novel during her adolescence that had an enduring influence on how she taught English. In the book, author Louisa May Alcott recollects childhood memories that are deeply evocative and rich with vivid descriptions and details. Today Sullivan suggests that students write most creatively when they have prompts that allow them to share important childhood memories, such as "Remember a time when someone really trusted you and you came through," or "When did you learn a valuable lesson from something that happened to you?"

Sullivan would engage students and jog their memories by having them keep journal notes on each topic. In the midst of this recall process, Sullivan assigned readings designed to inspire autobiographical writing: "Make Something of Yourself" by Russell Baker and "A Whole Society of Loners and Dreamers" by William Allen, for example. After recalling several childhood memories and reading parallel literature, each student selected two topics from which to develop process writing narratives. "I often pick topics from my own childhood to illustrate different stages of the writing process. I always select something to which students can relate. For example, once we get to the idea-development stage, I might use the story of my fourth-grade experience of being separated from my best friend because our behavior was considered disruptive. It was a painful but powerful lesson."

"By using childhood memories, I find that students get to know each other and themselves in new ways. It helps create an open and trusting sense of community. This is an aspect of teaching I really like."

This was particularly evident when students worked in peer conference groups. Using seven questions developed by Sullivan (see Exhibit B), small groups of four students critiqued one another's narratives. Sullivan systematically moved from group to group, listening, guiding when needed, and reinforcing effective critiques. Students took their roles quite seriously and typically provided positive and direct feedback. "I think you need better developed examples," "This part of your introduction is confusing," and "Why don't you try some dialogue here?" were comments frequently heard in the peer conferencing groups. Sullivan saw her role as helping students "discover and use all of their potential. I try to create a classroom environment where students feel they are valuable members who have opinions and important ideas. I want my students to realize that I see them as people, not just students. Furthermore, I want them to value and respect one another's work."

This teaching philosophy of caring was also apparent in Sullivan's informal relationships with students. She stood outside her classroom door at the beginning of each class, greeting each by name; her personal interactions contributed to students' sense of belonging in her classes. Typically, a group of between six and eight students could be found hanging out in her class before school, and students would frequently hail her with affectionate cries of "Sullivan" as they passed her room while changing classes.

"Sullivan" was her preferred nickname. For the last three years, she had played competitive volleyball, and her teammates used the term with great affection. The team approach, implicit in many of her strategies for teaching English, also spilled over into her extracurricular involvements. As sponsor of the debate team, for example, she frequently had students conduct group research on debate questions to increase involvement and mutual support. "These opportunities give students such an important way to get involved with each other and to develop their own interests," she explains. "For me, it's a great way to get to know students on an entirely different level. The students seem better able to relate to me on a personal level, and that makes all of the difference for later establishing rapport in the classroom."

Despite Sullivan's strong commitment to knowing students well, she was concerned about the inequity in the distribution of school responsibilities. "I do get frustrated when it seems like it's always the same teachers accepting responsibility for after-school programs. I'd like to see some of the teachers who don't teach English, and therefore don't have as many papers to grade, be in charge of *something*. A lot of teachers say they don't understand why we choose to give so many writing assignments, but they are also the same teachers who never take a single paper home."

SULLIVAN'S WRITING APPROACH

Sullivan's new approach to the teaching of writing was the direct result of her full-time participation in the state-sponsored Writing Project offered through the public universities. "My style of teaching has changed dramatically this year," she reflects.

"When I first began teaching, I focused primarily on grammar and literature. We were constantly using our grammar book, and I always had students diagramming sentences. I had students do autobiographical writing, but I never made the connection between what they were reading and the narratives they were developing. Now, practically every reading assignment includes their analyzing the writer's techniques and finding ways of incorporating them into their own writing" (see Exhibit C-1).

"Due primarily to reforms and the Writing Project, I have my students writing more now than ever before. I begin teaching the writing process as soon as school starts. Since I always require them to work on more than one piece of writing at a time, it's essential that students keep writing folders here in the classroom."

Sullivan attributed many of her innovations to her six-week immersion in the Writing Project. Comprised of teachers from both elementary and secondary schools, the purpose of the summer project was to provide an environment where teachers could not only work intensively on their own writing but also collaborate with other teachers on ideas for incorporating writing into the classroom. "The Writing Project was the most wonderful professional experience I ever had," Sullivan noted. "I walked away from the project with ideas that I knew I could use in the classroom, and I began using them immediately."

"For example, whenever my students read a novel, such as the one they just completed, *The Great Gatsby*, they complete a Reading Analysis (see Exhibit C-2). Instead of just answering study questions, this exercise allows them to generate their own reactions to the text, which we use as a basis for our classroom discussion. I also use 'Reader's Circle' in my classroom at least once a week. During this time, we literally create a circle, and students can choose a piece of writing that they are working on to share with the rest of the class. By this stage, the writing has already been through the small-group peer conferencing, so students are eager for a larger audience. Of course, they still receive helpful feedback, but this time it's from the entire class."

During a typical writing workshop one mid-October day, Sullivan explained the importance of good revision techniques to her students. After placing an anonymous example of student writing, "Disillusioned," on the overhead, she then guided the class through the process using a handout of specific revision questions (see Exhibit D). When it was obvious that students understood the task at hand, Sullivan had students read their personal narratives aloud to their writing partners, who used feedback sheets for their responses. When the bell rang, students were still absorbed in one another's stories.

Sullivan's participation in the Writing Project clearly changed her attitude toward teaching writing—her new approach focused on writing as a process and on students' ownership of their work: "I want students to feel what they are writing is truly theirs instead of just an assignment completed for the sole purpose of a grade. The entire feedback process, both from their peers and from me, is the key to ownership. Overall, I definitely spend more time conferencing with my students, and they must come to each conference well prepared. Rather than my leading the discussion, I expect students to have specific questions they are working on or to point to certain areas in their papers where they know they need help. Ultimately, to be independent learners, they must learn to be their own best critics."

SULLIVAN'S CLASSROOM

At first glance, Room 424 appeared to be a very traditional classroom. Although the 32 desks were arranged in perfectly straight rows, students frequently moved their desks together for peer revision of papers and whole-class discussions. Sullivan's desk was located in the back right corner of the classroom. She admitted that she liked this location for one simple reason: "I can watch everything that goes on in the classroom during any given time, and the students know that."

The desk reflected the dual emphases of her courses. Several stacks of papers were neatly arranged at one corner of the desk; in the opposite corner lay beautifully bound hardbacks of some books used in the course, including *The Great Gatsby*, *The Scarlet Letter*, and *Death of a Salesman*.

Sullivan taught five classes: two sections of junior honors classes and three sections of general level juniors. Her average class size ranged from 25 to 31 students. The wide range of ability levels within each class, consistent with the goals of reform, meant that she spent more time individually conferencing with students. Sullivan was eager to comment, noting that "conferences are essential to teaching writing, but it really adds to the increasing pressure of not having enough time to cover everything I want."

In addition to conferencing during the first semester of the year, Sullivan spent about 15 minutes on every major paper she graded for approximately 135 students; she also graded quizzes, tests, journals, and on a weekly basis, two pages from every student's reader-response evaluations.

Her students readily commented on what they were learning in class. One student said, "I just can't keep up with her! I wrote a story that was three pages long, and she wanted more details. My story ended up being nine pages long. Besides that, she always has us working on more than one piece of writing at a time. I don't even know how she can grade it all. My writing has definitely improved because of her, though. It seems like a lot of my other teachers didn't really care about what I was writing. Mrs. Sullivan really makes us work hard to improve our writing skills."

Throughout the year, Sullivan required students to work on writing assignments and to read an average of one novel per quarter. Her workload did not diminish and neither did her concern for smaller class sizes. After one late afternoon faculty meeting, she again emphasized the issue to her department chair.

"Ann, it's obvious I'm not the only one with this concern about class size. We are being asked to do far too much. We've got to deal with this problem, and I think it begins with hiring another English teacher."

"Christy, you know that's never going to happen," Ann responded.

"Why not, if reform and the teaching of writing are such high priorities?"

"We've been trying for the past few years to get another English teacher so all of us could work with fewer students, but where is that person? Every year Lloyd promises us smaller classes, but the reality is that our class size is increasing instead. He tried this past year to hire one additional English teacher, but once again the funding just wasn't there. If we wait for that to solve our problems, we will be waiting for a long time."

SPRING TERM: MORTON COUNTY HIGH SCHOOL

In the spring, there were three significant developments relevant to Sullivan's concerns: change at both the department and school level about communication with parents, her students' progress in writing skills, and her own new emphasis on time management.

As department chair, Ann Powers had supported Sullivan both personally and professionally throughout the year. After observing Sullivan's shock at the reactions of both Lloyd Carter and Pam's parents, Powers had several conversations with her in an attempt to resolve the dilemma. She commented, "In time, we both began to realize that the parent and the student should have been notified earlier. I realize Sullivan's paper load is burdensome, but I reminded her that what we are doing is essentially for the benefit of the students. I suggested that she write progress updates for all of her students on a regular basis."

Power's change in attitude coincided with a new school policy. Problems with parents had not been unique to the English department; it was the first of a string of complaints. Parents wanted progress reports earlier in the semester to inform them of their children's academic standing in every subject area. As a result, Carter required all teachers to send progress reports to all parents halfway through each nine-week grading period. This decision met with mixed reactions from the faculty. Most teachers were supportive, but several thought their time could be spent more productively. As feedback from parents was overwhelmingly positive, Carter maintained the policy.

By May, Christy Sullivan was seeing her own hard work and that of her students pay off. "Students work on writing pieces throughout the school year, and by spring they have plenty to choose from in their writing folders. They complete their writing portfolios by self-selecting the pieces they believe are the best reflection of their writing; then they improve those pieces one final time."

"When they read some of their writing from earlier in the year, they realize just what they have learned. Pam's writing had really begun to improve, and I think she noticed the difference, too. After apologizing to me for not accepting any of the blame for the grading incident, she realized her efforts in the class were going to determine her grade. She really started to apply herself and turned in all the assignments. Even though her overall grade at the end of the first semester was a C, she earned a B as her final grade for the year."

Although students worked on their writing portfolios right up to the last week of school, there was a certain tranquility in Sullivan's class that had not been present earlier in the year.

In her own words, "Using the process approach to writing is time-consuming, but I was determined not to give it up. At the same time, I had to do something to alleviate my stress level, so I've become a master at the art of time management. I've developed techniques for dealing more successfully with all of the writing turned in by students. I learned a great deal from the Pam situation. Now, as soon as papers are handed in, I have a check-off system and speak to a student immediately about any missing assignment. Also, by the day the assignments come in, I've formulated a clear plan for grading. I've blocked out time every day—typically two hours each weekday evening, a couple of hours on Saturday, and all day Sunday—so I know approximately how many papers I need to look at in each time frame. At the beginning of the year, I wasted a lot of time worrying about how everything was going to get graded rather than having a precise schedule to follow."

"The most important change is that I've realized I don't have to grade every piece of writing. I'll check to make sure that students are writing drafts of each assignment, whether essays or creative pieces, and give them credit accordingly—but in any given grading period, each student decides which writing assignment he or she will submit for a grade. Students decide for themselves which topics or prompts they want to develop further. By teaching students how to recognize the difference between strong and weak writing, they have far more responsibility. If they can't get to me for a conference, they have each other. Before this year, I saw my role as basically a director—now I'm convinced that students learn best and stay engaged when I'm their coach."

Given her new approach to time management, Sullivan responded to the question of whether the dilemma she experienced in the fall was now resolved: "No, I would say that is far from being true. The paper load is still enormous, and the stress level remains high. What has changed, however, is the way I've chosen to deal with the problem. I've found that I'm enjoying my students more because I'm not as overwhelmed with the amount of work involved. I still feel that smaller classes would alleviate some of the burden placed on English teachers; but until that change comes about, I guess I'll just continue working to see that these students have at least one successful writing experience in their lives."

EPILOGUE

During the summer, Ann Powers had the full support of her department colleagues in sending a strong letter to the superintendent. She requested additional support for the English department, noting that the school had received state recognition in the spring for its exemplary work with student writing portfolios: "In order to continue with this distinction, it is essential the department be assigned another teacher," the letter concluded. The superintendent did not reply.

On the first day of the fall term, an additional teacher was assigned to MCHS to teach junior English, a decision made by Carter. His decision was grounded in the fact that the previous year a teacher outside of the English department had taught three sections of sophomore English because of unexpected increases in enrollment. Carter hoped that the creation of a new teaching position would resolve that dilemma. The new teacher's schedule included four sections of junior English and one study hall, totaling 83 students in her English classes. As a result, Sullivan's total number of students decreased from 135 to 108. "The difference is tremendous: my smallest class is 17, and my largest is 24—it's actually possible for me to conference with everyone in a class within a couple of days. Of course I'm still grading practically every night, but the load is not as overwhelming. I now can give my students more focused help, and that is what's most important."

A friend and colleague of Sullivan reflected on their expanded department: "Sullivan was surprised when she was the only one who had a real change in class size this year. The rest of us are still working with 130 to 140 students. I am so envious . . ."

REFERENCES AND SELECTED BIBLIOGRAPHY

Applebee, A. (1981). *Writing in the secondary school*. Urbana, IL: National Council of Teachers of English.

Burns, R. (Ed.) (1993). *Parents and schools: From visitors to partners*. Charleston, WV: Appalachia Educational Laboratory.

Calkins, L. M. (1986). *The art of teaching writing*. Portsmouth, NH: Heinemann.

Danielson, C. (1996). Enhancing professional practice: A framework for teaching. Alexandria, VA: Association for Supervision and Curriculum Development.

Donahoe, T. (1993). Finding the way: Structure, time and culture in school improvement. *Phi Delta Kappan, 75*(4), 298–305.

Feeley, J. T., Strickland D. S., & Wepner, S. B. (Eds.). (1991). *Process reading and writing: A literature based approach*. New York: Teachers College Press.

Fishman, M., & McCarthy, L. (1998). *John Dewey and the challenge of classroom practice*. New York: Teachers College Press. (See chapter 3: Moral traits of character and Dewey's student curriculum.)

Graves, D. H. (1983). *Writing: Teachers and children at work*. Portsmouth, NH: Heinemann.

Lobin, T. (1993). *Writing relationships: What really happens in the composition class*. Portsmouth, NH: Boynton/Cook Heinemann.

Murray, D. (1985). Teaching the other self: The writer's first reader. In T. Newkirk (Ed.), *To compose: Teaching writing in the high school* (pp. 52–61). Chelmsford, MA: Northeast Regional Exchange.

Noddings, N. (1998). An ethic of caring and its implications for instructional arrangements. In E. L. Stone (Ed.), The feminist education reader. Berkeley, CA: University of California Press, pp. 37–46.

Powell, A., Farrar, E., & Cohen, D. K. (1985). *The shopping mall high school. Winners and losers in the educational marketplace*. Boston: Houghton Mifflin.

Sizer, T. (1992). *Horace's school: Redesigning the American high school*. Boston: Houghton Mifflin.

E X H I B I T   A

Contents of Eleventh-Grade Portfolios[1]

Any of the following portfolio entries may come from subject areas other than English/Language Arts, but a minimum of one piece of writing must come from other content areas.

1. Table of contents: Specify the title of each entry, the content area for which the piece was written, and the page number in the portfolio
2. Best piece
3. Letter to the review: A letter written by the student explaining why he/she selected the best piece and how the piece was developed
4. One persuasive piece
5. One poem, short story, or play
6. One piece of writing that will achieve any one of the following purposes:
   a. predict an outcome
   b. defend a position
   c. solve a problem
   d. analyze or evaluate a situation
   e. explain a process or concept
   f. draw a conclusion
   g. create a model

Portfolios will be due in Language Arts class on the last Friday in May. The completed portfolio will count as two (2) 100-point test grades during the fourth nine-week grading period. Incomplete portfolios will count as a zero.

A portfolio will be considered complete when:

a. it is in blue or black ink or typed
b. it has an accurate table of contents
c. the fringes are cut off
d. all pieces are revised to eliminate evaluation marks
e. all pieces are legible
f. it has page numbers
g. only the front side of the paper is used
h. all required pieces are included

---

[1]Adapted from Kentucky Department of Education. (1993). KIRIS writing portfolio assessment: Contents of the grade 12 portfolio. *Kentucky Writing Portfolio: Grade 12 Teacher's Handbook* (2nd ed.). Frankfort, KY: Author.

E X H I B I T   B

Peer Conference Questions

Name _____

Date _____

Group Member _____

Directions: As you listen to the writer's piece, ask yourself the following questions:

1. What things do I like about this piece?
2. What do I want to know more about?
3. What is the writer's main point?
4. What are some details that are especially interesting?
5. What suggestions can I offer?
6. Is any part of this piece confusing?
7. What can be eliminated without losing the author's intention (words, phrases, sentences, paragraphs)?
8. **Suggested Revision Notes**

E X H I B I T   C - 1

Reader's Response Prompts

You may use one or more of these questions to help you write the response to your reading.

1. What character(s) was your favorite? Why?
2. What character(s) did you dislike? Why?
3. Does anyone in this work remind you of anyone you know? Explain.
4. Are you like any character in this work? Explain.
5. If you could be any character in this work, who would you be?
6. What quality(ies) of which character strikes you as a good characteristic to develop within yourself over the years?
7. Overall, what kind of feeling did you have after reading a few paragraphs of this work? Midway? After finishing?
8. Do any incidents, ideas, or actions in this work remind you of your own life or something that happened to you? Explain.
9. Do you like this book? Why or why not?
10. Are there any parts of this work that were confusing to you? Which parts? Why do you think you got confused?
11. Do you feel there is any opinion expressed by the author through this work? What is it? How do you know this? Do you agree? Why or why not?
12. Do you think the title of this work is appropriate? Is it significant? Explain. What do you think the title means?
13. Would you change the ending? Tell your ending. Why would you change it?
14. What kind of person do you feel the author is? What makes you feel this way?
15. How did this work make you feel? Explain.
16. Do you share any of the feelings of the characters in this work? Explain.
17. Sometimes a work leaves you with the feeling that there is more to tell. Did this work do this? What do you think might happen?
18. Would you like to read something else by this author? Why or why not?
19. What do you feel is the most important word, phrase, passage or paragraph in this work? Explain why it is important.
20. If you were an English teacher, would you want to share this work with your students? Why or why not?

E X H I B I T   C - 2

Reading Analysis

Name _____ **Date** _____

Title of reading

_____

Response covers pages

_____

RESPONSE:

Reading Response   3—Needs Attention
Scoring Guide   4—Satisfactory
50 pts.   5—Satisfactory +

_____ 1. An appropriate response was chosen for the type of reading.

_____ 2. Response indicates that the reading was done.

_____ 3. Response reveals there was an attempt to gain from the reading/writing.

_____ 4. Ideas and thoughts are elaborated, supported, and explained.

_____ 5. Flow of thought is orderly and makes sense.

_____ 6. Signals of organization are evident.

_____ 7. Vocabulary/word choice is appropriate.

_____ 8. Sentences make sense.

_____ 9. Handwriting is legible.

_____ 10. Heading on paper is complete.

_____ TOTAL POINTS

E X H I B I T   D

Revision for Writers

1. Where and how do I provide signals of purpose throughout?
2. Have I justified the purpose? Where? How?
3. Where could I provide fill-ins, background? What can I do to help orient the reader to my purposes, my angle?
4. Where could I add examples, especially from my own experience? Where could I add hypothetical examples?
5. Where could I add even more information to inform and to "impress" the reader?
6. If a reader did not understand me or had trouble, where would it likely be and what could I add to help?
7. Where could I add quotes, comparisons, analogies, contrasts?
8. Where could I add "interpreting statements"?
9. Where might I include some visuals or some set of data?
10. Where could I add "what I mean" or "what I don't mean"?
11. Where could I include statements that address the reader or pose author reflective questioning?
12. Where could I address problems a reader might want me to deal with?
13. Where could I slow down and step back to reflect on what I am offering to the reader—to clarify importance, purpose, etc.?
14. Where could I pinpoint for the reader: the unusual, the new, the important?
15. Where could I help with "in other words" or "another way to put it"?
16. Where could I return to my overall idea or controlling point and bring it again to the reader's attention?
17. Where could I discuss HOW I know what I am saying?
18. Where could I be even more specific or SHOW the reader, not just tell?
19. What in my writing does a reader not already know? What could I add that the reader probably does not know or understand?
20. If a reader disagreed, where would it be and what would I say in response?

DISCUSSION QUESTIONS

1. Describe Christy Sullivan as a teacher.
   - How do you think Sullivan would describe herself at the beginning of the case?
   - What factors have influenced her professional development?

2. What is the main issue for each of the key players (Sullivan, Lloyd Carter, Ann Powers, Pam's parents, Pam)?

3. How does Christy Sullivan's new curriculum support the intellectual and personal development of her students?
   - It seems that for Sullivan, good writing should be linked to personal experience. Do you agree? Discuss the similarities and differences between a teacher's drawing upon students' prior knowledge and experiences and drawing upon their own prior knowledge and experiences.
   - Could this linking to personal experience pose any problems, and, if so, how? Do you agree with this approach? To what extent is it developmentally appropriate for this age group?

4. What specific techniques does Sullivan use to engage students?
   - What evidence is there for the effectiveness of these techniques?
   - Discuss specific ways she gives students responsibility for their own learning. Did she expect too much of Pam in this regard? How does a teacher gauge the reasonableness of her expectations?
   - Sullivan has made major changes in how she teaches writing. Now consider the various readings she requires of her students. Is there room for change here? If so, how and why?

5. Evaluate Sullivan's time-management strategies as an aspect of her planning.
   - At the beginning of the case, how did she attempt to handle her various responsibilities?
   - By the end of the case, what changes had she made? To what extent were they consistent with her philosophy? To what extent are the changes Sullivan made applicable to any teacher's effectiveness?
   - If you were Sullivan, what other possible time-management strategies would you use? What might be the consequences of each, including the compromises or changes in your teaching style?
   - What does Sullivan's experience teach us about the change process?

6. Discuss the role of extracurricular activities in Sullivan's professional life.
   - What positive or negative effects have these had on her teaching?
   - To what extent are these activities an integral part of her philosophy? Are there extracurricular activities that are integral to your philosophy?
   - If she were to relinquish some of these responsibilities, would it influence her effectiveness as a teacher? To what extent do you share her perspective on the value of extracurricular activities?

7. Sullivan has seen a significant reduction in the size of her classes. What are the pros and cons of the new situation?
   - If the reduction had not occurred, what other courses of action could Sullivan have taken to help alleviate the time-management and planning issues?

8. Discuss Sullivan's approach to assessment.
   - What is she trying to achieve through her methods? What other assessment approaches would be appropriate for Sullivan's goals? Are there specific modifications you would make?
   - Given Sullivan's philosophy of classroom community, should students have a role in designing scoring rubrics? Is it consistent on her part that they aren't?

9. During the course of the year, principal Carter made several decisions directly affecting Sullivan and the other faculty members. How might his decisions have been different and with what consequences?
   - How serious was Sullivan's slipup in not informing Pam's parents of her drop in grade? Did Carter get pushed around by a parent, or was his response appropriate? Discuss the issue of regular progress reports to parents. If you agree with Carter as to their importance, explain why.
   - In what other ways might Sullivan improve communication with parents? Are the possible benefits worth the additional demands on her time?
   - Were there other ways Carter could have eased Sullivan's workload without engendering the envy of her colleagues?

10. How have Sullivan's feelings about herself as a teacher changed from the beginning of the case to the end? To what extent is she a reflective practitioner? What criteria should be used to determine the quality of a teacher's reflections?

11. One of the characteristics of a thinker-friendly classroom is that the teacher focuses on depth of content over breadth. Using this criterion, discuss the extent to which Sullivan's classroom is thinker-friendly.
    - Are there specific steps she could take to make it more so?

12. For her short readings, Sullivan selected works "designed to inspire autobiographical writing." Is this an appropriate criterion given her goals?

- What criteria should a dedicated language arts/English teacher use in determining what students will read? Discuss how the criteria should differ among disciplines.
- Should teachers select readings based on their inherent relevance to students' lives or use classics and find ways to "make them" relevant?

13. According to Nel Noddings, "Teaching is filled with caring occasions." (See Noddings in case references.) Analyze Sullivan's classroom from this point of view—in general and with respect to Pam.

- When responsible professionals prioritize classroom goals, how high of a priority should Sullivan's goals of trust, valuing, and community have?

CASE 8

Discussion Question	Corresponding INTASC Principle
3, 11	2 The teacher understands how children learn and develop, and can provide learning opportunities that support their intellectual, social, and personal development.
4, 12	5 The teacher uses an understanding of individual and group motivation and behavior to create a learning environment that encourages positive social interaction, active engagement in learning, and self-motivation.
5, 8	8 The teacher understands and uses formal and informal assessment strategies to evaluate and ensure the continuous intellectual, social, and physical development of the learner.
10	9 The teacher is a reflective practitioner who continually evaluates the effects of his/her choices and actions on others (students, parents, and other professionals in the learning community) and who actively seeks out opportunities to grow professionally.
11, 12	4 The teacher understands and uses a variety of instructional strategies to encourage students' development of critical thinking, problem solving, and performance skills.

Will the Real Reform Please Stand Up?

TALKING IN THE LOUNGE

Cypresstown High School was humming at lunchtime. Jason Gordon slipped into the teachers' lounge out of breath, moments after dismissing his class on the other side of the building. He hated to be late for his intern, Mike, especially since this was only their second official meeting. Gordon, beginning his fifth year of teaching, had wanted to be a mentor for three years. He was convinced he would do an excellent job. As Gordon put his stack of National Geographics down, Mike was already talking.

"You know, all the department is talking about these days are the field trips."

Using detailed topographical maps, biology students visited several nearby tributaries of the Ohio River annually to measure oxygen levels and to document industrial and agricultural contaminants. It was part of the statewide "Water Watch" project that allowed students to monitor water quality and learn about water ecology at the same time (see Exhibit A). The department chair, Mrs. Meyers, had been instrumental in the department's decision to join the project. Mike was waving his hands in the air, clearly animated as he spoke.

"As everyone knows, Mrs. Meyers is convinced that the 'Water Watch' project really hooks students. She says they get so into collecting they come away truly appreciating the diversity of life forms. This emphasis on real-life applications is what education reform is all about according to Meyers. She thinks we are the leader in this area."

Gordon was stonily silent during Mike's description of the science department's pet project. He had struggled unsuccessfully to use the early field trip sequence in his first year of teaching. He felt the field trips were premature. There were many complex biological concepts and processes with which his students were either not yet familiar or knowledgeable enough for meaningful, accurate connection with fieldwork. Now he planned field trips primarily at the end of the year, when students had mastered the essentials necessary for guided discovery. For Gordon, the pure discovery approach, in which a teacher gives rules and only after a problem is defined, was an unfortunate holdover from the open classroom reforms of the 1960s.

Although he had not observed any of his colleagues teaching, based on field trips and department discussions, he saw this as the dominant teaching style within the department.

Mike continued without pausing for breath. "But I don't know . . . When I ask the others in the department how it helps kids learn and if the kids understand what they are seeing, they just say things like, 'We want them to see for themselves.' Sometimes I'm not even sure what I should be doing on these field trips besides taking roll."

Gordon nodded his head vigorously, and his voice rose several notches. "I am here to teach science, not just to 'get them hooked.' My students are going to know what they're looking at before they go mucking around in the water." Neither of them seemed to notice as the lounge door opened behind Gordon, who was still talking emphatically. "Look, it's pretty simple. When kids go on trips before they know what they're even looking at, how does that relate to science as a discipline? I don't see how that relates to helping kids learn concepts, and I don't even see that it functions well in this school's curriculum."

Catching an abrupt change in Mike's expression, Gordon turned around to Meyers and another colleague standing in the doorway with eyebrows raised in his direction.

The following week, Mike was reassigned to a different intern supervisor. After the fact, Gordon received a terse memo from the department chair saying that due to a scheduling conflict, it had been necessary to reassign Mike to a teacher who had fourth period free for conferencing.

THE SCHOOL

Cypresstown was considered a city high school, but the district's student assignment plan ensured that it drew from both city and suburban middle schools with widely varying characteristics. A large school, it had 2,200 students and 115 faculty, with at least 40 percent of them close to retirement age. Although 65 percent of the students went on to college in their first year after graduation, last year fully 20 percent of Cypresstown's student body never made it to graduation. Approximately 25 percent were on free lunch. In the last several years, the school employed additional social workers to address problems with teen pregnancy and substance abuse.

Cypresstown was better known for the success of its basketball team than for its academic accomplishments. The school was separated into three tracks: honors, regular, and low. The lower track included most of the school's special education students, as well as those who primarily took vocational classes.

Like many schools in the state, it was challenged by education reform to reevaluate programs for students who were not succeeding in school. For example, at least 20 percent of the freshman class generally failed their science course, but teachers passed them anyway to avoid further overcrowding. Three years into reform, the School-Based Decision Making (SBDM) Council began to explore solutions to such entrenched problems.

At the council's unanimous recommendation, the principal shepherded the process of piloting block scheduling with part of the freshman class. Competition to teach in the new program had been fierce, and Gordon was one of several applicants who had not been selected. With 90-minute blocks for each subject and reduction in the teacher-student ratio, teachers in the block formed interdisciplinary teams with the goal of creating thematic units. Most of the science teachers saw this as an affirmation of their self-defined mission: To teach a thematically organized, inquiry-based curriculum. A leader in the science department who was part of the block team offered his viewpoint: "As I worked on the interdisciplinary thematic units, it was energizing—I began to see science in the bigger picture, forcing me to really prioritize what I would teach. I began to understand what some reformers mean by 'less is more.' "

The principal, Jeff Danielson, had been at Cypresstown only a few years but inherited what many claimed were intractable problems. There was a community perception that discipline policies were lax and unenforceable. The high percentage of discipline problems compared to other schools in the area was often attributed to severe overcrowding. Knowing new facilities were at least three years away, Danielson had to find immediate solutions for the SBDM Council to consider. Quite knowledgeable about reform efforts, he knew block scheduling could help with the overcrowding. But his commitment to creative scheduling was derived from its potential for changing the curriculum and teachers' instructional strategies. One of the dilemmas he faced was how to ensure that the experimental block would do more than just tinker with time.

Faculty reactions to Danielson were mixed. Most everyone agreed that discipline problems had somewhat improved during his tenure, and he was respected for his ability to admit when he made a mistake. Several faculty and parents described him as "an idea person" capable of making reform happen. Others were concerned that he was not enough of a hands-on manager and delegated too much to assistant principals. For Jason Gordon, the principal was the only person at Cypresstown who really understood and appreciated his efforts.

THE DEPARTMENT

Cypresstown had a central core of experienced teachers who prided themselves on their commitment to the school. In the science department, four positions were held by relative newcomers while the other eleven teachers had been at the school for ten or more years. The long-timers were tightly knit by friendships that extended well beyond school life. The department culture emphasized the importance of being a team player and mentoring student teachers and interns.

A committee of senior science teachers planned the sophomore biology curriculum three years before Jason arrived. Their goal was to create a high-interest sequence, using a widely accepted strategy of "contextualizing." By participating in field trips, students would become immersed in topics such as water quality through direct experience. Once their interest had been captured, they would develop testable hypotheses, in the process learning the necessary steps in scientific investigation. Essential concepts would emerge from student inquiry. For example, testing water quality naturally evolved into a study of ecosystems. This approach enabled teachers to make science relevant to students' interests and to contemporary issues, such as pollution, AIDS, and teenage smoking. Gordon agreed with the need for engaging students' attention—his primary concern was what he considered to be an emphasis on process at the expense of content. He strongly objected to what appeared to be a prevailing viewpoint that very few students were ever going to become scientists so they did not need a wealth of content as long as they developed an interest in science and could replicate the scientific method. A university professor adamantly supported Gordon's statement that, "It's no wonder that the students don't become science majors in college—they've had a superficial foundation without a broad conceptual grounding." Nonetheless, the approach taken by Gordon's colleagues received more acclaim than criticism. In recent years, three department teachers won state or national awards for excellence in teaching. One recent student teacher said, "This is a fabulous department. I'd give anything to be a permanent member of it."

When department members began to study the state-adopted curriculum guidelines and learner expectations, there was general agreement that their existing curriculum exemplified the reform emphasis on real-world applications of knowledge. Several department members prided themselves on being ahead of the curve; as one said, "We had reformed our curriculum before it ever became required."

GETTING STARTED

A self-styled loner, Jason Gordon was passionately involved in his subject matter. "I have zero political skills. You might not believe it to see me in front of my class, but around other adults, I'm just shy." Some saw him as aloof rather than shy, perhaps because of his privileged background and extensive education. In addition, his no-nonsense manner and knowledge of scientific research probably made it hard to believe that he was still relatively new to teaching.

From the beginning, he was off to a difficult start. Given the number of applicants for science openings for that year, he had the feeling that he had not been the department's first-choice applicant. Having completed all but his dissertation in developmental biology and five years of research at a prominent medical institute, he realized he did not exactly fit the typical new teacher profile.

When he arrived at Cypresstown, Gordon found no available science materials, and those he requested were very slow in coming. As a new teacher, Gordon did not have his own room assignment. Instead, he shuffled between classrooms with all of his supplies on a cart, which involved navigating down a narrow winding corridor and through heavy swinging doors. He had mastered the art of getting through the doors without having them hit against the cart, potentially knocking over fluid-filled beakers or stacks of books and papers. It was a little harder when he also wrestled with a second cart of microscopes or a third cart containing video equipment borrowed from the library or another teacher. He solved the problem by soliciting help from students.

Early on, Gordon began asking around for resources and assistance with the curriculum. He often sought out Danielson, since he did not find his science colleagues eager to talk with him. He was able to get some useful feedback from a university supervisor with the state Teacher Internship Program. Also, as part of the program, the principal made three required observations and commented that Gordon seemed to have fresh ideas and promise as a teacher. But Gordon wanted more specific feedback and continued to ask for guidance and materials to support his work. He found a few colleagues in the social studies department who allowed him to visit their rooms and who visited his in return. Together, they created an interdisciplinary unit, combining history and science that focused on the theme of invention.

However, within his own department, Gordon's attempts to get help where futile. His several requests to the department chair for observations and feedback received no response. When Gordon asked other teachers in the department for help, they gave only brief answers—neither the detailed rationales for lessons nor the help with materials he was seeking. After what Gordon considered many rebuffs, he withdrew and began his private struggle to teach sophomore biology to five classes of the lowest track in the school. To his surprise, he found that he had a special talent with these students and was determined not to water down the curriculum for them.

Gordon knew his strong points as a teacher were his knowledge of the subject matter and his passion for making science accessible. Part of his motivation to teach emerged during his doctoral work in developmental biology at a prestigious university. There, he had been surprised at the "insider" culture he found in the field of science generally. He questioned whether only a privileged few should be involved in science—did the field have to be such an exclusive club? Disillusioned, Gordon eventually decided not to be a researcher in the "ivory tower."

As an undergraduate, he had studied in a special honors "college within a college" at another notable university. Cross-disciplinary seminars were common, and the catchphrase was "you have to get everyone up to speed." The high-level dialogue was egalitarian, not "insider" focused. To Gordon, this conveyed two important lessons: (a) it was both possible and desirable to communicate crucial and complex concepts to a very general audience, and (b) a foundation of basic understanding enabled a substantive discussion to take place. Of his classes now, he says, "I have to create a common knowledge base, then we can have that inductive discussion."

While his doctoral work—and what he considered to be the "elitism" of scientists—had propelled his interest in becoming a teacher, it had also given him a way of thinking about subject matter that framed his philosophy of teaching high school biology. In his specialty of developmental biology, the professors required students to demonstrate understanding of a complex natural process like ovulation or fetal development. When students knew the basic concepts thoroughly, down to the molecular and chemical level, they could adequately synthesize and explain the big picture. As Gordon became increasingly immersed in this process, he gained an entirely new perspective on his own high school science courses. While he had done exceptionally well in high school, he was able to remember little from one year to the next. He had successfully memorized a great deal of disconnected terminology and hands-on processes but never felt he had a conceptual foundation that would have enabled him to retain and expand upon his knowledge. The realization of what had gone wrong in his own secondary education fueled his determination to teach science for thorough understanding and to do so with high aspirations for all students. "They need the little pieces to understand the big ones. And there has to be logical progression. Once they really learn one process, then they can use it to understand another."

CHANGING THE CURRICULUM

Just after he began at Cypresstown, the state reform act was passed, and Gordon was enthusiastic about innovations in science teaching. He certainly wanted to make an improvement over the rote learning and lack of conceptual connections in his own high school experience. He had struggled during his first years to find ways of "really teaching" his students instead of "just talking at them." He wanted his students to talk and think biology in and out of class and to use the biological concepts and habits of scientific inquiry wherever they were relevant.

For the next four summers, he attended a series of seminars on problem-based learning. These emphasized extensive writing and discussion as an opportunity for students to reveal their reasoning processes to each other and to the teacher. Gordon came away committed to helping students find their own analogies for scientific concepts and processes. He also found support among other science teachers at the seminars.

After the first seminar, he energetically began to revise his curriculum (see Exhibit B). He maintained all the required content while changing the presentation sequence and built his new program around a series of "crucial" labs. In his new curriculum, each lab report was actually an extensive writing probe to gauge students' understanding of scientific ideas as they apply to real-life problems. But Gordon heard from a vocational teacher that other biology teachers were suspicious, noting that Gordon had reduced the number of labs required in his classes.

While the other teachers started with ecology and worked from the contextual "high interest" material into molecular biology later in the year, Gordon began with a rigorous hierarchical approach, emphasizing a logical sequence of concepts. He started with the smallest part, atomic structure, and worked his way throughout the year past molecular biology into larger and larger systems, culminating in ecology (see Exhibit B). As he explained, "It's true when they start, the kids don't see the point of any of this. Sometimes it's like pulling teeth in the regular sections to find a spark of interest, but it does come. I teach all of my sections, honors to the lowest track, the same concepts, the ones you have to be familiar with when you start college biology. But I'm teaching them more than just about DNA or ecology. I want them to know how to test a hypothesis, how to think critically and question what they're told."

Every year, Gordon found a recent first-run movie that presented a scientific dilemma. He used films to introduce the scientific method, to connect biology and real life, and to establish a shared context for learning crucial biological concepts throughout the course. For example, one September he showed *Awakenings*, an engaging story with well-known actors. He said, "I referred to this movie at least once a week for the rest of the year." The movie showed potential benefits and risks of scientific investigation and also demonstrated how living systems (including humans) may depend on essential processes or elements that are not obvious or quickly understood.

For his first assignment, Gordon had students write a review of the movie to elicit examples of student thinking as well as to draw their attention to each other's perspectives. He wanted them to start seeing that there might be more than one way to observe and describe a problem, situation, or experience. In their movie reviews, he asked them to discuss what they had learned and its potential relevance to their own lives. In addition, he required students to compose written reviews of each other's work and to respond in writing to their reviewers. He found that while this peer review process took time to teach, it paid off in helping students to see the value of each other's perspectives rather than directing all of their comments to him. This work was a foundation for later lab reports.

Gordon required students to rewrite any work he considered less than "A" quality. He focused on student understanding of a few key concepts in each lab. "It's true I don't do as many labs. But each one we do is really important, and we beat it to death. I won't let them just fill in blank answers on a worksheet." For each of these labs, he expected students to demonstrate understanding through a thorough write-up, including the purpose of the lab and steps of the scientific method with hypotheses and methods of investigation. As a part of their lab write-up, students had to describe a plausible dilemma or related life experience that could have generated the experiment or process (see Exhibits C-1 and C-2). After the lab, they discussed implications.

Often, he could see students making some connection from the lab to their own lives. One student noted that, "It would be pretty hard to always test carbohydrate composition with Benedict's solution, but in the future I'll probably read product labels." From a lab in a unit on genetics, another student proposed a more time-consuming plan. Students had learned to use a chart, the Punnett square, to analyze probability of dominant and recessive characteristics occurring in offspring. The student, whose family had a history of hypoglycemia, suggested that he could use a Punnett square with his future spouse to determine the probability of hypoglycemia in their children.

LEARNING THE BASICS: DNA

Gordon's dedication to thorough mastery was especially evident during the times when a class could not grasp key concepts. He would not consider moving ahead just to cover content. This past year, for example, one class period came to a halt during a unit on cellular functions. Building on the basic chemical composition, which he had reviewed during the first six-week unit, Gordon introduced the next building block of life, the cell.

Most of the class seemed to understand the periodic table, reading confidently from the frayed chart at the front of the room. The next step, though hard, was foundational for later material on human inheritance. Gordon showed them how various molecules formed the parts of a cell and how those parts functioned in making the cell a living organism capable of self-maintenance. He wanted them to understand basic processes as well as terminology.

As in previous years, the section on cellular functions was difficult for students. But Gordon knew from experience they could all understand the material with some real mental effort. In one lab, students made geometric paper cutouts to demonstrate key concepts; the cutouts represented the different molecules of DNA, and students arranged and rearranged them to demonstrate how DNA forms the code for production for proteins through the processes of transcription and translation. Gordon had almost always been able to teach the material in the week allotted so students were able to turn the lab in by week's end.

Early in the week, Gordon used Lego block stacks to demonstrate transcription and translation. He explained that in order for the DNA information to organize new protein, it had to have a way to send a message outside of the nucleus, and he demonstrated this by comparing a section of DNA to two interlocking stacks of white Lego blocks. The two (stacks) strands were perfectly complementary to each other. After pulling the two stacks apart, he replaced one stack with a similarly shaped stack of blue blocks. This blue stack was a new complementary strand, a complete and perfect copy now able to assemble next to the original strand. Like the white stack it replaced, the blue stack also interlocked with the other white stack to represent "messenger RNA," which was able to leave the nucleus. This was Gordon's process for visually illustrating how the new copy transmits the blueprint (mRNA) of the new protein outside the nucleus via a cell part called the ribosome.

Gordon attempted to reinforce this conceptual understanding with brief video clips from several well-made public television specials on DNA and cellular functions. For hands-on manipulation and examination, the class used large standard models of the DNA double helix with each chemical part color-coded.

By the end of the week, students in one of his regular classes were still responding only with rote memorization to his questions. The question "So, what are the chemical pairs that form the ladder of DNA?" would elicit an accurate answer from most students. However, when Gordon asked them to state in their own words, departing from the Lego block analogy, what these processes of transcription and translation were, students were tongue-tied. They muttered, "I just don't get it," or "Who cares about this stuff anyway?" And no one had turned in the paper cutout lab.

While his other regular biology class and honors class were able to move on, Gordon decided to have this class produce its own in-class drama demonstrating the DNA transcription and translation process. Although this would put them a week behind on the syllabus, Gordon considered the concepts essential. In addition, he felt increasingly confident about his teaching based on notes from students and positive feedback from Danielson and guidance counselors. In the next week, students worked in groups to develop their own analogies, such as "The spy (DNA) who can't leave the island (the cell nucleus) sends a telegraph message in Morse code (mRNA) to get the exact reinforcements needed (new proteins) . . . it's translated back out of code by the telegraph operator (ribosome) who calls transport vessels (tRNA) full of the exact troops needed," and then rehearsed their demonstrations of each step of the process.

Soon after the students performed the DNA drama in class, they completed the difficult DNA paper cutout labs, showing a much improved understanding of the concepts. Now Gordon was ready to move on to more complicated concepts, confident that the class understood enough of DNA's role in cellular functions.

MAKING CONNECTIONS TO STUDENT'S LIVES

Gordon kept a stack of student index cards for each class, listing hobbies and interests (as stated by students) and current issues he noted as they arose. He used the cards during class discussion to help students make meaningful associations. For example, when a student was struggling for an analogy to explain the abstract process by which DNA is expressed in the organism's actual features (phenotype) compared to the DNA code (genotype), Gordon referred to his cards. Since the student was a cooking enthusiast, Gordon asked, "Well, can you think of the phenotype as how the cake tastes and compare it to the recipe? What would the recipe be? Could there be things in the recipe you can't taste in the cake?"

In addition to his passion for helping students make science their own, Gordon empathized with his students as young people needing encouragement. Between classes and during cooperative learning assignments, Gordon used his resource of index cards to personally connect with several students one-on-one each week. His brisk, informal air had the ring of an athletic coach on the playing field: "Serena, I hear you've brought up your math grade—I knew you could do it." Explaining his emphasis on student contact, Gordon mentioned freely how difficult times in his own life had made him very sensitive to adolescents. "My parents insisted on perfection, so I would get punished if I wasn't doing 'A' work. If a kid is halfway trying, I'll try to at least let him or her know I notice." He is deeply committed to acknowledging efforts by students to whom learning does not come easily. His expectations are high; he will work hard with any student, and he expects students to help one another in keeping up with the material.

Soon after Gordon's first semester, students began to request his classes, a trend that continued in the following years. As one student explained, "He makes it easy. If we don't understand, he keeps working with us until we do, or he helps us find another way to figure it out so it makes sense." An honors student trying out the regular track said, "Sometimes I wish he would move on, but if the class doesn't get it, he keeps plugging away until we do."

A school counselor offered this perspective on why students were requesting Gordon's classes: "Gordon just seems to have a gift for knowing when to go the extra mile with a kid. Time after time I have seen him come in here and sit down with kids and parents. Or a lot of times, he'll just spot a few kids with something wrong and send a referral to get them in to see a counselor. It's no accident that those kids are ending up in his classes. And it's not just scheduling—a lot of kids come and ask for him."

After his rocky start, Gordon had more regular classes in his schedule, even two honors sections in his fourth and fifth years. He was encouraged by Danielson, who steadily lobbied for Gordon to teach the honors sections of biology. But he still did not have his own classroom and had watched three newly vacated rooms be assigned to more junior teachers. He continued to have the heaviest class load in the department and a disproportionate share of the most challenged students in the regular track. With all the difficulties, however, Gordon knew that he had found his niche as a teacher—nothing gave him greater satisfaction than engaging the hard-to-reach students. The philosophy driving the entire state reform effort was "All children can learn and most at high levels." For Gordon this was not a belief, but a conviction.

AN EXCEPTIONAL STUDENT

Many of the more challenged students responded well to Gordon's matter-of-fact style. One who captured his attention this past year was a student designated learning disabled who had requested several classes in the regular track for his sophomore year, including biology. Nick was a "regular guy," who typically wore jeans and an oversized tee-shirt. He was indistinguishable from the rest of his peers, except that he was failing and barely responded to teachers' attempts to draw him out verbally.

Gordon knew Nick had been diagnosed with difficulties in reading and was not surprised that he had not turned in any of the extensive writing assignments but had earned a C+ in quiz grades. Gordon had repeatedly encouraged Nick to write for substance and not to worry about spelling and grammar. He had also called Nick's parents and followed up just as he did for other students who seemed to have trouble. He tried to touch base with Nick one-on-one during class cooperative learning and writing time, but still Gordon watched Nick throw away every writing assignment handout and lab write-up guide he received.

Because the C+ quiz grade showed some content mastery, Gordon took a chance with Nick. He asked the special education team for permission to pass Nick after the first six-week period with a D− grade he had not earned. He received permission and gave Nick the grade.

Gordon watched out of the corner of his eye the day grades were given as Nick came into the class for biology. He sidled up to the lab station at the front of the room and waited patiently while several other students finished asking about their grades. Gordon was curious to see how Nick would respond to receiving a passing grade of D− when in fact he had done very few of the class assignments and had actually earned an F for the first six weeks.

"Mr. Gordon," Nick began, "can I ask you about my grade?"

"Sure, what's up?"

"Well," Nick said slowly, with a half-smile playing around his mouth, "I didn't think I was doing this well." He looked up at Gordon and then quickly away. Gordon was amazed by the length of response and wondered if he might finally be reaching this student.

"Well," Gordon replied, "you see what you can do if you work a little? And if you just turn in your assignments, you can make a decent grade."

"Well, thanks," Nick replied as a he ducked his head and headed for his seat.

Nick turned in the next writing assignment, and Gordon gave brief notes as feedback. Subsequently, Nick made revisions and continued to turn in assignments. Nick now maintained his mastery of concepts, and Gordon corrected Nick's work when he was off-track. Nick was also participating in the peer review process, reading other students' work and giving his write-ups to them for comment. Gordon heard Nick clearly explain concepts to classmates on several occasions.

Halfway through the second six weeks, Gordon chuckled at Nick's version of the "Cell Play" he had assigned. It was entitled "The Factory for Cells" and had a decorated title page. Gordon opened the second page and found it full of a detailed cast of characters (see Exhibit D); every part of the cell had been given an appropriate character. For example, security guards represented the cell membrane, which keeps what belongs in, in and what belongs out, out. Conveyor belts represented the tRNA, which moves specific parts together for assembly. As the play progressed, Gordon saw that the characters had dialogue and that all of the major processes taught in the unit were accurately described through the factory analogy. It definitely earned an A grade.

As the six-week period progressed, Nick diligently turned in all assignments but rarely spoke more than a few words to his teacher. Gordon made a special effort to acknowledge him in comments on his written assignments: "You're doing great; keep up the good work," and "Thanks for your help in class." Gordon noted that Nick continued to jump in and explain concepts to classmates to the point where he had come to think of him as one of the class tutors. Nick would pick up his returned papers, look up briefly at Gordon, smile, and then return to his seat. By the end of the second grading period, Nick had a solid A in regular biology.

DO I BELONG HERE?

Despite his successes with students, in the middle of his fifth year, Gordon was having serious concerns about trying to survive another year at Cypresstown. He had not been accepted to teach in the expanded block schedule for the following year although he was quite sure that structure would make the best use of his talents for reaching students with difficulties in learning. Gordon also knew he was unlikely to get his own classroom even as a sixth-year teacher. Feeling there was little left to lose, he reached out to an experienced colleague in the department who had not seemed quite as distant as the others. This teacher had a son in Gordon's class, which provided a reasonable excuse for communication, especially since Gordon made a practice of calling all parents at least once a semester.

After casually opening the conversation, Gordon went out on a limb: "Rhonda, I guess you know your son is doing fine in my class, but I really do want to talk to you. I know you're not just a concerned parent; you probably have an informed opinion as a science teacher. Do you have a problem with the way I teach? I really need some comments or feedback. I just don't know why everyone in the department turns the other way when I walk toward them down the hall."

Rhonda responded briefly. "Well, I have no problems. I think my son's learning a lot in your class." Gordon was discouraged and soon ended the phone call. But later that night, Rhonda called him back. Her comments were to the point: "Jason, you know word has gotten around that you are really negative about the department. That's why your intern was reassigned. There's a lot I really can't say . . . I think in many ways you're doing an excellent job. When your students did better than most on the performance assessment exams, that said something." Gordon thanked her for her candor and for the positive feedback on his teaching.

This call began a series of increasingly less guarded conversations between Rhonda and Gordon. Feeling ostracized by the department, he had sought counseling some months earlier and saw the need to improve his social relations with colleagues. Maybe this was a start. Also, he had made an effort to incorporate a few additional labs into his sequence. He did not think it would necessarily help students, but he was hoping that word would get around.

Other pluses included Gordon's confidence in Danielson's support and having his talents recognized by teachers in other departments. Teaching honors biology was considered a real plum, and the principal had made it possible for him to have two sections. Even though he was not part of the new block program, he had been solicited to help some of the teachers with interdisciplinary units. He was quite pleased with a unit he co-designed with an English teacher, and he had sent a copy of it to Rhonda. He was heartened by her positive feedback. These were promising signs.

Still, he was not sure Cypresstown would ever be a good environment for him. He realized that while he saw his building block approach to biology as totally consistent with reform, there were others who were convinced that the pure inquiry model was how students really made science there own. The school grapevine still produced occasional rumors that Gordon was successful with students because his classes were just plain easy. It was hard for Gordon to forget remarks like the one made by a department colleague the day he used coin tosses to demonstrate probability: "If you've got some spare change, you can ace Gordon's class." As spring drew to a close, Gordon wondered whether he should stay or try to find another school where his efforts would be more appreciated.

REFERENCES AND SELECTED BIBLIOGRAPHY

Arons, A. B. (1983). Achieving wider scientific literacy. *Daedalus*, 112(2), 91–122.

Bateman, W. (1990). *Open to question: The art of teaching and learning by inquiry.* San Francisco: Jossey-Bass.

Collins, A., & Stevens, A. L. (1982). Goals and strategies of inquiry teachers. In R. Glaser (Ed.), *Advances in instructional psychology* II (pp. 65–119). Hillsdale, NJ: Erlbaum.

Cruickshank, D. R., Banier, D., & Metalf, K. (1995). *The act of teaching.* New York: McGraw-Hill.

DeBoer, G. E. (1991). *A history of ideas in science education.* New York: Teachers College Press.

Dewey, J. (1998). *How we think.* New York: Houghton Mifflin.

Driver, R., Asoko, H., Leach, J., Mortimer, E., & Scott, P. (1994). Constructing scientific knowledge in the classroom. *Educational Researcher*, 23(7), 5–12.

English, F. (2000). *Deciding what to teach and test.* Thousand Oaks, CA: Corwin Press.

Fenstermacher, G., & Solits, J. (1998). *Approaches to teaching* (3rd ed.). New York: Teachers College Press.

Fullan, M. (1993). *Change forces.* Bristol, PA: Palmer Press.

Gardner, H. (1999). *The disciplined mind.* New York: Simon and Schuster. (See chapter 9.)

Orlich, D. C., Kauchak, D. P., Harder, R. J., Pedergrass, R. A., Callahan, R. C., & Keogh, A. J. (1990). *Teaching strategies: A guide to better instruction.* Lexington, MA: D.C. Heath.

Simons, P. R. J. (1993). Constructivist learning: The role of the learner. In T. M. Duffy & D. H. Jonassen (Eds.), *Designing environments for constructivist learning.* Heidelberg, Germany: Springer-Verlag.

E X H I B I T   A

Water Watch Assessment Report

KENTUCKY WATER WATCH BIOLOGICAL MONITORING ASSESSMENT REPORT

RIVER BASIN					DATE		TIME
STREAM NAME					SUPERVISING SAMPLER		
SAMPLING SITE					ORGANIZATION		
FLOW RATE 1. ___ Ponded 2 ____ Low 3 ___ Normal 4. ___ Bank Full 5. ___ in Flood					MAILING ADDRESS		
AREA SAMPLED IN SQUARE FEET		NUMBER OF PARTICIPANTS			TELEPHONE #		
GENERAL DESCRIPTION OF WATER CONDITIONS							

MACROINVERTEBRATE TALLY

GROUP 1 TAXA	CODE	GROUP 2 TAXA	CODE	GROUP 3 TAXA	CODE
WATER PENNY LARVAE		DAMSELFLY NYMPHS		BLACKFLY LARVAE	
MAYFLY NYMPHS		DRAGONFLY NYMPHS		AQUATIC WORMS	
STONEFLY NYMPHS		CRANE FLY LARVAE		MIDGE LARVAE	
DOBSONFLY LARVAE		BEETLE LARVAE		POUCH SNAILS	
CADDISFLY LARVAE		CRAYFISH		LEECHES	
RIFFLE BEETLE ADULTS		SCUDS			
OTHER SNAILS		CLAMS			
		SOW BUGS / ISOPODS			
Number of taxa present		Number of taxa present		Number of taxa present	
Times index value of (3) =		Times index value of (2) =		Times index value of (1) =	

Cumulative Index Value	

Biological Quality Assessment Scale

POOR   FAIR   GOOD   EXCELLENT

5   10   15   20   25

SEND REPORT FORM TO: WATER WATCH BIOLOGICAL STREAM ASSESSMENT TEAM
KENTUCKY DIVISION OF WATER
18 REILLY ROAD
FRANKFORT, KY 40601
502-564-3410 ATT: Ken Cooke

E X H I B I T   B

Gordon's Biology Course Outline

Q. How do cells synthesize molecules from building blocks and extract energy from their environment?

A. Metabolism

I. Protons/neutrons/electrons → elements → compounds

   A. Compounds—use electron dot pictures to show.

II. Biomolecules (what your body is composed of):

   A. Fats

      1. glycerol and 3FA's

      2. function → membranes, hormones, etc.

   B. Carbohydrates (sugars) [cell energy → ATP]

      1. polysaccharides—a chain of sugars

         a) glycogen—animals

         b) starch—plants

      2. disaccharide—a 2 sugar molecule (sucrose = glucose + fructose)

      3. monosaccharides—(end in suffix -ose) single sugars, 6C hexose

         a) glucose, fructose, galactose

         b) 5C pentose—ribose, deoxyribosec

         c) function

            (1) energy

         d) components of other molecules (glycerol in fats, ribose in DNA)

   C. Proteins

      1. protein synthesis—transcription & translation

         a) composed of a chain of amino acids (guanine, cytosine, adenine, thymine, DNA)

         b) peptide bonds/dehydration synthesis

      2. function of proteins:

         a) structural (hair, muscle)

         b) functional (enzymes, hormones, antibodies)

   D. Nucleic acids

      1. DNA—genes, nucleus, double stranded helix, etc.

      2. RNA (mRNA, tRNA, rRNA)

      3. nucleotides (sugar, nitrogeneous phosphate)

III. Cells are composed of organelles (whose functions depend on the biomolecules)
   A. Cell membrane
      1. made up of fats + proteins (fluid mosaic model)
      2. gives cell shape
      3. controls movement of molecules in & out of cell
         a) lipid bilayer—diffusion and osmosis
         b) active transport—protein channels, uses ATD
   B. Nucleus—contains DNA controls activities in cell
   C. Endoplasmic reticulum (smooth—without ribosomes, rough—ribosomes attached)
      1. organelle that transports newly synthesized protein to Golgi
      2. a membranous lipid bilayer "tunnel hallway" through cell
   D. Ribosomes
      1. synthesize proteins
      2. made of rRNA
   E. Golgi—package proteins in fat for transport out of cell
   F. Cytoplasm (network of tubules)
      1. gel/mesh substance in which organelles are suspended
      2. loose precursors—components of biomolecules float here
   G. Mitochondria
      1. site of cellular respiration
      2. supplies energy to cell (ATP)
      3. utilizes carbohydrates (glucose) to do this
         a) glycolysis—split glucose in 1/2
         b) Krebs cycle—load up electron carriers
         c) oxidative phosphorylation
            (1) ADP gets phosphorylated → ATP
IV. Cells divide (to produce an organism)
   A. Mitosis (body cells)
   B. Meiosis (reproductive cells)
V. Genetics
   A. Inheritance of traits (by offspring from parents)
      1. Why does the organism look the way it does?
      2. Why does the organism function the way it does?
   B. Via DNA expressed through protein function—everybody uses the same biomolecules in very similar ways
VI. Organisms
   A. Plants (chloroplasts, photosynthesis → ATP)
   B. Animals (organ systems)
VII. Ecology—the environment the organisms live in and how they interrelate

E X H I B I T   C - 1

Student Lab Write-Up

Carbohydrate Lab
Sample Student Lab Report: Sugar
September 15

1. Introduction: I am going to do an experiment to find out what kind of sugar certain elements might be. I want to find these things out because I want to know what ones to include in my diet. Also, I want to find out what foods are what kind of sugar so that I can balance my sugar diet. I already learned one thing from this experiment I am going to do. I learned that fruits have sugars in them. The four foods that my group will test are honey, oats, table sugar, and apple juice.
2. Hypothesis: My hypothesis for table sugar is disaccharide, because it takes two sugars to form sucrose, which is sugar. I hypothesize that oats are a polysaccharide because oats store their sugars in starches. Starches are polysaccharide. I think that honey will be a monosaccharide because it comes from the nectar, which is the fruit of a plant. The sugar is stored in fructose, which is monosaccharide.
3. Experimental Design: My lab group will test monosaccharide, disaccharides, and polysaccharides. We will observe their reactions to Benedict's solution and iodine color. Then we will record their reactions and compare that reaction to the reactions of our unknown substances. After that we can figure out what kind of sugars our unknowns are.
4. Materials List and Method:

    1. a monosaccharide
    2. a disaccharide
    3. a polysaccharide
    4. iodine color
    5. Benedict's solution
    6. honey
    7. apple juice
    8. table sugar
    9. oats
    10. droppers
    11. test tubes
    12. hot plate
    13. a beaker
    14. tube stand

Method: If you will look in the worksheets you will find a detailed description of my method.

5. Data: Once again please look in my worksheets to find the charts where my data can be found.

6. Discussion:

   1. The control in this experiment is the reactions of the monosaccharide, disaccharide, and polysaccharide to the iodine color and Benedict's solution. The independent variable is the unknown substance. These are honey, oats, apples, and table sugar. The dependent variable is the reaction to the Benedict's solution and to the iodine color. 2. and 3. My data show that monosaccharides turn yellow when Benedict's solution is put into it and that they have no reaction to iodine color. I learned that disaccharides do not react to Benedict's solution and to the iodine color. Polysaccharides react to the iodine color but stay the original color with the iodine color. With these data I figured that honey is a monosaccharide because it reacts to Benedict's but not the iodine solution. Oats is a polysaccharide because it only reacts to the iodine color. Table sugar is a disaccharide; it did not react to either of the solutions. The apple juice was proven to be a monosaccharide; it reacted only to the Benedict's solution. 4. A further study for this that I would like to know the results of would be to test the sugars to see what kind of sugars are better for your body or which ones you need more of. This would actually be a better experiment to do to find out about my diet, as explained in my introduction.

7. Conclusion: I accept my hypothesis. Everything said in my hypothesis was proven in my experiment and explained in my data.

Elements of Reasoning: Sugar Lab

1. Purpose of thinking: The purpose of this lab was to find what kind of sugars are in certain kinds of food. For instance, fruits are monosaccharides because they store their sugar in fructose, which is a monosaccharide. This lab also helped us learn how to figure out what sugars foods are without doing the Benedict's and iodine tests. Like honey, I know honey is a monosaccharide because honey comes from the nectar of a flower, is like the fruit of a flower.

2. Question at issue: What kinds of sugars make up table sugar, honey, oats, and apple juice? Are they monosaccharide, disaccharide, or polysaccharide?

3. Concepts: The basic concept of this lab is how you can tell what foods are monosaccharide, disaccharide, and polysaccharide.

4. Assumptions: An assumption that I made was that I could tell the difference between the sugars using the Benedict's solution and the iodine color.

5. Information: Some information was already given to me before I began the lab. It was that monosacchrides turn colors in Benedict's solution and stay the original color in the iodine color, that disaccharides stay the original color in Benedict's solution and iodine color, and that polysacchrides change colors in Benedict's solution but stay the original color in iodine color.

6. Interpretation and Inferences: I interpreted the changing or not of color in the unknown substances as facts to prove that the unknowns are certain sugars by looking at their color changes when mixed with Benedict's or iodine color.

7. Point of view: My point of view regarding this lab is that it will help me balance my sugar diet. While at the same time, Heidi and my friend Jessica would probably want to do this lab to help them understand about sugars because of their diabetes. My teacher's point of view on this lab is probably to get us to learn about sugars on our own and understand them.

8. Conclusion: My conclusions from this lab are that oats and plants like that are polysaccharide, apple juice, honey, and things that come from fruits are monosaccharide, and table sugar is a disaccharide.

9. Consequences and Implications: The consequence of this lab is that I learned about the different sugars and how to tell them apart and like doing the lab to figure this out. I learn a lot more in labs than in lecture, reading, and writing.

EXHIBIT C - 2

Peer Review of Lab Report: Sample Student Letter

Dear Beth,

Your introduction was good, but you need to tell a little story at the beginning to grab the reader's attention. Your hypothesis was good because it was an educated guess. Your experimental design, the materials and methods, and the data were also strong. Your discussion could possibly use a little more description. The conclusion was fine because you accepted or rejected your hypothesis.

Your paper raised a good question, which was, "What kinds of sugars are found in different kinds of food?" Your paper gathered and assessed relevant info. You came to a well-reasoned conclusion at the end of your paper when you accepted your hypothesis. You thought open-mindedly and were willing to accept new ideas. You communicated effectively throughout your paper and made it clear. Overall, this is a good paper.

Your friend,

Anonymous Fellow Student

E X H I B I T   D

Excerpts from Nick's Factory for Cells (TV Production Factory)

Parts of Cells	Place or Character	Description of Job or Function
Nucleus	Factory Supervisor Name John	He controls the whole company.
Cell Membrane/Wall	Security Guard	He keeps intruders out of the factory.
Endoplasmic Reticulum	Board of Directors	If a new product is made it must go through them.
Ribosomes	Work site	Where TV's are made
Golgi Bodies	Boxes	What the TV's are put into and stored in.
Mitrochondria	Oxygen tanks	They supply oxygen to the factory.
Chloroplasts/Plastids	Foremen	Manufactures TV's for people.
Vacuole	Storage	To store the TV's in.
Cytoplasm	Workers	The people who build the TV's.

DISCUSSION QUESTIONS

1. What is the immediate problem Gordon faces at the end of the case? How did this situation develop? What are some underlying issues in the case?

2. Describe Jason Gordon. What is his philosophy of teaching?

   • What do you think Gordon means when he states, "I am here to teach science, not just to get them hooked."

   • How does Gordon's background as a researcher inform his approach?

   • Gordon's professors emphasized knowing "the basic concepts, down to the molecular and cellular level" so students could "adequately synthesize and explain the big picture." How does this relate to Bloom's taxonomy of educational objectives?

3. Describe the particular strategies that Gordon uses. Give specific examples from the case.

   • Gordon considers his own approach to inquiry "guided discovery" (see chart below), where he provides the necessary rules and concepts for students to arrive at an informed solution. Compare and contrast this approach with the more pure discovery approach in which rules and concepts emerge during the discovery process. How do inquiry processes in other disciplines compare?

Classification of Inquiry–Expository Learning Modes[1]

Rule	Solution	Type of Teacher Guidance
Given	Given	Exposition
Given	Not Given	Guided discovery (deductive)
Not Given	Given	Guided discovery (inductive)
Not Given	Not Given	"Pure" discovery

[1]Note. From "Psychology and Mathematics Education" by L. Shulman, 1970. In E. G. Begle (Ed.), *Mathematics Education: The Sixty-Ninth Yearbook of the National Society for the Study of Education*, Part 1 (p. 66), Chicago, The University of Chicago Press. Reprinted by permission.

4. What are the strengths and weaknesses of Gordon's approach?

   • Gordon comments, "It's true, when they start, the kids don't see the point of this."

   • What might Gordon risk by using his approach?

   • Gordon's classes do better on the performance assessment exams than many others. What might be the reasons for and implications of this?

5. According to Fenwick English (see references at end of case), curriculum alignment "refers to the 'match' between the curriculum content to be taught and the test content to be used in assessing pupil learning" (English, 2000). To what extent would curriculum alignment by all of the biology teachers solve the problem?

6. We know from existing research that one of the most effective strategies for learners is to connect new knowledge with prior knowledge.
   - How does Gordon do this?
   - Does this seem different from the way his colleagues do it, and, if so, how?
   - We know Gordon's colleagues have engaged students in some very high-interest activities. Brainstorm ways in which such activities can be effectively connected to both previous and acquired knowledge.

7. How does Gordon shape his curriculum to accommodate diverse students?
   - Gordon states, "I teach all of my sections, honors to the lowest track, the concepts, the ones you have to be familiar with when you start college biology." Are Gordon's high expectations reasonable? What are possible consequences for less able students?
   - Recount Gordon's strategy with Nick. Do you agree or disagree with what Gordon did?
   - Was Gordon's decision about Nick's grade an instructional accommodation for a different kind of learner or a reasonable decision about grading or neither?
   - Was Gordon's decision about Nick's grade unfair to the other students? Why or why not?
   - What were alternatives Gordon might have used to motivate Nick, and what might have been the consequences?

8. At one point, Gordon spends time reteaching the DNA transcription and translation process to one class, while the other two classes move on. This seemed to be an instance when the entire class was having difficulty. Suppose just half the class was having difficulty with this concept. What would you do and why? Just five students? Just one student? Consider the implications in terms of content coverage.

9. How do Gordon's colleagues respond to him? What are possible explanations?
   - Do the differences between Gordon and his colleagues focus on philosophy or style? Do Gordon's colleagues understand his philosophy? How important is this?
   - What could Gordon do to improve his relationships with his colleagues?
   - How might Gordon's relationships with his department affect his teaching and, consequently, affect his students' learning?
   - What actions might Danielson take to improve the situation within the science department? What are the reasons for and against him taking on this responsibility?

10. According to Dewey (1998, pp. 29–33; see references at end of case), three attitudes are essential to reflective thinking: openmindedness, wholeheartedness, and responsibility. Assess the Cypresstown science department from this perspective on reflective practice.

11. What should Gordon do at the end of the case?

    • How might the principal see the situation?

12. If you were Gordon and you did transfer to another school, what would be your top three priorities in the new environment?

13. Discuss those pedagogical issues in Gordon's teaching that are relevant to your own discipline.

CASE 9

Discussion Question	Corresponding INTASC Principle
3	**6** The teacher uses knowledge of effective verbal, nonverbal, and media communication techniques to foster active inquiry, collaboration, and supportive instruction in the classroom.
6	**5** The teacher uses an understanding of individual and group motivation and behavior to create a learning environment that encourages positive social interaction, active engagement in learning, and self-motivation.
7	**2** The teacher understands how children learn and develop, and can provide learning opportunities that support their intellectual, social, and personal development.
7	**3** The teacher understands how students differ in their approaches to learning and creates instructional opportunities that are adapted to diverse learners.
9	**7** The teacher plans instruction based upon knowledge of subject matter, students, the community, and curriculum goals.
9	**10** The teacher fosters relationships with school colleagues, parents, and agencies in the larger community to support learning and well-being.
10	**9** The teacher is a reflective practitioner who continually evaluates the effects of his/her choices and actions on others (students, parents, and other professionals in the learning community) and who actively seeks out opportunities to grow professionally.

When Is Enough, Enough?

CLASSICAL HIGH SCHOOL, ROOM 47

Mark Mattioli looked down at his clenched fists as his face became more flushed. "I want out! Outta here right now! This reading is crazy, and you're making me crazy!"

Elaine Temkin quietly took Mark aside, pulling together two empty chairs near the windows on Broad Street, a congested urban thoroughfare along the east side of the high school. Surveying the classroom from over her shoulder, Temkin nodded to herself, reasonably confident that the other 27 students were on task in their work groups. As Temkin started to open Mark's copy of Roger Hilsman's *To Move a Nation*, Mark flipped the book closed and forcibly stated, "Look, I can't do it! You gotta let me outta this class!"

THE SCHOOL

Decades earlier, Classical High School had been the pride of Providence, Rhode Island. One of the city's four high schools, its reputation as a college-preparatory school engendered both admiration and envy well beyond district lines.

Classical was a grim, gray cinder block edifice in a highly diverse urban neighborhood. When the high school was rebuilt in 1949, landscaping was considered a luxury. Even in more recent years, nothing softened the plain concrete walls. The poorly maintained, sparsely seeded lawns were in striking contrast to the academic rigor for which Classical was known. One of the most civilizing influences on the environment was accomplished by a succession of student artists: indoors, vibrantly colored murals adorned the otherwise dreary labyrinthine corridors. Awards for both student achievements and outstanding teaching filled the walls outside the principal's office. A steady stream of state and national certificates recognizing student achievement and teacher excellence awards dated back a century.

Traditionally, any student in the region could choose to attend Classical with the understanding that he or she would be dropped if high academic standards were not maintained. For example, during the 1960s, 1,200 to 1,400 students might begin school in September. By second semester, stiff competition typically narrowed the enrollment to a manageable 900. In the mid-1970s, several local groups, bolstered in part by desegregation initiatives, challenged the school's admissions standards. Quotas were reserved for minority applicants; students who did not live within the city limits of Providence were excluded. Several teachers claimed that the challenges of the desegregation years and a burgeoning immigrant population prompted many traditional Classical families to move to suburban school districts.

By the 1990s, students from every economic class and ethnic group comprised the student body of Classical high school. The school was now more diverse than ever before, with more African American, Latino, first-generation Italian, and newly arrived Southeast Asian students. The school also continued to attract a steady stream of children of faculty from prestigious Brown University.

Classical had a large ESL population, a solid reputation, and was officially classified as an "urban magnet school." However, it was not uncommon to find Classical students with reading scores two to three years below grade level. Further, veteran teachers agreed that an acceptable score on the school's admissions exam was noticeably lower than it was even five years before. Despite the shifts, admission was still competitive.

ELAINE TEMKIN

Elaine Temkin began her teaching career at 40, when her children were in elementary school. As an undergraduate, she had been an honors political science major with a passion for history. This interest in history prompted her to complete a rigorous MAT (Master of Arts in Teaching) program before seeking her first teaching position. Raised in rural New Hampshire, Temkin recalled that the major event each day was the arrival of The New York Times. Dinnertime in Temkin's family always centered around a discussion of current events. "My father required my brother and me to take stands on issues and back up our opinions with supporting facts and examples. I really had to understand what I read to be able to support my ideas. Seeds were planted that have become essential to my own teaching."

The first teacher ever to receive an honorary doctorate from Brown University was wholeheartedly committed to Classical High School. The challenges of changing demographics and high numbers of students with English as a second language were not obstacles according to Elaine. Her unrelenting passion for U.S. history was, for the majority of her students, contagious.

"All but three of my twenty-three years of teaching have been spent at Classical High School. During that time, not a year has gone by that I haven't coached a student teacher. Initially, each is required to use my curriculum, which relies on different interpretations of history and primary sources rather than textbooks. New teachers must learn to teach thematically rather than just factually. Once they see that kids learn to think when they work with themes, they won't retreat to facts and lectures. Of course, thematic teaching can be chronological, too." While the majority of student teachers had felt it was a very demanding but exhilarating experience having Temkin as a mentor, a few students bristled because they could not experiment with their own curriculum and methods initially.

MARK MATTIOLI

Mark was 15 years old, and at 5′11″, tall for his age. Heavyset, Mark wore only oversized shirts and black cotton pants, low-slung and baggy. He tested well enough to be admitted to Classical High School as a freshman but had never gotten above a C in any course. This concerned Mark's parents, who moved to Providence from Milan, Italy, when Mark was in fifth grade. Italian, Mark's native tongue, was used almost exclusively in his home.

Mr. Bill Mattioli, with the reputation of "a very concerned parent," made several trips to the school. Because he wanted Mark to attend a good college, his visits were usually to discuss Mark's "poor" grades. On one occasion, Mr. Mattioli told two of Mark's sophomore teachers how difficult it was for him as a father to see Mark caught up in the tastes and values of American teenagers. When Mark told him "I hate you" for no apparent reason, he confided how hurt he was.

THE COURSE

Temkin began every class of her eleventh-grade U.S. History course with a five-week unit on the Vietnam War almost entirely based on historical analyses and some primary source materials. In addition to Hilsman's *To Move a Nation*, students read excerpts from Halberstam's *The Best and the Brightest* and Maxwell Taylor's *Response and Responsibility*. Guest speakers included Vietnam veterans like Dave Pritchard, who spent two years flying a helicopter over Vietcong territory.

Temkin leaned forward and firmly tapped the green desk blotter with her index finger. "I have two purposes in beginning with Vietnam. First, I don't think any history teacher has a right to teach without an overriding theme, a framework for looking at different periods of history. Students won't remember the small details, but they will remember the theme, because it gives them something to plug into and they will always have it as a way of sorting out current events in their lives."

"The theme for this course is conflict and consensus. On the face of it, conflict seems fairly self-explanatory, but there are different levels of conflict. During the Vietnam era, there was the physical conflict on the battlefield, as well as the ideological strife at home that included the protesters. In the post-war era, there have been many conflicting interpretations of that period. As for consensus, I mean the middle ground between two extremes. It's how democracy has been able to exist, and that's really what U.S. history is all about—an enduring democracy. So students learn about conflict studying the Vietnam era and realize that a consensus concerning the U.S. involvement has not yet been reached. These concepts form the basis for studying the rest of U.S. history, starting with the Revolutionary War, which becomes as controversial a subject as the Vietnam War. The conflict and consensus theme is continued throughout the course. For instance, was the New Deal a revolution, an evolution that brought just enough change to prevent revolution, or a conservative movement that merely enabled America to return from the Depression to the old status quo? I stick to one major theme per course, though I do vary the themes from year to year. Here is another theme I use: Ideas, such as democracy and communism, change our world more than any person or event."

"My other purpose is purely motivational—Vietnam still has some interest for these students. Not just because of all the movies, but most of them know or have heard of someone who was in Vietnam. It's not a totally distant event. Of course, I'm not sure how long it will be that way. Also, starting with Vietnam engages the students from Laos, Cambodia, and Vietnam."

In Temkin's classes, students were expected to understand the main ideas in the primary source materials and historical analyses. She accomplished much of this in small groups where students coaxed, prodded, and challenged one another. Temkin assigned groups to ensure mixed skill levels and appointed key roles such as facilitator and reporter. During the first several weeks of school, her students learned how important it was to participate and listen in the groups and to rely on one another to clarify and elaborate on main ideas. At the conclusion of an intense small group discussion on foreign policy, one student commented, "When we work in groups, we get practice sorting out ideas and coming up with our own conclusions. We really have to be prepared and show our understanding of the main ideas of the readings. At first, it's just Ms. Temkin saying, 'What's the evidence?' But pretty soon we are all saying that to each other in groups. All of us try hard to support our answers."

Temkin spoke further about her goals: "Students come away with some big themes—frameworks for looking at history. As far as major events or significant individuals—my students learn those—but listing them is never an end in itself."

"I am teaching them to read and write and to think through history. They will never have an objective test in this class (see Exhibit B). A quiz may have only one question, but it must be answered thoroughly and with supporting examples (see Exhibit D). I keep their papers, and at the end of the year, they have to go back and summarize the ways in which their skills have developed. Granted, some have come further than others, but all have improved their thinking and writing skills. Some have even learned to like history."

RELATIONS WITH OTHER TEACHERS

Temkin was perceived as a maverick by her six male colleagues in the social studies department. She taught for many years at Classical without ever developing a close personal or professional relationship with any of the other history teachers. Gradually she began to respect one of the younger members of the department who had become the girls' basketball coach. "He was different. I liked the fact that he didn't have the traditional macho sense of coaching." They frequently talked about their student teachers and shared materials. Occasionally, they shared recipes. Only once during Temkin's two decades at Classical High School did another woman, Eileen Chester, teach in the social studies department. But Chester left after two years, disappointed in teaching. Over the years, Temkin and Chester have continued to stay in touch.

Temkin had a very definite approach to her work with student teachers, which she was quick to explain. "OK, so student teachers are usually not very enthusiastic about getting students in groups to discuss conflicting interpretations of foreign policy—even though it's all laid out for them and the materials are there. Initially, they seem to have a hard time using groups, especially for this kind of purpose—they don't feel confident managing conflict. They need to understand that some of the best results come from conflict within the groups. Despite the grumbling, I often get letters two or three years later thanking me. Of course, there are those who choose not to stay in teaching. I can think of one student teacher I had—he was brilliant in history and somewhat creative, but he used my materials quite reluctantly. He loved to lecture, and nothing I said or did could convince him that when students are lectured to, they don't make history their own. After one year of teaching, he left the profession to join the foreign service."

BACK TO CLASSICAL HIGH, ROOM 47

Temkin explained what had happened in her classroom that September with Mark Mattioli. "I began my unit on Vietnam a few days after school started by assigning Chapter 1 of Roger Hilsman's *To Move a Nation*. I am always very open with the students, and I tell them about my philosophy of teaching and learning."

"They are going to be assigned things they can't do: readings that are scholarly and complicated like Hilsman, questions that require research and reflection, and written essays in which they support their ideas with a wealth of evidence. Through my coaching (which doesn't mean I will tell them 'the answer') and help from their peers, they are going to be able to do what they could not do when they came into the class. I tell them, 'If I give you merely tasks you can do, you have learned nothing.' "

"When I said this in September, Mark Mattioli, a husky linebacker on the Classical football team who had deliberately chosen a front seat, muttered something about being able to read already and 'big deal.' He appeared to be snickering at me while outlining football maneuvers on his desktop."

"The first homework assignment was to read Chapter 1 in Hilsman, identify the author's main idea about the making of foreign policy, and cite the evidence he uses to support his idea. On the due day, I walked about the room, checking students' homework. Those with some thoughts on paper or even just a glimmer of an idea were assigned to a group. They had made an effort and had shown some sign that they had read the material."

"A few others with nothing on their papers claimed they had read the chapter and could not understand it all. I was sympathetic to their problem. It was hard. However, I knew if I could convince them to try once more to sit back and relax, they might make it. I gave them a couple of basic questions: What does Hilsman say about the process of making foreign policy? Who is involved?"

"And then there was Mark Mattioli, with no paper and no sign of an attempt to understand Roger Hilsman. When I approached him, he asked politely if he might see his guidance teacher. I asked, 'Why?', and that was when I saw him lose his self-control. 'I want out. Outta here right now. This reading is crazy, and you're making me crazy. I always did good in history, but not this stuff. It ain't history.' "

Temkin pointed out that by this time she already had a hunch that Mark Mattioli was a student whose reading scores were below grade level. She did not, however, check his previous scores or past grades. As a matter of personal policy, she never consulted the guidance department before midterm and only used school records when she was deeply concerned about a student. "All these years at Classical High School, and I've only had two students drop a history course—I'm determined that Mark will not be the third."

"It's really a challenge, kids like Mark. Mark didn't 'not do' that assignment—he just didn't care enough to really work at comprehending the text. It's a risk keeping him in the class, but it's a risk I want to take. Mark has requested a transfer, but I'm fighting it. I know I can get him to do the work. Still his sharp words haunt me: 'This stuff makes me crazy.' "

TEMKIN RECOLLECTS

"I didn't pressure Mark to participate in class that morning. I did my best to calm him and allay his fears. I did this diplomatically so as not to embarrass him. We agreed to talk the next day."

"I met with Mark the next afternoon. 'Let's talk about it,' I said as I opened the book. Quietly I told Mark to relax. 'Put your feet up, lean back, and read that first paragraph to yourself. Read it a couple of times if you want to.' I watched attentively as Mark read the paragraph, well aware of the complexity of Hilsman's sentences. As Mark finished, I told him to close the book. I handed him a piece of paper and said, 'Now, in one sentence, write what you think Hilsman is saying.' Mark appeared pensive and then hastily jotted a phrase. I glanced at the paper—Mark hadn't gotten the gist of the paragraph, but he had understood one essential point. I was firm yet encouraging: 'OK, this is a start. You are going to do your homework just like this. If you don't get it all in the first reading, just read it again. But each time you finish a section, close the book and write down the main idea. At first it will take a lot of time, but soon you'll be galloping through readings that are as difficult as this one.' "

"I kept encouraging Mark and refused to react to his occasional antagonism. I wasn't really sure he could meet the challenge, but I never let him know that. I'd have him come in after school a couple of times a week, and we'd keep going over the same process: read a section, close the book, and write down what you understand. It didn't take him long. He wasn't ever stretched before; now he is, and he sees he has a contribution to make. But this is still new to him—he is not a wholehearted student yet. The progress we have made makes me feel good about my teaching."

"Despite a scheduled football practice, Mark hung around after class, waiting until the other students had left. He startled me as he approached my desk: 'Hey, Ms. Temkin, ya know what? Hilsman was a cinch compared to Halberstam.' He was holding out his quiz to me somewhat tentatively, seeming to want more than the half page of my written comments. The class had been asked to answer the following two-part question: 'What does Halberstam say is the essence of foreign policy? Give the evidence he uses to support his idea.' "

"I told him, 'Mark, your progress has been commendable! As far as this quiz goes, your answer to the first question was really super. You understood exactly what he was trying to say. However, you didn't answer the second question at all!' Mark nodded, 'Yeah, just didn't have enough time . . . you know how it is, Mrs. T.—Well, gotta go to football practice.' Mark seemed unconcerned with the second question and poor grade."

"I'll never figure that kid out—what a paradox! He is proud of his contributions to the class, and often his answers are well supported. I don't think the entire problem is reading—I also think he is just lazy. He has the capacity to do so much more—he has already taken the first step from being disinterested to involved. But like so many students, he is content with just passing. How do you move them to the next step of wanting to really ace the course?"

By mid-November, Mark had established himself as one of the more outspoken members of the class and a solid "B" student for that quarter. He expounded after class one day, "I originally wanted out of this class because it was going to be real tough. The reading was so hard; at first I had to read it two or three times. Now I'm not just reading to get it done, I'm focusing. I've learned how to concentrate."

"I don't like to study—I wouldn't do homework, except that I'd get killed by my father. My interest is music—playing rock guitar—that's what I want to do when I grow up. I don't take much else seriously. I study in this class because it's interesting, and I really like talking about it in class. The Vietnam War is really complex. Mrs. Temkin acts like she just learned this stuff yesterday. She's like one of us."

Mark elaborated that Temkin never acted as though she knew the answers but expected the class to find them. Opening his hands as though catching a football, Mark exclaimed, "She makes us feel like we are discovering the answers together."

When asked how U.S. History compared with his other classes, Mark commented that he was pretty sure he would get a B or B+, while his other grades were C's and D's. "History is my best subject, but I do OK in math, too. English isn't my thing—when Mrs. Temkin corrects my grammar, I tell her that if I start talking fancy, my friends will think I'm a geek."

Mark's outspokeness continued throughout the year and was evident spring semester during a unit on the Civil War. In this unit, Temkin made extensive use of cooperative learning. Her approach was based on what she referred to as "a very tight system of accountability." Before a student is allowed to join a specified group, the pupil must demonstrate in writing that the preassignment has been read and comprehended. Any student who does not demonstrate an attempt to meet this requirement cannot join a group until he or she has done so. In the Civil War unit, each student was required to study thoroughly one prominent historian of the era: Alan Nevins, Arthur Schlesinger, Charles Beard, James Randall, or Peter Geyl. Each student had to attempt to define the author's central thesis and to support it with key facts (see Exhibit A). Once students demonstrated this in writing, Temkin assigned students to five-member groups and assigned one author to each. She informed each group that all members were responsible for becoming experts on the assigned author's central thesis. In phase two of the assignment, the groups were reorganized. This time, each student was clustered with a representative from each of the other original groups so that all five historians were discussed within each new group.

In the first round, Mark was in a group that studied Arthur Schlesinger. His group's consensus on Schlesinger's position was that slavery could not have been abolished without the war and that the war was necessary. When Mark presented this idea to the representatives from other groups during the second round, he insisted they take careful notes on the examples he gave: (1) Lincoln's idea for compensated emancipation had absolutely no support in the South, and (2) the South had made no attempts to abolish slavery.

When Mark completed his presentation, it was Larry Michael's turn to report on historian James Randall.

"According to Randall," he began, "the war wasn't necessary—it was based on fanaticism."

"What do you mean?" Mark interrupted.

"You know, like crazies—a small group of ministers and others."

"Prove it!"

"How can I prove it?"

"What's the matter with you? You are supposed to have facts to support your hypothesis—you don't have any, so you're going to screw up our whole group," Mark finished.

Temkin, overhearing the conversation, moved quickly to another group to listen to Jessica Nelson, who had also been a member of the first-round Randall group. When Jessica gave the same answer as Michael's with no supporting facts, Temkin walked quickly to the front of the class. Her arms tightly folded, she announced, "I want to meet with all the Randalls here, right now—the rest of you may continue."

As the Randall group convened around Temkin, she looked at the their individual notes. Then lowering her voice so as not to interrupt the rest of the class, she began, "It's obvious you just don't have enough of Randall's evidence to support his hypothesis. You're selling an important, good historian short here—please work for ten minutes on your own, supporting Randall's thesis with some evidence. When you accomplish this, you can go back to your group. I know you're missing what's going on now. You'll just have to get it from someone else."

With only four minutes left in the period, Larry Michaels was one of the three Randall representatives who had gathered enough evidence to return to his second group where students shared their expertise. He had barely slid into his seat when Mark punched the air and said with a voice the whole class could hear, "It's about time, let's get down to business."

In early June, Temkin was asked about Mattioli's progress. "In three days, my students will take their final exam, and I'm sure Mark will pass. But it hasn't been an easy semester."

"Mark was out for more than two weeks in April on a family trip to Italy. For an entire month he was really lost, and his being away seemed compounded when a freshman in my homeroom turned him down for the junior prom. I was too busy to give him much time except for a few minutes snatched during class time. His grades went down, and his participation in class was mostly shooting from the hip. I was concerned that all the progress we had made was in serious jeopardy. But Mark proved me wrong. After receiving a deficiency slip, he seemed to pull himself together. Since his last two essay exams averaged a B+, he managed a B− for the semester."

"At this point, he considers himself a history buff and is quick to challenge his peers when they fail to support their ideas adequately. What excites me is how he has improved in his response to test questions—he is much more specific now (see Exhibit C). The big surprise came last week when he asked me if I would give him the recommendation required for Advanced Placement U.S. History. It's the hardest course I teach, a course students really brag about taking and surviving. Mark seems pleased as punch about his decision, and I'm delighted—maybe the candle that's been flickering is really going to burn."

EPILOGUE

Mark returned his senior year fifteen pounds lighter and with what appeared to be a new and quite colorful wardrobe. He seemed more outgoing than ever with his friends but was relatively quiet during the first few days of Advanced Placement U.S. History. On Thursday, he waited after class for Temkin.

"You know, this is interesting stuff, but I don't want to work this hard," he said.

"I wish you'd stay Mark—you'll add to the class."

"But Mrs. Temkin, it's my senior year and I want to have a good time. Don't worry, I'll stop by and see you."

Mark did stop by in April to tell Temkin he had been accepted to a small state college not too far from his home.

In recounting these final episodes with Mark, Temkin reflected, "Mark could have made it if he really wanted to—that I know. Was there something more I could have done?"

SELECTED REFERENCES AND BIBLIOGRAPHY

Beyer, B. (1997). *Improving student thinking*. Needham Heights, MA: Allyn & Bacon.

Brophy, J. (1992). Probing the subtleties of subject matter teaching. *Educational Leadership*, 9(7), 4–8.

Brophy, J., & Alleman, J. (1991). Activities as instructional tools: A framework for analysis and evaluation. *Educational Researcher*, 20(4), 9–23. (See also the Appendix.)

Chuska, K. (1995). Improving classroom questions: A teacher's guide to increasing student motivation, participation, and higher level thinking. Bloomington, IA: Phi Delta Kappan Foundation.

Cohen, E. (1994). Restructuring the classroom: Conditions for productive small groups. *Review of Education Research*, 64(1), 1–35.

Ducharme, E. R. (1991). The great teacher question: Beyond competencies. *Journal of Human Behavior and Learning*, 7(2), 127–134.

Fenstermacher, G. D., & Soltis, J. F. (1999). *Approaches to teaching*. (3rd Edition) New York: Teachers College Press.

Fishman, S., and McCathy, L. (1998). John Dewey and the challenges of classroom practice. New York: Teachers College Press. (See chapters 1 and 2.)

Gardner, H. (1998). *The disciplined mind*. New York: Simon and Schuster. (See chapter 9.)

Hostetler, K. (1997). *Ethical judgment in teaching*. Needham Heights, MA: Allyn and Bacon.

Kohn, A. (1999). *The schools our children deserve*. New York: Houghton Mifflin. (See chapters 7 and 8.)

National Research Council. (1999). *How people learn*. Washington, DC: National Academy Press. (See chapter 7.)

Paul, R., Binker, A., Martin, D., & Adamson, K. (1995). *Critical thinking handbook: High school*. Santa Rosa, CA: Foundation for Critical Thinking.

Rossi, J. A. (1996). Creating strategies and conditions for civil discourse about controversial issues. *Social Education, 60*(1), 15–21.

Torp, L. T., & Sage, S. M. (1998). *Problems as possibilities: Problem-based learning for K–12 education*. Alexandria, VA: ASCD.

Whitehead, A. N. (1967). *The aims of education and other essays*. New York: Free Press.

EXHIBIT A

Cooperative Learning—Expert Technique
Topic: Civil War

I. Required reading for all students: Textbook reading in *The American Pageant*, Chapter 21, "Drifting Toward Disunion."

II. Individual reading required of each student: In *The Causes of American Civil War*, edited by Rozwenc, prepare a reading by one of the following authors you have been assigned.

Charles Beard   Alan Nevins
James Randall   Arthur Schlesinger
Peter Geyl

III. Objective—to gain an in-depth knowledge of the historical explanations of the causes of the Civil War.

Directions for the individual student:

A. Carefully read your article.

B. In a sentence or two, cite the author's hypothesis on the cause of the Civil War.

C. Below your hypothesis statement, enumerate the facts and ideas the author uses to support his hypothesis.

Directions for groups:

First-Round Groups

Each group is to be made up of students who have read the same article. Share your ideas on the causes of the war according to your author. Alter or add to your own ideas.

Second-Round Groups

A. Each group is to be composed of students who have read different rather than similar monographs. Appoint a facilitator.

B. A thorough knowledge and understanding of the reading will enable each to assume the "role" of "his or her historian" for this second round.

C. A student must be able to explain his or her point of view to the satisfaction of the group.

D. Be able to defend "your hypothesis" against the scholarly assault of the other "historians."

Required material:

The group (second round) as a whole must submit a single written hypothesis, arrived at by consensus, on the causes of the Civil War. A student who truly feels unable to support the group consensus must write a "dissenting opinion" supported by facts and ideas from the reading.

E X H I B I T   B

The Midterm Exam
Topic: Civil War

Required Material:

- Chapter 20 & 21 in *American Pageant*.
- Your assigned historian in *Causes of the American Civil War* and the other three authors that were assigned to your classmates. Know the authors' theses and the evidence they use for support.
- Chapter 13 in *The Negro in the Making of America* by Benjamin Quarles.

Write a scholarly essay on the causes of the American Civil War in which you integrate the facts from your text and from Quarles with the historical monographs you have read. You will have read a number of opposing and often controversial viewpoints. What do you think are the causes of the war or what is the cause of the war that tore apart our country and the reverberations of which are still felt today? Support your hypothesis with evidence from the readings. Remember to bolster your argument by discussing your reasons for questioning the validity of some of the theses.

E X H I B I T   C

The following are excerpts from two of Mark Mattioli's short-answer tests:

October 6

Green Berets are a military force which are the most powerful of the rest. These guys are the craziest of them all. The government calls these guys out in crucial times.

May 23

Fourteen Points

Wilson's moral diplomacy can be clearly seen in his Fourteen Points. These points that Wilson wanted to see in the Treaty of Versailles were to provide an easier way of dealing with Germany. Three of the Fourteen Points are:

1) Open seas to all countries
2) No economic barriers
3) No secret treaties

E X H I B I T   D

The following exam shows how Elaine Temkin has students use hypotheses and evidence.

U.S. History   Name _____
E E. Temkin

Read the following excerpt from *The Epic of America* by James Truslow Adams. Plan to spend at least one-half the time you devote to this question reading and one-half the time preparing short and precise answers to Parts A and B.

"The merchant and other wealthy and conservative classes had been chiefly anxious to avoid trouble and merely to get the obnoxious acts (Sugar and Stamp Acts) rescinded. On the other hand, there was a mass of smoldering discontent among the poorer people everywhere in America."

"Opinions will differ regarding Samuel Adams, but there can be no difference of opinion as to his consummate ability as a plotter of revolution. As he surveyed the field of public opinion in which he would have to operate, he saw clearly the two classes of rich and poor and realized that their interests were different . . . the rich were desirous of as little change as possible, the poor clamored for any change that would benefit their condition; . . . . if these two classes could be brought together, public opinion would be a unit . . . It is a great mistake to think of public opinion as united in the colonies and gradually rising against the British tyranny. Public opinion is never wholly united, and seldom rises to a pitch of passion without being influenced—in other words, without the use of propaganda. From about 1761 until independence . . . Adams worked ceaselessly for the cause to which he had devoted his life, manipulating newspapers and town meetings, organizing committees for correspondence, even bringing about happenings that would inflame public opinion. At one period it looked as though his efforts would be in vain, but in the end the stupidity of the British government won the day for him . . . the British government gave the India Company what was practically a monopoly of selling tea in America which eliminated profits of the American merchants and resulted in the Boston Tea Party. 'The die is cast,' wrote George III to Lord North, 'the colonies must either triumph or submit.' "

"With the stating of the Declaration of Independence, the upper classes were thinking of their independence as against the exercise of legislative power by Parliament. The lower classes were thinking not only of that, but of their relations to the colonial legislature and governing class. 'No taxation with representation.' If that were true between England and America, why not also between poor Western frontier counties and rich European ones, as between town mechanic and the rich town merchant, as between the laborer and the planter?"

A. State the author's hypothesis. (13 pts.) (Use lined paper)
B. Cite the facts and/or ideas used to support his hypothesis. (13 pts.) (Use lined paper)

DISCUSSION QUESTIONS

1. Describe Elaine Temkin's personal development as a teacher.
   - What factors have influenced her teaching style?
   - What knowledge and skills are necessary for Temkin to teach as she does?
   - Is she rigidly stuck in her ways, an innovator, neither? Give specific examples.

2. Discuss Temkin's relationships with her colleagues from an ethical perspective.
   - According to Nel Noddings, "From the care perspective, we ask what our actions will mean for each party involved and how we can best respond as carers" (Hostetler, 1997, p. 60; see references at end of case). What, if any, responsibility does she have for building productive relationships?

3. Temkin decides to keep Mark in her class. What are the underlying issues here?
   - Is she acting out of her own pride or in Mark's interest?
   - What factors may be influencing Mark's apparent lack of motivation?
   - Should Temkin have checked Mark's record before making this decision? What are the pros and cons of this?
   - To what extent is her action a caring one, using Noddings' perspective?
   - What other actions might she have taken before making this decision and with what consequences?

4. How does Temkin accommodate Mark's learning needs?
   - Discuss the pros and cons of her high expectations for students.
   - To what extent should teachers be expected to give this kind of individualized attention to students? What if Temkin had many students like Mark? Should she be using these specific strategies with the entire class?
   - What other alternatives did Temkin have when she decided to keep Mark in class, and what are the consequences of each?
   - How might Temkin structure her curriculum to fit the needs of different students? What would be the advantages and drawbacks of such changes?

5. Howard Gardner (1999) states, "The disciplined thinking of the historian is crucial if individuals are to draw their own inferences about what happened in an event, decide what historical analogies are apt and which are not, and express opinions and cast votes on issues of import in terms of reasonable criteria rather than sheer whim" (p. 154; see references at end of case).
   - To what extent are Temkin's goals and philosophy consistent with Gardner's statement?
   - Discuss the appropriateness or not of teaching secondary social studies students the disciplined thinking of historians.

6. Using Gardner's theory of Multiple Intelligences, could Temkin expand her teaching of both the Civil War and Vietnam without compromising her position on the use of evidence? How so?

7. It is important to Temkin that students become experienced with using themes "as a way of sorting out current events in their own lives." This goal is consistent with the research on transfer of learning. Specifically, how to solve a problem within a classroom should be transferable to an out-of-classroom context (National Research Council, 1999, p. xiii; see references at end of case). How could Temkin determine the extent to which such learning is actually occurring outside her classroom?

8. Using the table that follows, analyze specific examples of how Temkin has or has not created a thoughtful classroom. (These criteria were developed by Beyer [1997; see references at end of case] and are excerpted from page 20 of his book on student thinking.)

Typical Behaviors or Condition	Thoughtful Classrooms	Traditional Classrooms
Curriculum	In-depth study of a limited number of topics Integrates learning with students' experiences Incremental, conceptual, integrated learning Utilizes multiple sources of information	Superficial coverage of many topics Information learning is an end in itself Fragmentary, episodic, entity learning Utilizes single sources of information

© 1997 Allyn & Bacon, Needham Heights, MA. Used with permission.

• What, if anything, could Temkin do to create a more thoughtful classroom? Should she? Defend proposed changes based on their potential effect on student motivation and learning.

9. Compare and contrast a chronological approach versus a thematic approach to teaching history. How would you describe Temkin's approach?

10. Identify and analyze Temkin's teaching strategies.
    • How, specifically, does she cultivate critical thinking and incorporate problem solving in her history class? If she were to make the thinking processes she is teaching more explicit, discuss the pros and cons for student learning.
    • Analyze Temkin's approach to reading, writing, and understanding. What motivates students to engage in such demanding work?

- Temkin uses cooperative learning extensively and states, "Some of the best results come from conflict in groups." Elaborate upon how cooperative learning functions in Temkin's class.

- Is Temkin justified in spending so much time on Vietnam? Discuss the pros and cons of such in-depth study of one war.

11. How do you account for Mark's progress? Identify the various factors.

- In the eleventh grade, Mark wanted to leave the history class but did not. In the twelfth grade, Mark did drop out of class. Discuss the differences in Mark's motivation.

12. What more might Temkin have done to keep Mark in the advanced placement class? What do her actions suggest about her philosophy?

13. Discuss those pedagogical issues seen in Temkin's teaching that are relevant to other disciplines, especially her use of major themes around which content is organized.

CASE 10

Discussion Question	Corresponding INTASC Principle
1, 10	**1** The teacher understands the concepts, tools of inquiry, and structures of the discipline(s) he or she teaches and can create learning experiences that make these aspects of subject matter meaningful for students.
3	**10** The teacher fosters relationships with school colleagues, parents, and agencies in the larger community to support learning and well-being.
9	**3** The teacher understands how students differ in their approaches to learning and creates instructional opportunities that are adapted to diverse learners.
11	**4** The teacher understands and uses a variety of instructional strategies to encourage students' development of critical thinking, problem solving, and performance skills.
11	**5** The teacher uses an understanding of individual and group motivation and behavior to create a learning environment that encourages positive social interaction, active engagement in learning, and self-motivation.

Activity-based instruction With this teaching method, activities are used as instructional tools rather than adjuncts or enhancements to instruction. Activity-based instruction involves extensive use of direct student interaction with materials or tasks to achieve learning goals. Proponents emphasize that active participation of the learner promotes student ownership and engagement.

Adaptive switch A device for a computer or other technology that allows a user to access and activate the technology without using the standard method (for example, if the user cannot easily work a flip switch, perhaps a button switch can be substituted). Adaptive switches come in many varieties and can be designed to fit a specific person's needs.

Alternate keyboard Any keyboard that replaces the standard keyboard for computer access. It does not necessarily have the same features as a standard keyboard but allows access based on an individual's abilities.

Ambulate The ability to move from one place to another.

Anecdotal record A classroom observation strategy that provides descriptive information about (a) students' behavioral patterns or (b) the extent to which students have mastered or applied specific concepts or techniques. The teacher/observer provides a brief description of the student's behavioral pattern or learning experience. For example, several brief anecdotes might be used to illustrate how a student reacts to a particular situation such as a cooperative learning group. Alternatively, sketches might also show how a student used knowledge from a math lesson to solve a problem in another subject. Anecdotal records differ from "running records" or "behavioral checklists." Anecdotal records are a distinctly narrative and illustrative method, as contrasted with an enumerative or systematic recording of a student's behaviors, such as a checklist of skills. Anecdotal records generally require less of the teacher's time and are often completed after the event has occurred.

Appalachian crafts The Appalachian region of the eastern United States extends along the Appalachian Mountains from areas of western Virginia northward through Kentucky, West Virginia, Pennsylvania, and the southern tier of New York. Rugged and isolating, the mountainous terrain shapes the culture of the region in unique ways. On the one hand, the isolation has given rise to rural poverty and educational equity issues. On the other hand, the seclusion has strengthened a folk culture rich in family traditions and handwork, which has produced some of the most cherished examples of existing Americana. Quilts, woodworking, hand-crafted musical instruments, and myriad other crafts are produced by Appalachian artisans.

Assessment A broad term for the various methods to determine a student's (or school's) academic progress. Assessment is integral to instruction regardless of the pedagogical approach. For example, assessment of didactic instruction may include testing for recognition and recall, while inquiry or holistic instructional approaches may use portfolio scoring with performance rubrics to assess the application of concepts or knowledge. Performance-based assessment as used in a number of states and local districts has met with varying results.

Assistive technology services   An agency, individual, or program that directly aids an individual with a disability in the selection, acquisition, or use of an assistive technology device.

Attention Deficit Disorder (ADD)   "A persistent pattern of inattention and/or hyperactivity-impulsivity that is more frequent and severe than is typically observed in individuals at a comparable level of development. Inattention may be manifest in academic, occupational or social situations. Individuals with this disorder may fail to focus on details or may make careless mistakes in schoolwork and other tasks. Hyperactivity may be manifested by fidgeting or squirming in one's seat, by excessive running or climbing in situations where it is inappropriate or by experiencing difficulty when playing or engaging in leisure activities." (From *Diagnostic and Statistical Manual of Mental Disorder* (4th ed.), by American Psychiatric Association, 1995, Washington, DC.)

Authentic assessment   Assessments that are designed to correspond as closely as possible to real-world experiences. Problems selected for authentic assessment tasks can be generated by teachers or students and often make use of rubrics to clarify, communicate, and evaluate expectations. Assessing skills in authentic contexts is thought to promote students' capacity for self-monitoring and awareness of personal problem-solving styles and relies on five critical stages. First, a student must have a genuine situation or experience to initiate thought. Second, the case must

provide enough data to help the learner deal with the specific difficulties that this empirical situation presents. Third, the difficulty of new problems must be large enough to challenge thought but contain enough familiar material to shed light on potential solutions. Fourth, the learner is responsible for developing his or her own solutions to the problems through critical thinking. Finally, the learner must have an opportunity to test his or her ideas to make their meaning more clear and to measure validity .

BAT keyboard   A type of assistive technology consisting of a keyboard used with one hand. Individuals use different combinations of keys, not unlike "chords" of multiple keys on a piano, to represent the keys on a standard keyboard.

Block scheduling   A change strategy at the secondary school level that makes use of alternative scheduling to increase the amount of instructional time per class and to decrease a student's total number of classes per day. The school day is organized into large blocks of time rather than the more traditional 55-minute classes. Block scheduling accommodates a variety of instructional strategies and generally allows time for more team planning and interdisciplinary collaboration.

Case method teaching   This pedagogical approach uses real-life situations often through scenarios or narratives as the basis for analytical reflection. What actions did the teacher take and with what consequences? What were alternatives and with what consequences?

Cerebral palsy   A neurological disorder that affects specific muscles of the body. It ranges from very mild to severe impairment of muscle control, depending on the extent of neurological damage.

Collaboration   See **Team teaching**.

Collegiality The sharing of educational knowledge, insight, and vision among members of a teaching faculty. Collegial interactions can be effective for continuous professional development.

Constructivism A term that refers to a collection of educational theories, including (among others) discovery learning, generative learning, situated learning, and problem-based learning. These approaches are characterized by a focus on the learner, who actively constructs knowledge and understanding through collaborative, realistic problem solving.

Contextualizing Conceptual knowledge is not independent of the situations in which it is learned and used. Any presentation of fundamental (and sometimes abstract) theories or concepts in ways that relate to students' everyday life or to their prior knowledge contextualizes learning. This approach allows students to "situate" knowledge within a particular activity, skill, or knowledge base. Knowledge is then useful rather than disconnected from its applications.

Continuous assessment Evaluation of students' progress occurs intermittently throughout a learning experience rather than as a single test or performance event following instruction. Continuous assessment benefits both the learner and the instructor. Through incremental evaluation, instructors can gauge student understanding or progress and strategically redesign the approach to meet the needs of the learners. Students' misconceptions or difficulties can be identified early in the learning process; thus, difficulties can be avoided or addressed as they occur.

Cooperative learning A learning activity in which the instructor structures the assessment and delegates responsibilities to student peer groups to achieve specific tasks. In optimal cooperative learning situations, students are assigned to mixed-ability groups (generally of four to five people) and are given a multifaceted task. Each group member has a designated role to fulfill (for example, facilitator, recorder, timer, or reporter), and all work together to ensure all members complete the instructional goals.

Critical thinking Examining information from multiple perspectives before making a decision or coming to a conclusion. One example is the analytic habit of mind that involves defining the key thesis of an argument, evaluating evidence, and assessing appropriate conclusions or logical outcomes.

Curriculum sequencing A systematic analysis of concepts, materials, and activities that builds upon previous learning and challenges students to use existing knowledge to acquire new understandings. Effective curriculum sequencing connects various concepts and ideas to support thorough understanding.

Disability The reduction of function of some part of the body (for example, loss of sight), or a learning disability.

Due process rights In Special Education, the rules that ensure the informed participation, consent, and adequate procedures for parents and students regarding the child's evaluation, program placement, and educational plan in special education.

Experience-based instruction Based on the work of educational philosopher John Dewey, experiential education emphasizes the central role of the student as active learner in the instructional process. Dewey emphasized that experiences can be cognitive as well as physical in nature and that, most important, grounding concepts in experiences contextualizes their meaning and promotes complex understandings and the desire to continue learning.

Firewall Software that serves as an electronic barrier for a networked or desktop computing system. Firewalls are used for information security, particularly in school systems. For example, a firewall may prevent students from accessing Internet sites that may contain objectionable materials. Firewalls have limitations, and many students who are proficient with technology can circumvent the strictures.

Free and appropriate education   The federally mandated right of all students regardless of disability to an education that is appropriate and provided free of any costs to the parents or guardians.

Full inclusion plan   The placement of a student with disabilities in a regular education classroom for all of his or her classes.

Guided discovery   An instructional approach that focuses on the acquisition of knowledge through exploration that is grounded in an understanding of previously acquired basic concepts of the subject. Proponents of this approach claim students draw on a foundation of knowledge to apply learning to specific examples through personal exploration and discovery.

Hands-on activities   See **Activity-based instruction**.

Heterogeneous grouping   A method of assigning students to instructional activities or classes by varying abilities rather than by similar characteristics or same-level abilities. The rationale in support of multiple-ability grouping is that each student has the opportunity to contribute to the group and to learn to value the unique contributions of others.

Inclusion   A term that refers to the practice of placing a special education student in a regular education classroom setting. Specific services or supports that enable the special-needs student to fully participate in the class (such as a signer for a deaf child) must also be provided in an "inclusive" setting.

Individualized education plan (IEP)   A mandatory written plan that must be developed for each student in special education every year. The IEP outlines the student's educational goals and objectives as well as the special education services that will be provided, and it incorporates a time line for providing services.

Individuals with Disabilities Education Act (IDEA)   Federal legislation regarding individuals with disabilities, which guarantees them the following from birth to age 21: due process rights, an education in the least restrictive environment, nondiscriminatory assessment, an individualized education plan (IEP), confidentiality, the right to privacy regarding records, the services of a parent surrogate if needed, and a free and appropriate education.

Integrated software program   Commercially available computer software package that contains several types of programs such as a word processing program, a spreadsheet, a database, and a graphics or drawing program. Examples of such integrated packages include Microsoft Works, Microsoft Office, and Corel Suite.

Inquiry approach   An instructional approach that allows students to explore a situation, make inductive judgements, and, through discovery, define underlying concepts. In pure inquiry, these concepts are explained, labeled, or defined by the teacher after students have worked independently to describe the phenomena. By contrast, in guided inquiry, students are taught basic concepts prior to exploration.

INTASC   The Interstate New Teacher Assessment and Support Consortium is sponsored by the Council of Chief State School Officers. Most states now use the INTASC standards or adaptations of the standards as part of teacher-preparation program requirements.

Integrated instruction   An individual classroom teacher draws on theoretical or conceptual perspectives from a variety of disciplines. For example, students reading *The Great Gatsby* might explore the use of irony in the plot while also studying the social or political implications of Prohibition on the events in the novel.

Interdisciplinary instruction   Curriculum that integrates the perspectives of different content areas into instruction on a common topic. Working as a collaborative team, teachers present students with the themes or concepts that connect knowledge within the different subject areas. For example, history and science teachers might collaborate on the theme of inventions that changed America.

Internship   Several states have comprehensive support programs for new teachers. Teachers involved in internship programs generally hold initial certification and are assigned to a faculty support team. This specialized support assists the teacher during the initial year with instructional planning, assessment strategies, and periodic performance reviews. Successful completion of an internship usually culminates in enhanced certification status, depending on individual state certification requirements.

KERA   Passed in 1990, the Kentucky Education Reform Act is an example of systemic reform because of its simultaneous emphasis on major change in the areas of finance, governance, and curriculum. In the late 1980s, 66 property-poor Kentucky districts sued the state superintendent for inequities in education and won (*Rose v. Council for Better Education, Inc.*). The Kentucky Supreme Court's ruling that the state's public school system was unconstitutional prompted the legislative and executive branches of state government to reconstruct the entire educational system.

Kidworks   An integrated software package designed specifically for use by children. In addition to a word processor, a spreadsheet, a database, and a drawing program, the package is often bundled with educational software such as an interactive phonics program and reading and writing tutorials for young children (http://www.mwcdrom.com).

Learning disability (LD)   Problems in learning that do not directly result from a disadvantaged background, mental retardation, sensory impairments, or behavioral disorders are termed learning disabilities. Extremely varied and complex, these deficiencies include specific difficulties in learning to read, write, calculate, or solve problems. More students are identified for special education services for LD than any other disability. Blackhurst, A. E. and Berdeine, W. H. (Eds.). (1993) An introduction to special education (3rd ed.). New York: Harper Collins.

Least restrictive environment   The federally mandated right of students with disabilities to be placed in the least restrictive education setting that will meet their needs.

Mainstreaming   The practice of including students with disabilities in the regular education setting as much as is appropriate during the school day.

Mastery level   A term for proficiency associated with the mastery learning approach, which emphasizes individualizing instruction. Mastery learning is made possible by goal specification and incremental assessment. Since intended outcomes are made clear and their assessment sought, the need for self-pacing and other forms of individualization becomes apparent. In mastery environments, students do not progress to the next level of knowledge or skill acquisition without demonstrating full proficiency at the previous one.

Mathematics manipulatives   Math manipulatives are physical objects that represent a mathematical idea or concept. Students can observe or arrange the physical objects for inductive or deductive activities that help them understand complex mathematical ideas or concepts.

Mentor A master teacher who works with a novice teacher or in a peer review or professional development capacity to facilitate the acquisition or refinement of teaching skills. A mentor can function in either an informal (at a peer's request) or formal capacity (as in some internship programs) and takes the role of knowledgeable guide vis-à-vis the learner.

Moebius syndrome A rare genetic disorder that is characterized by several factors, including facial paralysis resulting in the inability to smile, frown, or move the eyes from side to side. Sometimes blinking is also impaired.

Multidisciplinary transition team A team composed of individuals with personal or professional relations to a special-needs student who work together to make plans and address issues related to the successful transition from one environment to another (for example, from elementary school to middle school).

Multiple intelligences According to educational theorist Howard Gardner, measuring human potential solely by linguistic and mathematical/logical assessments is limiting. He identifies several different "human intelligences," including verbal/linguistic, musical, spatial, interpersonal, bodily kinesthetic, intrapersonal, and naturalist. Supporters of Gardner advocate the importance of using all the intelligences when developing curriculum and instruction.

Multiage/multiability classroom The philosophy stems from a position statement of the National Association for the Education of Young Children. It promotes the importance of teachers working with the whole child—his or her physical, social, emotional, and cognitive dimensions—within an integrated curriculum. Children engage in hands-on active learning rather than passive, paper-and-pencil activities (as described in *The Review of Education Research on* KERA by Frankfort Ky: Kentucky Institute for Education Research McIntyre & Kyle, November 1996).

NBPTS Founded in 1987, the National Board for Professional Teaching Standards consists of a 63-member board of directors, the majority of whom are classroom teachers. The board's mission is to recognize accomplished teachers who can effectively enhance student learning and clearly demonstrate what they know and are able to do based on rigorous standards. To date, hundreds of K–12 teachers have become nationally board certified through a strictly voluntary process.

O'Keefe, Georgia Prominent American painter (1887–1986) known for her close-up, colorful paintings of flowers.

Outcome-based instruction Related to competency-based education, this is a teaching approach in which teachers first develop a clear definition of what is consequential for students to learn and then plan curriculum according to the desired end results. All students must demonstrate their mastery of the specified outcomes.

Pattern blocks Geometric mathematics manipulatives that are uniformly color coded. Triangles are green, trapezoids are red, squares are orange, rhombuses are tan, and hexagons are yellow. Children can learn to conceptualize not only the shapes but also higher order concepts such as sorting and categorizing.

Pedagogy The art or method of teaching. Pedagogy is defined by choices involving the selection or combination of the basic underlying psychological, social, and philosophical theories and methods of teaching.

Peer review An evaluation process that uses review and commentary by "equals" (for example, classmates) rather than external judgements to assess the value of work. Used by teachers and students alike, peer review has often been implemented as a major component of the evaluation process.

Performance-based assessment The assessment of understanding and/or mastery of a given concept, skill, or procedure is demonstrated through direct application to a specific, demonstrable task rather than through interim exams that measure declarative knowledge.

Physical disability Any physical or health problem that impairs an individual from completing a task or activity so that specialized equipment is necessary to function normally in society.

Pollock, Jackson American abstract expressionist (1912–1956) noted for his vibrant use of color and drip technique of painting.

Problem-based learning (PBL) First developed some 20 years ago to address the complexities of applying knowledge in preclinical medicine that, at the time, primarily used traditional lecture-style teaching. Using PBL, learning is organized around realistic tasks in a field, and students explain, define, or apply knowledge in the context of true-to-life or simulated situations.

Professional development The process of continuous study, evaluation, and improvement performed by an educator to refine and enhance his or her performance.

Prosthetic legs Artificial devices used when an individual has lost or been born without all or part of his or her legs.

RAM There are two types of computer memory: random access memory (RAM) and read only memory (ROM). RAM is specifically used by the computer to store new data (such as a word processing file document you may be typing) and to run specific programs (such as your word processing program). Data and program instructions are entered into the computer's central processing unit, and then they are "accessed" by RAM when instructed to do so by the user (that is, one double-clicks on a program icon on the desktop, and the RAM executes the command).

Reading Recovery Program An early intervention program designed by Marie Clay to assist children in first grade who are having difficulty learning to read and write. The program's goal is to train teachers to make skilled teaching decisions that enable the at-risk reader to make accelerated progress and to become a competent, independent reader in approximately 12 to 20 weeks.

Reflective practitioner This term, the title of Donald Schoen's (1986) book *The Reflective Practitioner*, now commonly refers to the practice of constantly reviewing and evaluating one's own effectiveness as a teacher and continually improving or adapting teaching methods. A philosophical basis for reflective practice is found in John Dewey's (1934) book *How We Think*.

Renoir, Pierre Auguste French impressionist painter and sculptor (1841–1919).

Resource teacher A special education teacher who gives instruction to a variety of students for part or all of the day.

Restructuring In recent years this term has become so widespread in its reference to reform efforts that its meaning has become ambiguous. However, early advocates of school restructuring contend its original meaning is that decisions should be made by those closest to the problems needing to be resolved. For example, curriculum decisions once reserved for administrators should be based on shared decision making involving faculty and parents.

Rubric   A clearly defined set of standards used to operationalize criteria for achievement of skills at various levels of proficiency. For example, criteria to demonstrate skills at beginning, advanced, or fully proficient levels comprise a basic rubric. Rubrics appraise performance rather than assign grades. While rubrics can delineate a performance scale that can fairly assess achievement, their use in some contexts has been controversial because of inconsistent application of the performance indicators.

School-based decision making (SBDM)   An increasingly popular method of school governance that assigns a key role in school decision making directly to a council composed of administrators, parents, teachers, and community members. Proponents of SBDM feel the faculty and parental involvement results in a more effective schooling for students through shared responsibility for education.

Self-contained program   A special education program in which students receive all of their instruction in a single classroom and are not mainstreamed into regular education classes.

Team teaching   Teachers work together in pairs or groups to develop integrated lessons drawing from their knowledge and experience. The lessons may then be taught by each teacher individually in his or her own classroom or by several teachers to one common class, with each teacher presenting the material from his or her particular discipline in a team environment.

Thematic teaching   Focusing the curriculum around a group of themes, often linking each new theme to the previous one, and presenting each skill or concept to be learned within the context of the theme being studied. For example, the use of the theme "conflict and consensus" can tie together historical events over the course of several decades and political contexts in U.S. history.

Tracking   This practice creates disparate schooling for individual students. It occurs by assigning students to a particular long-term educational program for a set level of academic ability based on an early general assessment of students' learning capacities. Many educational reformers seek to eliminate tracking from school programs based on the belief that tracking permanently labels students and does not provide equitable opportunities to learn.

Transcription   The genetic process in which a strand of the genetic material DNA (which cannot leave the nucleus of a cell) is "read" and copied by a strand of RNA (which can travel freely).

Translation   The genetic process in which the RNA has copied genetic information from the DNA and travels out into the cell. Following the code of molecules it has copied, it creates a new strand of genetic material identical to the DNA in the nucleus.

Wide-area network (WAN)   A communications network that connects computers at geographically separate locations. For example, all of the computers and printers in a school building may be connected on a local area network (LAN), but to use the Internet, those computers must be connected to a wide area network (WAN) that links to communication servers and electronic information (such as the World Wide Web) outside the school building.

Writing portfolio   A volume of written work (including a variety of genres as well as writings from multiple academic disciplines) that is complied, edited, and refined by the student. The portfolio is designed to show the student's best products as well as to give evidence of the process by which those products were developed.

Writing process   Initiated by James Gray in 1974 at the University of California, Berkeley, the Writing Project consisted of a series of 6-

or 8-week workshops. The approach concentrated on teachers writing with and for other teachers, thereby teaching each other. The concept has enjoyed widespread adoption in numerous states. Local writing projects serve as a nexus for writing teachers to network about the writing process. The term writing process now generally refers to an instructional approach in which teachers give structure while providing students with the freedom to express their own ideas. Using techniques such as freewriting or guided discussion, students develop details and construct multiple drafts that are evaluated through peer review and/or teacher conferences prior to the construction of a final draft.

Wyeth, Andrew Newell   Famous American painter born in 1917 and son of the illustrator N. C. Wyeth. He is noted for a highly realistic style and attention to detail in his landscape paintings.